Oxford Archaeological Guide

General Editor: Barry Cunliffe

Southern France

Henry Cleere was for eighteen years Director of the Council for British Archaeology. Since 1992 he has been a consultant to the International Council on Monuments and Sites (ICOMOS) in Paris, coordinating its work as adviser on cultural heritage to the UNESCO World Heritage Committee. He is also Visiting Professor in Archaeological Heritage Management at the Institute of Archaeology, University College London.

Barry Cunliffe is Professor of European Archaeology at the University of Oxford. The author of over forty books, including *The Oxford Illustrated Prehistory of Europe* and *The Ancient Celts*, he has served as President of the Council for British Archaeology and the Society of Antiquaries, and is currently a member of the Ancient Monuments Board of English Heritage.

Oxford Archaeological Guides

Southern France

An Oxford Archaeological Guide

Henry Cleere

OXFORD
UNIVERSITY PRESS

UNIVERSITY PRESS

Great Clarendon Street, Oxford OX2 6DP

Oxford University Press is a department of the University of Oxford.
It furthers the University's objective of excellence in research, scholarship,
and education by publishing worldwide in

Oxford New York

Athens Auckland Bangkok Bogotá Buenos Aires Calcutta
Cape Town Chennai Dar es Salaam Delhi Florence Hong Kong Istanbul
Karachi Kuala Lumpur Madrid Melbourne Mexico City Mumbai
Nairobi Paris São Paulo Shanghai Singapore Taipei Tokyo Toronto Warsaw

with associated companies in Berlin Ibadan

Oxford is a registered trade mark of Oxford University Press
in the UK and in certain other countries

Published in the United States
by Oxford University Press Inc., New York

British Library Cataloguing in Publication Data

Data available

Library of Congress Cataloging in Publication Data

Data available

ISBN 0–19–288006–3

1 3 5 7 9 10 8 6 4 2

Designed by First Edition, London
Typeset by RefineCatch Limited, Bungay, Suffolk
Printed by Book Print S. L.
Barcelona, Spain

Series Editor's Foreword

Travelling for pleasure, whether for curiosity, nostalgia, religious conviction, or simply to satisfy an inherent need to learn, has been an essential part of the human condition for centuries. Chaucer's 'Wife of Bath' ranged wide, visiting Jerusalem three times as well as Santiago de Compostela, Rome, Cologne, and Boulogne. Her motivation, like that of so many medieval travellers, was primarily to visit holy places. Later, as the Grand Tour took a hold in the eighteenth century, piety was replaced by the need felt by the élite to educate its young, to compensate for the disgracefully inadequate training offered at that time by Oxford and Cambridge. The levelling effect of the Napoleonic Wars changed all that and in the age of the steamship and the railway mass tourism was born when Mr Thomas Cook first offered 'A Great Circular Tour of the Continent'.

There have been guidebooks as long as there have been travellers. Though not intended as such, the *Histories* of Herodotus would have been an indispensable companion to a wandering Greek. Centuries later Pausanias' guide to the monuments of Greece was widely used by travelling Romans intent on discovering the roots of their civilization. In the eighteenth century travel books took on a more practical form offering a torrent of useful advice, from dealing with recalcitrant foreign innkeepers to taking a plentiful supply of oil of lavender to ward off bedbugs. But it was the incomparable 'Baedekers' that gave enlightenment and reassurance to the increasing tide of enquiring tourists who flooded the Continent in the latter part of the nineteenth century. The battered but much-treasured red volumes may still sometimes be seen in use today, pored over on sites by those nostalgic for the gentle art of travel.

The needs and expectations of the enquiring traveller change rapidly and it would be impossible to meet them all within the compass of single volumes. With this in mind, the Oxford Archaeological Guides have been created to satisfy a particular and growing interest. Each volume provides lively and informed descriptions of a wide selection of archaeological sites chosen to display the cultural heritage of the country in question. Plans, designed to match the text, make it easy to grasp the full extent of the site while focusing on its essential aspects. The emphasis is, necessarily, on seeing, understanding, and above all enjoying the particular place. But archaeological sites are the creation of history and can only be fully appreciated against the *longue durée* of human achievement. To provide this, each book begins with a wide-ranging historical overview introducing the changing cultures of the country and the landscapes which formed them. Thus, while the Guides are primarily intended for the traveller they can be read with equal value at home.

Barry Cunliffe

Acknowledgements

I am deeply grateful to the many people who brought me safely through the long travail of writing this Guide. In particular I want to express my thanks to those sympathetic professionals from the Press—George Miller, Rebecca Hunt, Shelley Cox, Nancy-Jane Rucker, and Mary Worthington—who have guided me skilfully and patiently through the processes of book production throughout the long period of gestation. My family has demonstrated its usual tolerance of the long hours that I have spent in front of my computer. I am especially grateful to my daughter Jo for her assistance in preparing the maps and plans.

Several professional friends and colleagues have encouraged and assisted me in collecting material for this Guide. Barry Cunliffe, who shares my deep affection for the Midi, began by recruiting me to write it and discussed it with me over several leisurely lunches in Oxford. The late Barri Jones generously shared his own notes and other materials with me. One of the most succinct but nonetheless crucial contributions came from Christian Goudineau, who resolved my first and most difficult problem, that of defining the Midi (see Introduction, p. 2). I also benefited greatly from discussions in Paris with ICOMOS colleagues, in particular Carole Alexandre.

Contents

How to use this Guide

The entries in the Gazetteer (pp. 31–189) are arranged under the five French *Régions* that are wholly or partly covered by the Guide:

Aquitaine
Midi-Pyrénées
Languedoc-Roussillon
Provence-Alpes-Côte d'Azur
Rhône-Alpes.

Within these regions, the sites are listed in alphabetical order; where the name is preceded by an article (*le*, *la*, *les*) the entry appears under the first letter of the next word in the name.

The heading of each entry contains the name of the site, a brief description of its nature, and the name and number of the *Département* in which it is located.

This is followed by short information about the exact location. First comes the number of the familiar yellow Michelin 1 : 200 000 map, with the fold of the map identified. Thus, the entry for **Arles** is *Michelin 83/ 10*—the town appears on fold 10 of Michelin map 83.

For major towns no additional information is provided, since these are quickly identified from the maps. However, for smaller and less well-known sites more detailed instructions are given, tracing the location from a larger town by means of identified roads (the numbers are preceded by N for *Routes nationales* and D for *Routes départementales*). This section of the entry also contains the street addresses of museums and other important cultural features in some of the larger towns.

The main text begins with the historical background, and this is followed by a description of the site and its main features (identified in **bold type**).

Within the texts, cross-references to other sites covered in the present Guide are shown in SMALL CAPITALS. Terms for which there are entries in the Glossary (pp. 192–6) are indicated by means of a dagger (†).

At the end of each entry there is information on published material that is suggested as additional reading. Five sources are quoted, where appropriate, identified as follows:

GAF In certain cases, there are volumes in the excellent series of *Guides archéologiques de la France*. So far over thirty of these have appeared, published by the Imprimerie Nationale on behalf of the Sous-Direction de l'Archéologie of the Direction du Patrimoine, part of the French Ministère de la Culture. They are obtainable at larger bookshops in the major towns of Southern France.

GB Each of the *Régions* is the subject of one of the fine series of *Guides Bleus* published by Hachette over the past decade. These are among the finest guide-books available for any part of the world. Whilst the strictly archaeological information is limited, they contain much information about the other aspects of the heritage of Southern France. The page numbers in the relevant volumes are given where appropriate.

Bromwich The Roman Remains of Southern France: A Guidebook by James Bromwich (1993: Routledge, London and New York) is the most exhaustive treatment in English of this historical period (although slightly less broad in its geographical coverage than the present Guide). It is intended for the more quali-fied visitor, but it is essential reading for all those with special interests in Roman antiquities. The relevant pages are indicated where applicable.

Rigaud For those with a special interest in the prehistoric heritage of Southern France (in this case following the French usage of *préhistoire* to cover the Palaeo-lithic and Neolithic periods), *Les Haut Lieux de la Préhistoire en France* edited by Jean-Philippe Rigaud (1989: Bordas, Paris) is indispensable.

PBSAF The Guide-Album *Les Plus Beaux Sites Archéologiques de la France* (1993: Eclectis, Paris) weighs around 2 kg. and so hardly qualifies as a pocket guide. It is, however, well illustrated and informative, and hence useful to keep in the car or the caravan to assist in planning excursions.

Over thirty sites and monuments have been given special ratings, by means of one or two stars. One star indicates a monument that is worth visiting if you are in the area, whilst two stars are awarded to those that should be considered as essential components of any tour. For the single-star group the selection is a personal one, that of the author, but those accorded two stars are universally recognized as being of outstand-ing importance.

The section on 'Museums' (pp. 197–200) gives brief details of the museums within the region that contain relevant archaeological collec-tions. The list is arranged in alphabetical order of towns; some of these do not contain significant remains and so are not in the main gazetteer, but the museums contain collections that illustrate the archaeology of Southern France and are therefore adjudged to be worth visiting.

Maps

Aquitaine

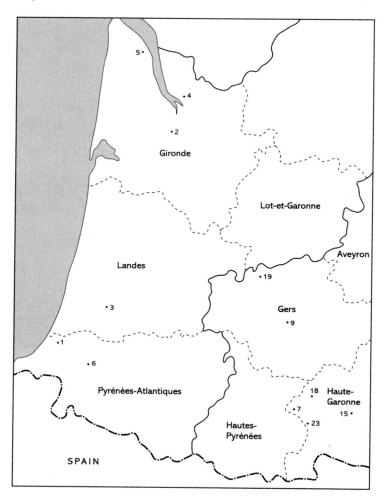

1 Bayonne
2 Bordeaux
3 Dax
4 Prignac-et-Marcamps★
5 Saint-Germain-d'Esteuil
6 Saint-Martin-d'Arberoue★

Midi-Pyrénées

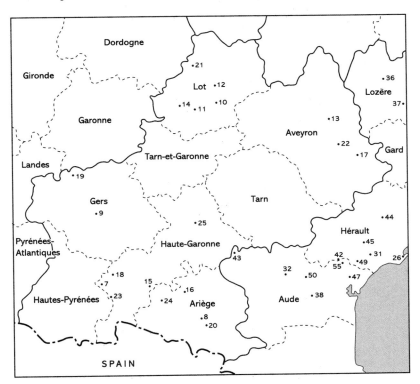

7	Aventignan: Grotte de Gargas	18	Montmaurin★
8	Bédeilhac-et-Aynat★	19	Montréal: Séviac
9	Biran	20	Niaux★★
10	Cabrerets★	21	Payrignac: Grottes de
11	Cahors		Cougnac
12	Cras: Murcens	22	Saint-Beauzély
13	Laissac: Montmerlhe	23	Saint-Bertrand-de-
14	Luzech: L'Impernal		Comminges★★
15	Marsoulas	24	Saint-Lizier
16	Le Mas d'Azil★★	25	Toulouse★
17	Millau: La Graufesenque★		

Languedoc-Roussillon

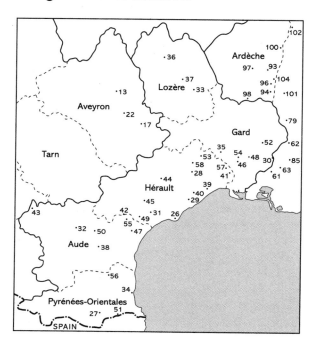

26 Agde
27 Amélie-les-Bains
28 Argelliers: Boussargues
29 Balaruc-les-Bains
30 Beaucaire
31 Béziers
32 Carcassonne★★
33 Le Cham des Bondons
34 Château-Roussillon
35 Gailhan: Plan-de-la-Tour
36 Javols
37 Lanuéjols
38 Laroque-de-Fa: La Clape
39 Lattes
40 Loupian: Villa des Près-Bas★
41 Lunel-Viel
42 Mailhac: Le Cayla

43 Montferrand
44 Mourèze: Les Courtinals
45 Murviel-lès-Montpellier
46 Nages-et-Solorgues: Les Castels★
47 Narbonne
48 Nîmes★★
49 Nissan-lez-Ensérune★★
50 Pépieux: Les Fades
51 Le Perthus
52 Le Pont du Gard★★
53 Rouet: Dolmen de Lamalou
54 Saint-Dionizy
55 Sallèles-d'Aude
56 Tautavel: La Caune d'Arago★★
57 Villetelle: Ambrussum
58 Viols-en-Laval: Cambous★

Provence-Alpes-Côte d'Azur

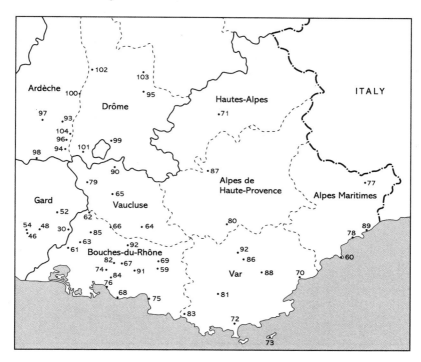

Rhône-Alpes

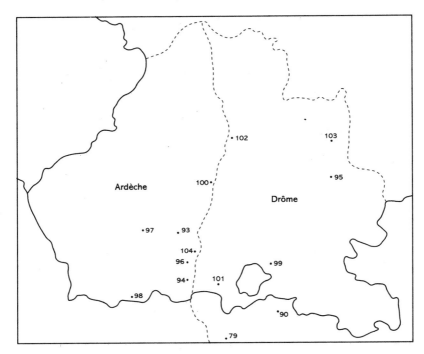

93 Alba-la-Romaine
94 Bourg-Saint-Andéol
95 Die
96 Donzère
97 Lussas: Plateau de Jastres
98 Orgnac-l'Aven
99 Le Pègue
100 Le Pouzin
101 Saint-Paul-Trois-Châteaux
102 Valence
103 Vassieux-en-Vercors
104 Viviers

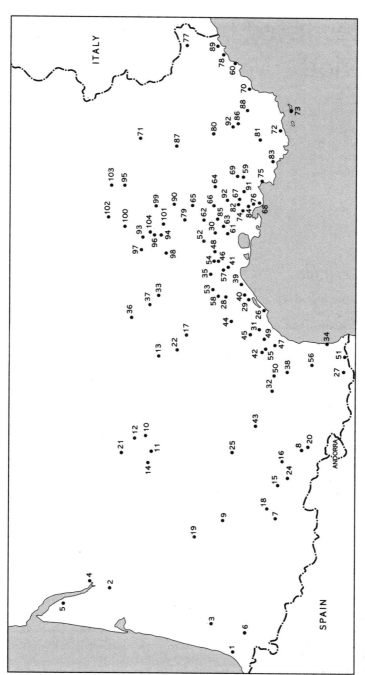

▲ Sites and monuments in Southern France

Sites listed by archaeological period

Many of the archaeological sites of Southern France span several periods: Iron Age fortified hilltop settlements (*oppida*) became Gallo-Roman towns, as did the Greek towns. In the table below sites are allocated to the period of the major surviving remains.

A = Aquitaine; LR = Languedoc-Roussillon; MP = Midi-Pyrénées; PC = Provence-Alpes-Côte d'Azur; RA = Rhône-Alpes. The numbers in *italics* refer to the Maps and the main gazetteer.

Palaeolithic

Aventignan: Grotte de Gargas [MP] *7*
Bédeilhac-et-Aynat: Grotte de Bédeilhac [MP]★ *8*
Cabrerets: Grotte du Pech-Merle [MP]★ *10*
Marsoulas [MP] *15*
Le Mas d'Azil [MP]★★ *16*
Niaux: Grotte de Niaux [MP]★★ *20*
Orgnac-l'Aven: L'Aven d'Orgnac [RA] *98*
Payrignac: Grottes de Cougnac [MP] *21*
Prignac-et-Marcamps: Grotte de Pair-non-Pair [A]★ *4*
Saint-Martin-d'Arberoue: Grottes d'Isturitz et d'Oxocelhaya [A]★ *6*
Salernes: Grotte de Fontbrégoua [PC] *86*
Tautavel: La Caune d'Arago [LR]★★ *56*

Neolithic

Argelliers: Boussargues [LR]★ *28*
Le Cham des Bondons [LR] *33*
Laroque-de-Fa: La Clape [LR] *38*
Mourèze: Les Courtinals [LR] *44*
Pépieux: Les Fades/Le Palet-de-Roland [LR] *50*
Rouet: Dolmen de Lamalou [LR] *53*
Saint-Germain-d'Esteuil: Barbehère-Brion [A] *5*
Viols-en-Laval: Cambous [LR]★ *58*
Vassieux-en-Vercors [RA] *103*

Bronze Age

Mont Bégo: Les Vallées des Merveilles et de Fontalba [PC]★★ *77*

Iron Age

Constantine [PC] *67*
Cras: Murcens [MP] *12*
Entremont [PC]★★ *69*
Gailhan: Plan-de-la-Tour [LR] *35*
Istres [PC] *74*
Laissac: Montmerlhe [MP] *13*
Lussas: Plateau de Jastres [RA] *97*
Luzech: L'Impernal [MP] *14*
Mailhac: Le Cayla [LR] *42*
Martigues [PC]★ *76*
Murviel-lès-Montpellier: Castellas [LR] *45*
Nages-et-Solorgues: Les Castels [LR]★ *46*
Nissan-lez-Ensérune [LR]★★ *49*
Le Pègue [RA] *99*
Saint-Dionizy: Roque-de-Viou [LR] *54*
Taradeau [PC]★ *88*
Velaux: Roquepertuse [PC] *91*

Greek colonial period

Agde [LR] 26
Antibes [PC] 60
Hyères: Olbia [PC] 72
Marseilles [PC]★ 75
Saint-Mitre-les-
Remparts: Saint-
Blaise [PC]★ 84
Saint-Rémy-de-
Provence: Glanum
[PC]★★ 85

Gallo-Roman period

Aix-en-Provence [PC]
59
Alba-la-Romaine [RA]
93
Amélie-les-Bains [LR]
27
Arles [PC]★★ 61
Avignon [PC]★ 62
Balaruc-les-Bains [LR]
29
Barbégal [PC]★ 63
Bayonne [A] 1
Beaucaire [LR] 30
Béziers [LR] 31
Biran [MP] 9
Bonnieux: Le Pont
Julien [PC] 64

Bordeaux [A] 2
Bourg-Saint-Andéol
[RA] 94
Cahors [MP] 11
Carcassonne [LR]★★ 32
Carpentras [PC] 65
Cavaillon [PC] 66
Château-Roussillon
[LR] 34
La Couronne [PC] 68
Dax [A] 3
Die [RA] 95
Donzère [RA] 96
Fréjus [PC]★★ 70
Gap [PC] 71
Île Sainte-Marguérite
(Îles de Lérins) [PC]
73
Javols [LR] 36
Lanuéjols [LR] 37
Lattes [LR] 39
Loupian: Villa des Près-
Bas [LR]★ 40
Lunel-Viel [LR] 41
Millau: La
Graufesenque [MP]★
17
Montferrand [LR] 43
Montmaurin [MP]★ 18
Montréal: Séviac [MP]
19
Narbonne [LR] 47
Nice [PC]★ 78
Nîmes [LR]★★ 48
Orange [PC]★★ 79

Le Perthus: Les Cluses
and Col de Panissars
[LR] 51
Le Pont du Gard [LR]★★
52
Le Pouzin [RA] 100
Riez [PC] 80
La Roquebrussane:
Grand-Loou [PC]★
81
Saint-Beauzély: Les
Bariols [MP] 22
Saint-Bertrand-de-
Comminges [MP]★★
23
Saint-Chamas [PC] 82
Saint-Cyr-sur-Mer: Les
Lecques [PC] 83
Saint-Lizier [MP] 24
Saint-Paul-Trois-Chât-
eaux [RA] 101
Sallèles-d'Aude [LR]★
55
Sisteron [PC] 87
Toulouse [MP]★ 25
La Turbie [PC]★ 89
Vaison-la-Romaine
[PC]★★ 90
Valence [RA] 102
Vernègues: Château-Bas
[PC] 92
Villetelle: Ambrussum
[LR] 57
Viviers [RA] 104

Text boxes

There is a number of 'boxes' throughout the text dealing with different aspects of the archaeology and history of Southern France.

Introduction

The Scope of the Guide

'The South of France' has strong resonances for contemporary travellers. These are compounded of the heady herbal aroma of the *garrigue* borne on the harsh *mistral*, the soft lapping of the Mediterranean on the beaches of the *calanques* along its coast, the herds of horses on the Camargue under its endless skies, the soaring peaks of the Pyrenees, the dramatic gorges of the Tarn, the delights of *bouillabaisse* and *pastis*, and much more. Alongside its natural beauty, the Midi also confronts the visitor with abundant evidence of its long and often turbulent history, from caves painted by Stone Age man through its wealth under Roman rule and the Middle Ages when it was fought over by many kings and princes to the elegance of its C17 and C18 towns and beyond.

A guidebook that did justice to the rich historic heritage of this region, encompassing the decorated *grottes* of Languedoc, the Roman remains of Arles and Nîmes, the medieval splendours of Carcassonne and Avignon, and the elegance of Aix-en-Provence, would be unwieldy in the extreme. The objective of this volume in the Oxford Archaeological Guides is therefore to provide in a relatively handy form an introduction to the prehistoric and classical remains of the Midi, from the arrival of Stone Age man some thirty centuries ago to the end of Roman rule in the C5 AD. It is confined to those sites and monuments that are still visible and which can be visited. Regretfully, a number of important sites to which access is not possible have been omitted from this guide.

In preparing the guide, it was necessary to define the area to be covered. This proved to be more difficult than had at first appeared. Standard works of history and geography supplied a number of conflicting boundaries. In his monumental work, *L'Identité de la France* (*The Identity of France*), the great French historian Fernand Braudel dates the emergence of two regions, the Midi and the North, to the Neolithic period in the fifth millennium BC, but his definition is somewhat vague. He describes the prehistoric Mediterranean cultural region as covering the southern half of the Massif Central and the lower Alpine region, but qualifies this in dealing with later periods. Other authors see the region as starting from the mouth of the Garonne in the west and crossing to Savoy, skirting the south flanks of the Massif Central. For the geographers the boundary excludes Lyons, starting at Montélimar and curving towards the Garonne. An appeal to no less an authority than Christian Goudineau, Professor of National Antiquities at the Collège de France, was equally imprecise: in a note to the author he wrote 'historians and

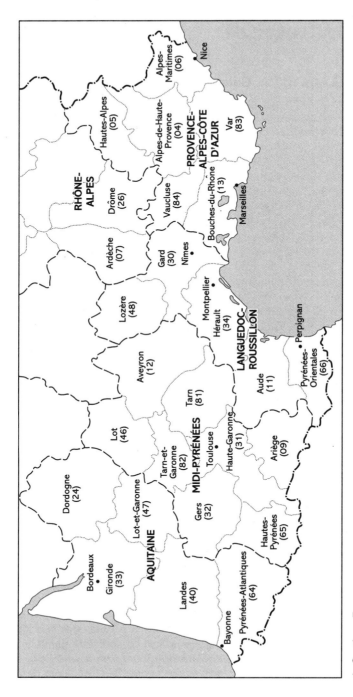

▲ Southern France

archaeologists have conceptions [of the Midi] that vary arbitrarily. Everyone does what he wants [*chacun fait ce qu'il veut*]!' The coverage of the present guide has therefore been determined equally arbitrarily, though respecting ancient cultural groupings. It covers the modern *Régions* of Languedoc-Roussillon, Midi-Pyrénées, and Provence-Alpes-Côte d'Azur in their entirety, all of Aquitaine with the exception of the *département* of Dordogne, and the southern part of Rhône-Alpes.

The Natural Environment

Southern France is made up of three mountainous areas—the Pyrenees in the west, stretching from the Atlantic to the Mediterranean, the Massif Central, and the southern parts of the Alpine massif in the east. Between the Pyrenees and the more southerly parts of the Massif Central lies the alluvial corridor of the Garonne, whilst a flat fertile strip stretches between Perpignan in the west and the wide delta of the Rhône. The Alps sweep down to the sea further east, the lower ranges known as L'Esterel and Les Maures ending in steep cliffs.

The three mountainous areas consist of large cores of igneous rocks (granites and basalts) surrounded by larger areas of metamorphic rocks, mostly schists and gneiss. Folding and erosion have created soaring peaks and ridges, with deep valleys between them. To the south of the Massif Central are the arid limestone plateaux of the Causses intersected by the dramatic gorges of the Tarn and its tributaries. The foothills of the Pyrenees are composed of sedimentary Jurassic and Cretaceous limestones which favour the creation of natural cave systems.

Along the Atlantic coast to the north of the Pyrenees is the brooding landscape of sand dunes known as Les Landes, which stretches from Bayonne nearly to the Gironde and extends inland nearly 100 km. at its greatest extent. It is surrounded by the fertile valley of the Garonne and the great floodplain of the rivers flowing down from the Pyrenees to the Bay of Biscay.

To the east of the Pyrenees is the fertile Plain of Roussillon, and further up the coast comes the equally rich alluvial area around Narbonne. A phenomenon of the coastline between the Pyrenees and the Rhône delta is the series of long narrow lagoons (*étangs*) parallel to the mainland, formed by the deposition of sands and gravels brought down by the Rhône and deposited to the west by the prevailing currents.

By virtue of its geological diversity and the wide variations in its relief, the natural vegetation of the region is rich in species. The high mountains support typical evergreen forests of firs and cypress, whilst on the lower slopes are to be found such trees as pines, chestnuts, and cork oak. The natural vegetation of the sedimentary and alluvial plains has long ago been felled, to be replaced by arable fields, olive groves, orchards, and vineyards.

However, in certain areas where climatic deterioration in the early-medieval period led to the abandonment of agriculture, regeneration took place in a form characteristic of the shores of the Mediterranean. Areas of granite and sandstone became colonized by *maquis*, a low, dense cover of ilex, briars, broom, tree heathers, and laurels. Its virtual impenetrability made it a relatively safe haven during the Second World War for resistance fighters, and its name will always be associated with them. Where the base rock is limestone, the secondary cover is known as *garrigue*†. Here the stunted holm oak and juniper are common, but the *garrigue* is especially memorable for the profusion of aromatic plants that it supports, such as lavender, rosemary, sage, and thyme.

The climate of the region is equally varied. Along the coast and in the southern lowlands it is typical of the Mediterranean, with hot dry summers and warm, wet winters. To the west the Atlantic makes its influence felt, with higher rainfalls and cooler summers, whilst the mountains, especially the Pyrenees and the Alps, are snow-covered in winter and temperate in summer, supporting lush grasslands.

This varied landscape provided many opportunities for human settlement. The early hunter-gatherer societies had abundant game at their disposal, as shown by the rich cave art. With the advent of farming, the alluvial and sedimentary areas provided excellent soils for agriculture, whilst flocks and herds could be driven up into the mountains for summer grazing (a practice still current in the Pyrenees). Although there are numerous mountain ranges in Southern France, the valleys of the Garonne and the Rhône made it possible to trade with the hinterland and into northern Europe, whilst the many natural harbours along the coast facilitated sea-borne trade with the whole of the Mediterranean.

The Prehistory and Early History of Southern France
The Earliest Men

There is fossil evidence that the ancestors of modern man (*Homo sapiens sapiens*) roamed the region as far back as the last Ice Age (known to archaeologists as the Lower Palaeolithic and to geologists as the Lower Pleistocene period) more than a million years ago. Sites have been recognized in the eastern Pyrenees and on the coast near Nice. Neanderthal man is also known to have inhabited the region, in the southern parts of the Massif Central) from around 55,000 BC, but he had been superseded by *Homo sapiens sapiens* by 35,000 BC.

It was at the end of the last Ice Age that Southern France saw more permanent human occupation, during what is known as the Magdalenian period of the Upper Palaeolithic. The hunter-gatherer communities of this period (20,000–10,000 BC) were responsible for the remarkable flowering of cave art, well represented in the region at sites such as BÉDEILHAC, ISTURITZ, LE MAS D'AZIL, NIAUX, AND PECH-MERLE in the western part of the region. There was some Upper Palaeolithic occupation further east, but very few examples of the outstanding rock art that distinguishes Languedoc and Aquitaine have been found. An exception is the Grotte Cosquer, near Marseilles, which has produced some remarkable paintings and engravings, but the entrance to this cave is now below sea-level and it cannot be visited. The GROTTE DE FONT-BRÉGOUA at SALERNES is of great archaeological importance but is undecorated.

Neolithic Farmers

As the climate steadily improved, from the eighth millennium BC onwards, the hunter-gatherer way of life was progressively replaced by a culture based on farming, coming from farther east, known as the Neolithic. By the sixth millennium BC sedentary communities were planting and harvesting cereals and pulses and keeping flocks of domesticated animals, such as sheep, goats, cattle, and pigs, in the fertile lands of Languedoc and Provence. At the beginning of the Neolithic, a form of 'slash-and-burn' agriculture was practised: cleared land would be cultivated intensively until its fertility was exhausted, whereupon it would be abandoned, the small community moving to another part of the forest. As a result these early Neolithic villages were occupied for relatively short periods of time—perhaps some thirty years.

However, as the population grew, an awareness of the value of artificial fertilization, using animal manure and other natural materials, led to settlements becoming more permanent. Increasing population pressure led to settlement being extended northwards into the foothills of the mountain massifs. The Neolithic peoples began to send their flocks and herds to feed in the lush upland pastures in summer, bringing them down again when winter closed in, a practice known as transhumance. The droveways (*drailles*) that they used can still be discerned in the modern landscape.

The sites of their settlements, such as CAMBOUS, are known partly because of the first appearance of pottery, but more spectacularly from the impressive remains of their communal burial mounds, known as passage graves† or dolmens†: there are some fine examples in the region at PÉPIEUX, ROUET, and SAINT-GERMAIN-D'ESTEUIL. This was a peaceful society and there is little evidence of conflict: weapons are rare finds and the small villages were only rarely enclosed by banks or ditches, and then only to prevent domestic animals from straying. The small fields were enclosed by means of banks and ditches or by low stone walls in the highland areas.

The Coming of Metal

This way of life was to change when metal became available for making tools and implements, in the latter part of the third millennium BC. First came copper, used in an unalloyed form, and then the superior alloy of copper and tin known as bronze. During the Bronze Age, the earliest traces of which have been found in the Rhône valley, defences began to be erected around settlements (e.g. MAILHAC) and weapons are common finds. Bronze Age religion was elaborate and complex, as illustrated by the remarkable rock engravings in the Vallée des Merveilles at MONT BÉGO. It was during this period that the earliest evidence of long-distance trade has been revealed by excavation, in the form of amber from the Baltic, coming down the Rhône valley, and glass brought from the eastern Mediterranean by coastwise shipping. It is not inconceivable that tin was also being brought in for bronze production from distant Cornwall or Brittany, down the Garonne to the Mediterranean.

Iron came to Southern France from the north in the C7 BC, and transformed the culture of its inhabitants. It was brought by warrior groups belonging to what is known to archaeologists as the Hallstatt culture (called after the site in Austria where it was first identified). At the beginning of the C3 BC they were followed by Iron Age peoples with a more advanced material culture, usually described as 'Celtic' (although this appellation has been called into question in recent years); archaeologists prefer to use the term 'La Tène', derived from the type-site in Switzerland. It is unlikely that there were mass immigrations of people: it is considered more probable that small bands of warriors with superior weapons and knowledge of warfare were able to seize power in the Bronze Age communities. They would have brought with them craftsmen with skills in the production of iron, the ores of which occur in profusion in most parts of the world, unlike those of copper.

Because of its abundance and its consequent cheapness by comparison with copper and bronze, weapons made of iron became very common, encouraging a warlike disposition in the peoples of Southern France. This is manifested in the elaborate defensive works of banks and ditches erected to fortify dominating hilltops. These hillforts† were probably used initially only as refuges when danger threatened, but they gradually developed into permanently occupied proto-towns (*oppida*†), many of which survive to the present day (e.g. CONSTANTINE, ENTREMONT, MURCENS, NAGES-ET-SOLORGUES, NISSAN-LEZ-ENSÉRUNE, LE PÈGUE, SAINT-BLAISE, TARADEAU).

The availability of inexpensive iron also had a profound effect on the landscape. The region had been deforested gradually since the beginning of the Neolithic, but there is evidence that much of it was still covered with woodland at the beginning of the Iron Age. Strong iron axes, with steel cutting edges, made it much easier to fell large trees, whilst iron plough shares were more effective in cultivating the soils resulting from woodland clearance. Continuing population growth led to the settlement of areas hitherto not cultivated because of their vegetal cover or their altitude.

The incoming Iron Age peoples quickly integrated with the indigenous inhabitants, who adopted their tribal structure, centred on a strong hillfort or *oppidum*. In the east of the region the second group of immigrants amalgamated with the Ligurians, who occupied a strip of coast stretching from the Arno to the Rhône; they are known to archaeologists and historians as Celto-Ligurians. Among the main tribal groups were the Allobroges, Cavares, Deciatae, Oxubii, Salyes (Saluvii), Segobrigii, and Vocontii. Because of their links with peninsular Italy by sea and with the north of Europe along the Rhône, they quickly began to increase their trade with the Etruscan and Greek settlements from further south in Italy, with Phoenicia, and with the Greek cities of the Aegean and Asia Minor.

In the west the Iron Age tribes—Bituriges Vivisci, Helvii, Ruteni, Tarbelli, Tolosates, Volcae Arecomici, and Volcae Tectosages—also established strong trading links, in their case with the Iberian peninsula and with north-western France and the British Isles, using the Garonne in the way the eastern group used the Rhône.

The Greeks in the South

The earlier Greek traders did not establish permanent settlements, but this was all to change with the arrival of Phocaeans from Asia Minor. They established a trading post at MARSEILLES in 600 BC, and this quickly developed into a Greek city (*Massalia*), similar to those founded by Phocaean traders in southern Italy (*Magna Graecia*). Daughter towns soon followed—on the coast at AGDE, ANTIBES, HYÈRES/OLBIA, and NICE, and inland at ARLES—and the Etruscan and Phoenician traders were driven out of this market.

It was not part of the Massaliote policy to colonize the hinterland (although there was limited agricultural exploitation in the neighbourhood of OLBIA, to meet local requirements), and at first relations with the Iron Age tribes were peaceful and mutually profitable. However, as the volume of trade increased, these relations deteriorated and Marseilles came under attack, first from the Deciatae and the Oxubii in 154 BC and then from the powerful Salyes, with their capital at ENTREMONT, in 125 BC. The Salyes attacked the Massaliotes both on land and by sea, where their pirates preyed on Greek merchant ships. Intervention on the part of the Roman allies of the Massaliotes ensured the future safety of the city and its dependencies, but it marked the end of Greek influence in Southern France. Marseilles retained a considerable degree of autonomy with the arrival of the Romans, but sacrificed this by choosing the wrong side, by supporting Pompey in the Civil War.

The Origins of Roman Rule

From the beginning of the Second Punic war in 218 BC Rome was almost continuously involved in military operations in the Iberian peninsula. Its troops moved from Italy to Spain along the coastal area of Southern France, and were supplied by Massaliote traders *en route*.

With the defeat of the Salyes and their allies in 123 BC Roman policy changed abruptly. A Roman *colonia*† was set up close to the ENTREMONT *oppidum* after it had been taken, named *Aquae Sextiae* [AIX-EN-PROVENCE] after its founder, C. Sextius Calvinus. It was the capital of a new province known as Gallia Transalpina, which covered an area between the Alps and the Cevennes.

Aix was the base from which Cn. Domitius Ahenobarbus launched his campaign in 121 BC against the Arverni and the Allobroges in the upper Rhône valley. Once their power had been broken, he turned his attention to the area west of the Rhône, and gradually brought it under Roman control. He established a *colonia* in 118 BC at NARBONNE, at the strategically significant point where the routes from Italy to Spain and southwards down from the Gironde intersected, and installed a garrison at TOULOUSE. Despite several military interventions—the incursions of the marauding Cimbri and Teutones between 122 and 101 BC, an uprising by the Volcae Tectosages in 107 BC (during which the Toulouse garrison was massacred), and the upheavals occasioned by the campaigns of Julius Caesar in the mid-C1 BC—the *pax Romana* slowly took firm root in Southern France, in the new province of Gallia Narbonensis created in 27 BC by Augustus, with its capital at NARBONNE. The western part of the region formed part of the province of Aquitania.

The Roman Provinces

One of the most obvious signs of Roman control was the creation of a network of roads across Southern France. Ahenobarbus had begun this with the construction of the Via Domitia, which linked Italy with the Iberian peninsula through his colony of NARBONNE. Soon other major communications arteries were built, linking the main towns such as ARLES, NÎMES, and ORANGE with one another and with the northern provinces of Gaul, and up from NARBONNE to TOULOUSE and BORDEAUX, supplementing the river traffic on the Garonne. From these main routes there were lesser roads, piercing the hinterland and encouraging the growth of small towns such as JAVOLS and SISTERON.

It was, however, its large and prosperous towns that gave Narbonensis its special quality. In the opinion of Pliny it was 'more than a province, rather another Italy'. The dignitaries of the *coloniae*† established at ALBA-LA-ROMAINE, ARLES, FRÉJUS, NÎMES, ORANGE, SAINT-PAUL-TROIS-CHÂTEAUX, and VALENCE vied with one another in the erection of impressive public buildings, such as temples, fora, theatres, and amphitheatres, as well as elaborate and ornately decorated private residences. In this competition, ARLES was the unquestioned victor, earning the appellation of 'the little Gallic Rome'. Others did not fare so well: TOULOUSE found itself replaced by Lyons as a major centre with the subjugation of the whole of Gaul, whilst MARSEILLES went into a slow decline after it incurred the wrath of Julius Caesar.

In the countryside, tribal chiefs eagerly adopted the Roman way of life, and their lofty *oppida* were replaced by small towns laid out on the strict Roman chequer-board plan. Romanization brought with it an elaborate system of taxation, to support the creation and maintenance of these new towns and to fill the Imperial coffers. The upper classes in the new towns, whether retired legionaries or romanized members of the indigenous aristocracy, appropriated large areas of land and created vast estates for themselves. At the start these were run by managers from relatively modest villa establishments. These were to be vastly extended and decorated when external and internal pressures led to the progressive abandonment of urban life from the late C3 onwards: there are some exceptional examples in the region, such as LOUPIAN, MONTMAURIN, LA ROQUEBROUSSANE, and SÉVIAC.

The province of Narbonensis remained intact until 375, when the Emperor Diocletian carried out a radical reform of the entire administrative structure of the Roman Empire. It was split into several provinces of the Diocese of Gaul: Narbonensis Prima, with its capital at NARBONNE, Viennensis with its capital at Vienne (with ARLES designated as an Imperial residence), and Narbonensis Secunda in the east with its capital at AIX-EN-PROVENCE.

Aquitania, with its capital at *Burdigala* (BORDEAUX) had been created by Augustus after the subjugation of the Aquitanian tribes in 27 BC, and had been extended to include the ethnically different tribes up to the Loire. Like Narbonensis, it was broken up into several provinces in the C3. The territory of the original Aquitanian tribes, now coalesced into nine, was given autonomy as the province of Novempopulana, with its capital at *Elusa* (Eauze), excluded from the new provinces of Aquitania Prima and Secunda created by Diocletian.

The peace and prosperity of the region was first threatened in the later C3, when there were barbarian raids that penetrated deep into Gaul. It was at this time that defensive ramparts were first constructed around towns such as BORDEAUX, DAX, and TOULOUSE. The major towns further south were not affected at this time, continuing their prosperous way of life until well into the C5. However, this was to come to an end with the barbarian invasions of the C5. The Vandals swept through Aquitania on their way to Spain and North Africa, and they were followed by the Visigoths, who incorporated it into their kingdom of Spain. By 476, when the Western Roman Empire formally came to an end, the entire region was under the rule of barbarian kings—Visigoths over most of the area, Burgundians in the north-east.

Natural Resources

For the earliest inhabitants of Southern France, practising a hunter-gatherer way of life, the natural resources were abundant and more than adequate for a sparse population. This is demonstrated amply by the wealth of Palaeolithic cave paintings and engravings. During the colder periods there would have been herds of reindeer, bison, aurochs†, horses, and even woolly mammoths which could survive on a largely treeless tundra. In warmer periods the reindeer and mammoths would withdraw northwards, but they would give place to deer and wild pigs, which prefer a wooded environment. Wild goats (ibex) are tolerant of considerable extremes of temperature and would most likely have been a source of food for most of the post-glacial period. All these animals would provide food, skins, and bone and antlers for tool-making. Small mammals such as beavers and hares and a bird population that changed according to the climatic conditions would be other sources of food and materials.

The diverse soils of the region would support a rich and varied flora, even during cold periods. Berries, nuts, and grains of all kinds would provide a richly varied and highly nutritious diet, comparable with the 'bush tucker' that has sustained the Aborigines of Australia for many centuries in an apparently hostile environment. The plants and trees would have been hosts for many species of insects and invertebrates which would also doubtless have been a source of food: snail shells recovered in archaeological excavations have shown that the Gallic taste for *escargots* dates back to remote times! Fish figure in some rock art, especially from the warmer period at the end of the last Ice Age, and there can be little doubt that Palaeolithic man would have had techniques for catching them; even seals are depicted in one cave in the Pyrenean foothills. Cave paintings have also shown wild bees' nests being raided for honey by intrepid Palaeolithic men.

With the advent of farming in the Neolithic, a number of animal species were domesticated, starting with sheep, goats, pigs, and cattle. Horses were late to be domesticated, and they were in all probability first herded as food sources, only later being used for draught purposes and later still for riding. Wild asses are not native to Europe, and they are unlikely to have been introduced into Southern France until the Roman period. Dogs fall into a different category: they appear to have developed a symbiotic relationship with humans during the hunter-gatherer stage, repaying scraps from slaughtered animals by helping in the chase, using instincts inherited from their close relatives, wolves.

Analysis of pollens found in excavations suggest that the earliest vegetal species to be cultivated were pulses—wild peas, lentils, and chick peas. These were followed by early forms of barley, wheat, and beans. Oats, millet, opium poppies, and flax were also being cultivated by the end of the Neolithic period. The later Iron Age saw the introduction of grapevines, olives, peaches, and figs, brought in by Greek traders, whilst the Romans are credited with the introduction of walnuts, chestnuts, melons, almonds, and apples.

The mineral resources of the region are enormous, because of the nature of its geology. The southern part of the Massif Central is rich in copper ores, and these were being exploited from the middle of the third millennium BC, as were those of the Hérault, in the Cabrières area, where ancient mine shafts have been discovered. By the end of the millennium copper was being produced across the western part of the region. The mountain massifs to the east of the Rhône, however, were less rich in metal ores. Although there is no tin ore in the region, this was brought into the region from Cornwall and Brittany, down the Garonne. Throughout the Bronze Age high-quality bronze artefacts were being manufactured in Languedoc and exported to other parts of Gaul.

Gold was also produced by the placer technique, using washing and panning to separate the grains and nuggets eroded from solid deposits in the Massif Central. There is no evidence of mining for gold, as in Spain in the Iron Age and the Roman period. Argentiferous ores of lead were mined opencast in the Roman period in the Aveyron, producing substantial quantities of lead and silver.

Iron ore is even more common in the region, and its resources were being exploited from the C7 BC onwards. During the Roman period the production of iron in the Montagne Noire was on an industrial scale. Enormous slagheaps—one at Les Martys is estimated to have contained more than a million tonnes—demonstrate that this was one of the largest iron-producing areas in the Roman Empire, on the same scale as those in Noricum (modern Austria) or the Weald of south-eastern England. All metalliferous minerals were the personal property of the Emperor, and it is not unlikely that the Montagne Noire was an Imperial estate, exploitation of the ore being leased to private companies or individuals.

With the arrival of Greek and Roman colonists, bringing with them an architecture based on dressed stone, many quarries were opened up, to exploit the wide range of good building stone in Southern France. It is not always easy to identify early quarries, since the best stone continued to be quarried in subsequent centuries and the traces of early workings were obliterated. However, quarries at GLANUM and LA COURONNE have confidently been dated to the Roman period, and it is possible there to gain some impression of the extraction techniques in use.

There is plenty of good clay, suitable for making pottery, in most parts of the region, and kilns have been found on sites from the

Neolithic onwards. However, it was not until the Gallo-Roman period that the region began industrial-scale ceramic production. The clays in the neighbourhood of MILLAU proved to be ideal for the production of the fine red slip-coated pottery that had been developed in the C1 BC by potters from the Arezzo region of central Italy. The finest examples of this pottery are decorated with elaborate motifs in relief, reproduced from stamps impressed on the interiors of the moulds in which they were formed, from which is derived one common name for this ceramic type, *terra sigillata* (stamped pottery). However, a high proportion of the ware was plain, and so archaeologists prefer to use the term 'red slip ware'. The products from these kilns, the best known of which is LA GRAUFESENQUE, were traded widely in the western Roman provinces.

The growth of wine and oil production in Southern France created a need for containers in which to transport this valuable export. At SALLÈLES-D'AUDE a manufacturing centre that was established to produce brick and tile changed its output to amphorae† in the course of the C1 AD. This site and that at La Graufesenque provide a full picture of the processes involved, from opencast and underground extraction of the best clays through to the kilns in which the ceramic materials were produced.

Communications and Trade

The mountain ranges of Southern France—Pyrenees, Massif Central, and Alps—are separated by two great river basins. The Rhône flows down from the north to the Mediterranean and the Garonne from the foothills of the Pyrenees to the Atlantic. The narrow valley of the Rhône and the broad flood plain of the Garonne provided the main communications arteries for early man, either by boat or along tracks that followed the courses of the rivers. In the south, progress was not difficult by land on the alluvial belt that stretches from the eastern slopes of the Pyrenees to the Rhône delta, and the many inlets and lagoons along the coast made coastal navigation in small boats relatively safe for long periods of the year.

From the Neolithic period onwards, these routes, and in particular that down the Rhône valley, saw a continuous two-way transfer of cultures and materials. Knowledge of farming and metals technology travelled from the Danube basin into central and northern Europe and then down the Rhône. Precious materials such as amber followed the same route, whilst with the discovery of bronze the Garonne route brought the tin of north-western Europe and the British Isles, and along with them cultural influences.

In return, the fertile lands of Southern France were able to supply food in great quantities—grain from the farms of the alluvial plains, meat from upland pastures in the foothills of the mountain massifs, and later oil, wine, and dried fruits from the coastal strip. Oil and wine also travelled down the Garonne to its mouth and then by boat to north-western Gaul and the British Isles. With the arrival of the Greeks, more exotic products moved northwards: high-quality Greek jewellery, pottery, and other luxury goods have been found in many Iron Age sites in northern Europe. Greek ships took grain and metal from the Massaliote ports to Italy, to Greece, and into the eastern Mediterranean. All this can be confirmed by the careful study of finds from archaeological sites, including the many wrecks along the coast.

During the Roman period this traffic grew and intensified. It should not be thought, however, that the network of roads that followed the Roman annexation in any way led to the traditional waterborne routes being supplanted by overland traffic. Analysis of the economics of the Roman Empire shows that the cost of road transport was many times higher than that of river and sea transport; this is especially well demonstrated by the Price Edict of Diocletian (301), in which the Emperor attempted in vain to control inflation by pegging all forms of pricing, including transport costs.

The pattern of trade most likely took the form of the licensing of small markets, located initially at or near the pre-Roman *oppida* and later at the small Roman towns that replaced them. Goods would be brought by producers to them using pack animals or simple carts drawn by oxen and there purchased by traders, who would then ship them by river barge to the major river and coastal ports and mercantile centres, such as AGDE, ARLES, BORDEAUX, MARSEILLES, TOULOUSE, or VIENNE. Here they would be sold and transhipped for transport by river or sea to other markets, within the province or to more remote destinations. Only relatively small high-value goods would have been moved overland, most likely in protected convoys (as was the gold produced by the mines of north-western Spain).

The construction of the main Roman roads was carried out under military supervision and to a high standard; they are instantly recognizable because of the long straight alignments that were adhered to in all but the most mountainous terrains. They were about 8 m. in width, usually with a rammed surface of small stones or gravel on a foundation of larger stones and with ditches on either side. Only rarely were they paved with stone slabs or cobbles; this form of surfacing was reserved for the towns, and there are good examples visible at VAISON-LA-ROMAINE and elsewhere.

Rivers and streams along the routes of the Roman roads were crossed by bridges. These were usually pontoon bridges over the wider rivers, and little remains of them, but the smaller streams were traversed by sturdily built stone structures with single or multiple arches. The finest surviving examples are unquestionably the Pont Julien at BONNIEUX, the small bridge at LE POUZIN, the Pont Flavin at SAINT-CHAMAS and the bridge at VIVIERS. Only one of the original nine arches of the AMBRUSSUM bridge survives, and the upper part of the bridge at VAISON-LA-ROMAINE is a modern reconstruction.

Along the entire lengths of the major roads were to be found cylindrical milestones at distances of one Roman mile (1,481.5 m.) or in some cases the Roman or Gallic league (2,200 or 2,400 m. respectively). A good example is preserved on the north side of the N102 some 5 km. from ALBA-LA-ROMAINE. Evenly spaced along the roads at intervals equivalent to one day's journey on horseback were posting stations or inns (*mansiones*) with accommodation for both men and beasts; an example is known from MONTFERRAND, on the main route between NARBONNE and CARCASSONNE. Some of these grew into small towns, such as LUNEL-VIEL and SISTERON on the Via Domitia.

The minor roads were generally less wide (5–6 m.) and frequently followed natural contours rather than driving across natural features. However, for the most part they were equally well constructed. In the Montagne Noire area iron slag was used for road metalling, providing a very hard surface that was resistant to any kind of degradation.

Continuous occupation of the main urban centres of Southern France since the Roman period, and in particular the intensive development of the past two centuries, have meant that most of the traces of the early ports and harbours have disappeared. Only at ANTIBES, MARSEILLES, and FRÉJUS can they be identified with certainty. The Vieux Port of Antibes may confidently be identified as that of the Greek town, because of its relationship with the site of the town. Expansion in the Roman period led to the creation of a second set of harbour installations, the remains of which were discovered (and destroyed) when the Port Vauban was constructed in the northern part of the natural inlet. Excavations around the Vieux Port of MARSEILLES have shown that it was lined with large warehouses in antiquity; part of one of these forms the basis for the Roman Docks Museum. Another harbour has been revealed in the Jardin des Vestiges. The Roman port of Fréjus is still clearly discernible, with its lighthouse or harbour marker, the Lanterne d'Auguste.

Testimony to the important role played by boatmen is provided by the many funerary inscriptions by *utricularii* (members of the guild of river boatmen) to be found in many of the museums in the region—for example, at ARLES, the Île-Saint-Honorat (ÎLE-SAINTE-MARGUÉRITE), and VAISON-LA-ROMAINE. The Arles Museum also contains tombstones commemorating boat builders (*navales*) and captains of seagoing vessels (*navicularii marini*). Of especial interest is the funerary relief from Cabrières-d'Aigues, now in the museum at AVIGNON. This depicts a barge bearing two large barrels with the helmsman manipulating his steering oar; it is towed by men straining on ropes fastened to its stern.

There has been a great deal of underwater archaeology along this

▲ Roman tombstone from Neumagen showing a river boat carrying barrels

▲ Roman *amphorae* in the Madragues de Gien wreck

coast since the pioneer work of Jacques-Yves Cousteau in the 1950s. A large number of ancient shipwrecks have been systematically recorded and excavated. They show that the merchant vessels ranged in size from as long as 40 m., capable of carrying cargoes up to 400 tonnes (in the case of the Madrague de Giens wreck, near Hyères) to small craft less than 15 m. overall, with carrying capacities of no more than 20 tonnes (the Cavalière wreck, near Le Lavandou). Their cargoes graphically illustrate how they were used. The large vessels travelled long distances in the Mediterranean, conveying large cargoes of wine and oil in *amphorae* and other bulk products, such as metal ingots or fine pottery. The smaller vessels, by contrast, carried more varied cargoes, with small quantities of many commodities: they were the 'tramp steamers' of antiquity, moving goods short distances from one urban centre to another.

The museums of Southern France, such as those at ANTIBES, MARSEILLES, and NICE, contain extensive collections of material from shipwrecks.

Warfare and Defence

Warfare as such did not exist in the Palaeolithic period. The region was sparsely populated, by small extended family or clan groups, who ranged widely in search of game and edible plants. Skeletal evidence of wounds that might have been inflicted by humans rather than savage animals has suggested that there may have been clashes between these bands on occasion, but deliberate and sustained aggression did not form part of the way of life in the Palaeolithic.

In the Neolithic period similar conditions applied. There was plenty of land for cultivation and pasturage, and the small settlements were defended with banks and ditches, walls, or wooden stockades only to protect their flocks and herds against wild predators and to prevent them from straying. Among the wide range of stone artefacts that developed during this period, none can be assigned a function that is unambiguously associated with inflicting injury upon other human beings.

At the end of the Neolithic in northern France, with the coming of metal as a material for manufacturing tools and implements, specialized weapons begin to emerge, principally in the form of daggers and swords. At the same time, more elaborate defences appear around settlements, with what are clearly defensive towers erected to deter attackers. There is a striking example of the new defensive enclosure at Champ-Durand at Nieul-sur-l'Autize (Vendée). This practice did not reach Southern France until the third millennium BC, when a hexagonal defensive enceinte was erected at BOUSSARGUES with towers at each of its six corners. Collective tombs from this period produce skeletal remains that bear incontestable evidence of conflict, such as skulls with sword cuts and bones with arrowheads embedded in them.

There can be no doubt that this new phenomenon resulted from increasing demographic pressure. Conflicts resulted from disputes over territory, perhaps coupled with social changes associated with the emergence of hierarchical structures. This is confirmed by the appearance of occasional larger structures in Bronze Age settlements, indicating the houses of members of a ruling class.

This process was intensified in the Late Bronze Age and the Iron Age, when the warrior 'Celtic' societies of northern and central Europe penetrated into Southern France, bringing with them a wholly new social structure, headed by a powerful aristocracy. Intertribal warfare became common as strong aristocratic rulers gradually extended their control over their weaker neighbours and then came into direct conflict with one another. This period saw the establishment of a number of strongly defended forts on strategically placed high points all over the region. Most of these were probably intended initially as refuges in times of danger, since the earlier Iron Age warrior groups lacked the resources for prolonged sieges. However, as intertribal rivalries intensified and improved weapons and techniques of warfare were developed or imported, these hillforts† became permanent settlements (oppida†), with rectilinear internal layouts influenced by the Greek towns that had been established along the shores of the Mediterranean.

The sequence is well illustrated at the small hillfort of ROQUE-DE-VIOU. The small settlement was established in the Late Bronze Age (mid-C8 BC), but not fortified until the C4 BC. It was abandoned some two centuries later when the massive oppidum of LES CASTELS was constructed by the powerful Volcae Arecomici, who now ruled this area. The new fortress had massive walls up to 15 m. thick and still surviving in places to a height of 4 m., with bastions at intervals. Inside the enceinte the houses were laid out on a rectangular plan.

There is a group of oppida surrounding the Étang de Berre, of which the best preserved are CONSTANTINE and MARTIGUES. These, too, have bastions along their walls. There is also a concentration of oppida in the territory of the Salyes, near MARSEILLES, of which the best known is that of ENTREMONT. Its internal layout is rectilinear and, like its neighbour, CONSTANTINE, it has massive walls lined with bastions. Farther west there is a number of oppida, among them LUZECH and MURCENS, at both of which the earthen ramparts are constructed using timber-laced reinforcement in the technique known, following Caesar's term, as the murus gallicus (see p. 41).

The majority of the hillforts of Southern France are defended by walls or ramparts and ditches encircling hilltops which overlook important commercial or military routes. However, in some cases they are sited on dominant spurs jutting out from prominent ridges, and are known as 'promontory forts'. At JASTRES in the territory of the Helvii the two forms exist side by side: Jastres-Nord is a promontory fort and Jastres-Sud a hilltop site. The Roman annexation of Southern France in the C2 BC has left little evidence of military intervention. There are no legionary fortresses, and the remains of auxiliary forts of the type that are common in frontier provinces, such as Britain or Germany, are very rare (one dating from the C3 has been located near SAINT-BERTRAND-DE-COMMINGES). Military establishments were doubtless set up, but they would have been temporary in nature and their sites have been obliterated by subsequent town building and intensive agricultural exploitation in the centuries that followed. Since Narbonensis was a senatorial province, no military units were permanently stationed there, as was the case with Imperial provinces such as Britannia. The only evidence of the barbarian menace that led to the decline and disintegration of the Western Roman Empire from the later C3 AD is the construction or refurbishment of town defences, to be observed at, for example, BORDEAUX, DAX, FRÉJUS, and TOULOUSE.

Domestic Life

Few traces exist of the settlements of the earliest Palaeolithic hunter-gatherers in Southern France. It is likely that for much of the year they would lead a nomadic existence, following the herds of game, and so they would build only temporary encampments, which leave no more than slight traces of their way of life. However, during the winter and in colder periods, they would have occupied cave and rock shelters for longer periods of time. There is striking evidence of this in La Caune d'Arago at TAUTAVEL, where *Homo erectus* ancestors of modern humans lived intermittently between 500,000 and 100,000 BC. The excellent Musée de Préhistoire there illustrates this long occupation.

The Upper Palaeolithic sites are best known for their remarkable wall paintings. However, excavations have been carried out over many years in the caves in which these are to be found and, as at Tautavel, have produced abundant evidence of the way of life of the people who lived in them. There are very good displays in the museum at CABRERETS, based on finds from the nearby GROTTE DU PECH-MERLE, and at ORGNAC-L'AVEN. These have shown that specific areas were allotted for eating, sleeping, and craft activities. Low stone walls were built to protect the inhabitants from marauding wild animals and in some cases the caves were roughly floored with stone. In some cases evidence has been found of simple round tents of skins and branches having been erected at the mouths of caves, of a type known from excavations in other parts of France, notably the Paris Basin, to have been occupied in lowland areas at this time.

This pattern of habitation appears to have continued in Southern

France after the arrival of farming at the beginning of the Neolithic period. The evidence for this continuity is sparse, but good examples are known from the cave of La Madeleine near Villeneuve-les-Maguelonne (Hérault) and at the Font-Juvénal, near Carcassonne. Further north, more substantial rectangular houses made of wood and earth were being built in the sixth millennium BC, as part of what is known to archaeologists as the Chassey culture. This gradually spread to the south during the fifth millennium BC, and a number of sites have been excavated, including two near Toulouse, Saint-Michel-du-Touch and Villeneuve-Tolosane.

The transition to the Bronze Age is well illustrated by the settlements at BOUSSARGUES and VIOLS-EN-LAVAL. The houses are roughly rectangular in plan, with rounded ends; those at Boussargues are built up against the defences, a feature that begins to appear at around this time. The discovery of lines of postholes on the axes of the buildings suggests that they had pitched roofs that were in all probability thatched. In the interior, sleeping and living and working areas were separated by a central hearth.

Settlements of this type gradually grew in size throughout the Bronze Age, and defences became common. The houses also grew in size, as shown by what are believed to be house plans among the engravings at MONT BÉGO. Contact with Etruscan and Greek traders on the coast led to the importation of luxury goods in the form of fine pottery and personal ornaments, whilst wine and oil were being brought in, as witnessed by finds of *amphorae*†.

The introduction of new influences and peoples from the north at the end of the Bronze Age and the early Iron Age saw a major transformation in the social structure of the inhabitants of Southern France. The relatively small, dispersed settlements with their fields and pastures around them were progressively replaced by much larger groupings. Communities were created that lived in large settlements, with fortified refuges close at hand, as at MAILHAC, MARTIGUES, MURCENS, and ROQUE-DE-VIOU and the earlier phases of towns such as ENSÉRUNE, SAINT-BLAISE, and SAINT-RÉMY/GLANUM. At this time, houses were still small and usually single-roomed, as in the preceding period, and were built using the materials closest at hand—stone in the upland areas and wood and clay on the lowland alluvial and sedimentary plains.

The impact of the Greek settlements on the coast on the native settlements with which they were trading was great. As the prosperity deriving from trade with the Greeks grew, earlier notions of house design and urban layout were discarded in favour of Hellenistic models. This is to be observed in its most developed form at ENSÉRUNE and GLANUM, where the elaborate houses from the later period are built of stone and decorated with wall paintings and mosaic floors, and the town is laid out on a regular chequer-board urban plan.

This process continued and intensified with the advent of Roman rule. There are fine examples of large Roman town houses or urban villas in VAISON-LA-ROMAINE. The House of the Dolphin there is on the classic Italian model, with fine rooms disposed round an *atrium*†, a suite of baths, gardens, and porticoes. Even more lavish is the House of the

▼ Reconstruction of the House of the Messii at Vaison-la-Romaine (pp. 168 ff): 1 vestibule, 2 courtyard, 3 main reception room, 4 garden, 5 large building of uncertain use, 6 courtyard, 7 corridor, 8 latrines.

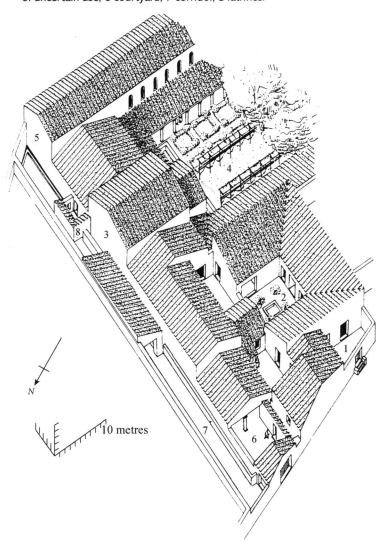

N

10 metres

Messii, with the magnificent marble floor in its main reception room. Vaison also provides examples of the homes of the less affluent classes: the row of tenements in the Puymin quarter are more representative of the majority of Roman town dwellings, with small rooms that would have been used by entire families for eating and sleeping. Less pretentious houses are also to be found at GLANUM, which survived into the Roman period. Many more have been found during excavations in the major towns of Narbonensis, but only the major public buildings are still visible. The houses of the less affluent citizens are also well in evidence in the smaller towns, such as LATTES or LUNEL-VIEL.

The most striking features of the Roman countryside are the villas. These often began as relatively modest farms, with unpretentious buildings in the Roman style: a good example is the establishment known as the Grand-Loou at LA ROQUEBRUSSANE, where the original wooden buildings were designed as the residence of a working farmer, not an urban grandee. Similarly, MONTMAURIN was originally the centre of an indigenous farm, which was then enlarged and embellished, though not lavishly, when its owner came under Roman influence, and SÉVIAC, though somewhat grander, was still essentially an agricultural establishment. By contrast, LOUPIAN was conceived from the start on a grand scale, with marble facings and mosaic floors.

The villa generally consisted of two parts, the *villa rustica* and the *villa urbana*. The former was the working section, with granaries, presses for oil and wine, stables and animal sheds, and accommodation for workers, servants, and slaves. The *villa urbana* was the residential part, with fine rooms ranged round a central colonnaded *atrium*†, and invariably a suite of baths, the symbol of good living. The focal point was the reception room (*triclinium*), often with a fine view over the surrounding countryside.

It is tempting to think of these early villas as the homes of indigenous landowners; however, it is more likely that the estates were owned by absentee landowners in the form of wealthy townsmen, who rarely ventured into the countryside. Their basic economic function as centres of agricultural production is well illustrated by the wine and oil presses that are an important feature at LA ROQUEBRUSSANE and DONZÈRE. There are similar structures such as barns and animal sheds at all the villas.

All this was to change in the C4, when the burden of taxes in the towns drove the wealthier citizens to their country estates. Loupian and Montmaurin in particular were enlarged and completely remodelled, with more lavish decoration and facilities for gracious living such as gardens and pools. They were to survive until abandoned by their owners after the barbarian invasions of the C5 and C6.

Little is known of the less grandiose dwellings of the peasant farmers of Narbonensis. It seems likely that much of the fertile lands of the Garonne corridor and the coastal strip were in the hands of rich

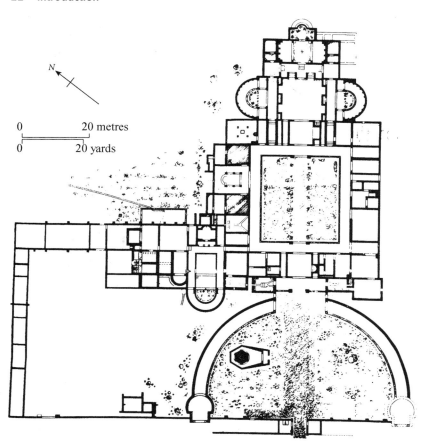

▲ Plan of the C4 Roman villa at Montmaurin (p. 47)

proprietors, who owned vast estates. Only in the less fertile areas, such as the foothills of the mountain massifs, does the land seem to have been parcelled out among small proprietors. Isolated farms are virtually non-existent, since urbanization had such a strong hold on the inhabitants of Southern France; the owners of the modest plots round the smaller towns are thought to have lived within the towns rather than on their lands.

Leisure in the Roman Period

Whilst the growth in material prosperity in Southern France from the Bronze Age onwards and the consequent development of an hierarchical society would undoubtedly have resulted in the emergence of a ruling class with ample leisure, there are no indications from the archaeological record about how that leisure would have been used. It is likely that, by analogy with the similar feudal societies of the Middle Ages, a great deal of time would have been spent in hunting in various forms, for sport rather than for food.

The Romans introduced more sophisticated forms of entertainment, and extended these to all classes. All the large towns had amphitheatres† (examples can be seen at ARLES, FRÉJUS, NÎMES, and TOULOUSE) and theatres (ALBA-LA-ROMAINE, ARLES, FRÉJUS, MARSEILLES, ORANGE, SAINT-BERTRAND-DE-COMMINGES, and VAISON-LA-ROMAINE), and there are traces of the latter in some of the smaller towns. These were designed for public performances—gladiatorial contests and other spectacles in the amphitheatres, plays and mimes in the theatres—and were accessible to all classes of Roman society.

The centres of social life in Roman towns were the public baths (*thermae*). In the larger towns, these were enormous establishments, with a number of rooms heated to different temperatures and with exercise areas and other facilities attached to them (e.g. the Constantine Baths at ARLES or those at GLANUM). Less grandiose sets of baths have been recognized in some of the smaller towns such as LUNEL-VIEL, comparable in scale with the bath suites attached to large town houses or rural villas, such as MONTMAURIN or LA ROQUEBRUSSANE.

The Romans had a special fondness for mineral spas, visiting them

▼ Plan of the bath house at Drevant (*Derventium*): Pr *praefurnium*, A *apodyterium*, Al *alveus*, C *caldarium*, T *tepidarium*, F *frigidarium*, Pi *piscina*, B *basilica thermarum*, P *palaestra* (after Inge Nielsen, *Thermae et Balneae*, vol. ii, Fig. 93; 2nd edn. 1993: Aarhus University Press, Denmark)

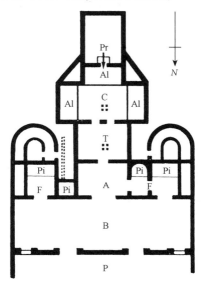

for medicinal and recreational purposes. The Roman baths at AMÉLIE-LES-BAINS have been incorporated, like those of Bath, into the modern thermal establishment. It seems likely that there would have been similar baths at BALARUC-LES-BAINS, where the remains of a Roman structure have been found in this contemporary watering place.

Ritual and Death

Magic and Religion

Nothing is known of the religious beliefs of prehistoric man, but tantalizing fragments of information have come down to us. It is difficult to interpret the abundant cave art, with its thousands of depictions of animals. Did these have a symbolic meaning, designed to make edible prey more abundant and vulnerable, or were they merely records of hunting achievements? The fact that they are found in association with representations of human beings, such as the four 'ghosts' at PAYRIGNAC or the stylized 'bison women' at CABRERETS, suggests that they may have had magical significance. This view is supported by the frequent stencilled outlines of human hands, often mutilated, which are to be seen at AVENTIGNAN and CABRERETS.

There is little that survives to give any clues to the beliefs of Neolithic man in Southern France. The standing stones that are prominent features of some of the upland landscapes, as at LE CHAM DES BONDONS, for example, are less spectacular than the stone alignments of Carnac or the henges of the British Isles, but they are equally enigmatic. The same may also be said of the Bronze Age; however, Southern France can lay claim to one of the largest assemblages of the art of this period at MONT BÉGO. The elaborate disposition of some of the motifs engraved on the rock faces here is strongly indicative of some form of ritual act. Some of the rare human figures are fantastically attired or in seemingly hieratic poses, which again suggests that they are depictions of individuals with special functions, such as priests or shamans. Other human figures bear weapons, and there are many depictions of the weapons themselves, which may indicate the existence of a warrior cult. However, the true spiritual meaning of these remarkable examples of prehistoric art remains hidden.

This uncertainty about prevailing religious beliefs persists throughout the succeeding periods. Ritual significance is assigned to the remains of structures and to artefacts that do not fit easily into other categories, but this is invariably unproven and speculative. It is not until the arrival of the 'Celtic' influences from the north, in the later Iron Age, that more reliable evidence becomes available. Classical writers such as Caesar, Strabo, and Tacitus produced accounts of the spiritual beliefs and religious ceremonies of the Iron Age peoples of central and northern Europe, and these can be discerned at some sites in Southern France.

Most sensational is probably the 'severed head' cult, which is widespread in the art of France and the British Isles. One of the structures at ENTREMONT, where carved heads and fragments of human skulls are common finds, has been tentatively identified as the centre for this cult. It is believed that the sanctuary at LA ROQUEPERTUSE was also associated with this cult.

One of the skills of the Roman colonialists was the toleration that they displayed towards indigenous religions. They adopted a synergetic approach, assimilating native deities with gods or goddesses from their own pantheon. The temple on the Castellas *oppidum* at MURVIEL-LÈS-MONTPELLIER is a good example of this practice. By contrast, the Iron Age inhabitants of Les Castels at NAGES-ET-SOLORGUES destroyed their small square temple when they abandoned their *oppidum* some decades after the Roman annexation, seemingly as a conscious act of defiance.

The large new Roman towns, such as ARLES, NÎMES, and ORANGE, eagerly adopted the Roman religion, along with its urban plan, and were graced by stately temples in the full Mediterranean style. What must have been a very imposing structure was built in RIEZ dedicated to Apollo, and there are several temples in GLANUM. The most outstanding of these is without question the Maison Carrée at NÎMES, which has preserved its original form intact, thanks to having been converted to a Christian church. This was the centre of the Imperial Cult, which was an essential element of Roman provincial administrative policy; its spiritual content was subordinated to a political purpose. The foundations of similar temples are to be seen at DAX, GLANUM, and SAINT-BERTRAND-DE-COMMINGES. However, oriental religions seem to have provided the spiritual qualities that were conspicuously absent from the official state religion. The worship of the Persian deity, Mithras, is testified by the bas-relief and temple at BOURG-SAINT-ANDÉOL.

A number of smaller shrines and sanctuaries are known from the region, such as those at LA ROQUEPERTUSE and SAINT-BEAUZÉLY. However, most of these are in a very ruinous state, and only rarely is it possible (as at VERNÈGUES) to identify the cults that they served.

Death and Burial

The practice of the deliberate interment of the dead is of great antiquity: burial pits containing human bones have been found on several habitation sites of Neanderthal man in France, dating back to before 35,000 BC. The presence of animal bones in these pits has raised the question of whether these represent offerings for the deceased in the underworld. None of these sites is known from Southern France, but there are several Upper Palaeolithic sites inhabited by *Homo sapiens sapiens* in the region where the same practice has been recorded. In these there is clear evidence of the interment of what are known to archaeologists as grave goods, including worked and unworked bone and flint, beads fashioned from shells or human teeth, and items of food. The bones were in some cases painted with red ochre. The condition of some of the human skeletal material indicates that corpses were exposed after death, the bones being collected later for interment in specially prepared cists made of flat stones.

In the Neolithic period burial rituals and practices became more elaborate and what can be identified as cemeteries, set apart from habitation sites, become increasingly common. The simple receptacles for human remains of the Upper Palaeolithic were enlarged, and often covered with piles of stones to form cairns, within which a burial chamber was fashioned using stone slabs or boulders. A number of the burials contain evidence of some form of ritual fire, perhaps associated with a mourning feast, having been built on top of the tomb.

At first, these tombs only contained single skeletons, but from the later fifth millennium BC multiple burials are recorded, the bodies having been added at different times; these probably belonged to a single family group. In north-western France these multiple tombs grew considerably in size, to form chambered tombs† of imposing proportions. This practice spread southwards, and a number of examples survive, usually in the form of dolmens†, the massive slabs that form the central burial chamber of these collective tombs. Among the best preserved examples in the region are those at LAROQUE-DE-FA (where there are several different forms of tomb in the small Neolithic cemetery), PÉPIEUX, ROUET, SAINT-GERMAIN-D'ESTEUIL, and VIOLS-EN-LAVAL.

The practice of multiple burial began to die out around the beginning of the second millennium BC in response to changing social patterns. The rise of chieftainship led to the building of imposing burial mounds on distinctive sites as the last resting places of warrior rulers, surrounded by their weapons and other rich grave goods. These burial mounds are less common in Southern France than they are in the north, but several have been excavated.

Also from the north came the use of cremation instead of inhumation, around 1200 BC. More than 400 cremation burials have been excavated in the cemetery below the Late Bronze Age settlement of Le Cayla at MAILHAC. This continued into the Iron Age, and cremation cemeteries have been excavated at ENSÉRUNE and other *oppida* in the region.

The Greeks, and in particular the Romans, brought a new dimension to the disposal and commemoration of the dead. Under Roman law burials were not permitted within the boundaries of towns, and so their cemeteries are always to be found along the roads leading into them. The most spectacular example is probably the many splendid mausolea† that line the Old Appian Way (*Via Appia Antica*) outside Rome.

The more illustrious and affluent dead were interred beneath mausolea in the form of temples or domestic houses, commemorative arches, and columns. These are to be found both in urban cemeteries and in the countryside, on villa estates. The most notable and best pre-served mausoleum is that dedicated to members of the Julian family just outside GLANUM. At LANUÉJOLS the substantial remains of a large cruciform-plan structure with architectural detailing and a dedicatory inscription give an idea of the nature of these monuments. There is another ruined example of what must have been an impressive monument at BIRAN.

The graves of the poorer citizens are not visible nowadays, but these come to light whenever the land in which they were dug is disturbed for new buildings or road-making. Such operations also from time to time reveal the catacombs in which the bodies of Christians were buried.

Archaeological sites in Southern France arranged by Région

Aquitaine

1 Bayonne Roman town walls *Pyrénées-Atlantiques (64)*
Michelin 78/18.

When internal unrest and barbarian incursions threatened the security and economy of southern Gaul in the C4 AD, a fortified settlement was created on a plateau overlooking the confluence of the Adour and Nive rivers, to cover the major route between the Iberian peninsula and Gaul. The D-shaped area enclosed by the walls, which centred on the site of the present-day cathedral, covered some 10 ha. The walls were equipped with twenty-four semi-circular solid bastions, and there were at least three gates. Nothing is known of the layout of the town itself, since this lies beneath the contemporary town of Bayonne. The walls were to serve as the defences of the town throughout the succeeding centuries and were much modified and strengthened. However, substantial remains of the Roman walls and bastions can still be seen incorporated into the later defences, such as the medieval Château-Vieux.
GB Aquitaine 188–201; PBSAF 273.

Berbehère-Brion *see* SAINT-GERMAIN-D'ESTEUIL.

2 Bordeaux Museum with important Roman collections *Gironde (33)*
Michelin 71 or 75. Musée d'Aquitaine: Cours Victor-Hugo; Musée Paléochrétien: Place des Martyrs de la Résistance.

Archaeological finds over many years have shown that this promontory site, on an alluvial terrace that provided the only firm ground in the marshy land at the confluence of the Garonne and Dordogne rivers, was first settled as early as the C6 BC. *Burdigala* lay at the northern end of the Aude-Garonne trade route that was of great importance in the pre-Roman economy of the region. Of especial importance in this trade was the tin of Cornwall. However, it appears to have been a small trading station, no more than 6 ha. in extent.

It was to expand enormously following the Roman conquest, and in particular after the middle of the C1 AD, when it succeeded *Mediolanum Santonum* (Saintes) as capital of the rich province of Aquitania. By the end of the C2 it is estimated to have covered more than 150 ha. When the barbarian incursions at the end of the C3 obliged Bordeaux, along with many other Gallo-Roman towns, to erect strong defensive walls, the circuit of which survived into the C18 and C19, an area of 32 ha. was enclosed, but the extra-mural areas were still very substantial.

Burdigala eventually fell to the Visigoths, but it retained its administrative role. The wealth of the city attracted the attention of marauding groups, among them Saracens (731) and Vikings (848), and it was not until the C11 that it recovered its pre-eminence in the region, thanks largely to the growth of the wine trade.

Although continuous occupation and development over the past two thousand years have obliterated virtually all traces of the Roman city, chance finds, plus some intensive urban excavations over the past decade, have produced indications of its street grid and of some public buildings, such as a mithraeum (temple of the cult of Mithras), a market (*macellum*†), at least one temple, baths, and an amphitheatre, although the site of the forum† had not been identified at the time of writing.

The only visible Roman remains in Bordeaux are some arcades of the C3 amphitheatre, known as the **Palais Gallien**, close by the church of Saint-Seurin. It has been possible to calculate that the amphitheatre measured 133 × 111 m. and had seating for at least 15,000 spectators. It was burned during the barbarian incursions at the end of the C3 and reconstructed; what remained was incorporated in a Renaissance building that was finally demolished during the French Revolution.

The **Musée d'Aquitaine** has excellent collections of archaeological material from Bordeaux and its environs, including some outstanding statuary and rich grave-goods from the Roman cemeteries around the town. Post-Roman material is to be found in the **Musée Paléochrétien**, which is situated beneath the Basilica of Saint-Seurin.

GB Aquitaine 238–60; PBSAF 274–5.

3 Dax   Roman temple remains   Landes (40)

Michelin 78/6–7. Musée de Borda and Crypte Gallo-Romaine: Rue Cazade.

The Gaulish tribe of the *Tarbelli* established a settlement on this low alluvial terrace on the left bank of the Adour river, but it was the Roman passion for thermal springs that ensured its prosperity from the C1 BC onwards. It is thought that it was they who first controlled the famous *Fontaine Chaude*, with its waters gushing out at a constant 64°C, that now stands in the centre of the town. It was to attract many famous visitors in search of health: Augustus is known to have brought his daughter Julia here in the hopes of curing her rheumatism with the aid of the therapeutic water and mud of the town that inevitably received the Latin name *Aquae*. The town became famous and benefited from the munificence of those it helped in the form of fine public buildings.

The ancient town lies beneath the present-day one, to which it bequeathed its street pattern, and so little is visible. It is known that the Roman thermal establishment is immediately below the *Fontaine Chaude*, but nothing of it can be seen now. However, the **Gallo-Roman**

Mithras

An ancient Aryan god of light and truth whose mystery cult is first known from south-eastern Asia Minor in the C1 BC. Mithraism became very widespread throughout the Roman Empire from the second half of the C1 AD, especially among soldiers and merchants. Fine examples of *mithraea* (the shrines and temples dedicated to Mithras) are known from frontier forts as widely separated as Dura-Europus on the Euphrates to Hadrian's Wall. It also flourished in most of the major cities of the Western Empire such as Rome, Aquileia, Bordeaux, and London.

Mithraism, which was confined exclusively to men, had an elaborate ceremonial, and initiates progressed through seven grades to the highest, that of *Pater* (Father). Few details are known of the initiation and other rites, but they are known to have included a form of baptism by immersion, a ceremonial meal, and various forms of ordeal.

Mithraic temples were constructed in the form of artificial caves, partly underground, to evoke the cave in which Mithras slew the bull, symbolic of the victory of life over death. They were rectangular in plan, with a central aisle flanked by raised benches. At the narrow end facing the entrance was a carved or painted depiction of the slaying of the bull. Mithras is shown kneeling on the victim and flanked by his two torch-bearers, Cautes and Cautopates. A dog and a snake drink the animal's blood, corn ears sprout from its tail, and a scorpion is shown attacking its belly.

Although small, judging by the size of the *mithraea*, the cult was influential, adopted by army officers and well-to-do merchants. It is reminiscent in a number of ways of Christianity, to which it was a formidable competitor in the C1 to C4 AD.

Crypt contains the remains of part of what must have been an impressive temple in standard classical style (cf. the Maison Carrée in NÎMES), measuring 30 × 20 m. It is dated to the Severan period (early C3 AD). The Roman ramparts, built in the troubled years of the barbarian incursion in the mid-C3 AD, survived intact until they were demolished over most of their extent in the C19; however, a well-preserved stretch is to be seen in the Parc Th. Denis.

The prehistoric and Gallo-Roman collections of the **Musée de Borda** in the C17 Hôtel Saint-Martin-d'Ags are especially worth visiting.

GB Aquitaine 300–6; PBSAF 278.

Isturitz, Grotte de *see* SAINT-MARTIN-D'ARBEROUE.

Oxocelhaya, Grotte d' *see* SAINT-MARTIN-D'ARBEROUE.

Pair-non-Pair, Grotte de *see* PRIGNAC-ET-MARCAMPS.

4 Prignac-et-Marcamps: Grotte de Pair-non-Pair

Prehistoric cave paintings *Gironde (33)* ★

Michelin 71/8. 20 km. N from Bordeaux on N 10 to Saint-André-de-Cubzac, then 6 km. on D 669.

The remarkable rock engravings in this cave date from the Perigordian phase of the Upper Palaeolithic (*c.*25,000 BC). The forty animal representations are in four main panels—three to the right on entering the cave and one to the left. Most numerous are ibex†, of which there are twelve carvings, followed by horses, aurochs† and other bovines, deer, and mammoths.

GB Aquitaine 268; Rigaud 165–6; PBSAF 297.

5 Saint-Germain-d'Esteuil: Barbehère-Brion Neolithic

dolmen and native settlement *Gironde (33)*

Michelin 71/0. N 20 50 km. N from Bordeaux to Lesparre-Médoc, then D 204E.

The impressive late Neolithic dolmen†, which is all that remains of a chambered tomb (*allée couverte*†), at Barbehère was carefully constructed of small limestone blocks. It has two sections: a short entry area and the funerary chamber proper.

The settlement site at Brion, on the Gironde estuary, was first occupied in the Late Bronze Age, but was abandoned shortly afterwards. It was resettled in the C3 BC, during the Iron Age, and continued in use

▼ General view of site of Saint-Germain-d'Esteuil

until the C3 AD. The native settlement was reconstructed in the early C1 AD as a typical Roman small town, covering more than 10 ha.; a number of examples of a characteristic house layout, consisting of three or four rooms round a small courtyard and probably rising to two storeys, were revealed during the excavations. Among the public buildings identified are a temple and a theatre, both of modest dimensions. It is known that vines were cultivated in the Bordelais region during the Roman period, particularly after the Emperor Probus, who reigned from 276 to 282, ended the restrictions on wine production throughout all the Gauls. The poet and scholar Ausonius, writing in the second half of the C4 AD, praised the wines from his native Bordeaux. It is highly probable that the economy of the town at Brion was linked with viticulture.

PBSAF 298–9.

6 Saint-Martin-d'Arberoue: Grottes d'Isturitz et d'Oxocelhaya Prehistoric cave paintings *Pyrénées-Atlantiques (64)* ★

Michelin 83/3. D 312 from Bayonne to Briscous, D 21 to Hasparran, D 22/D 14/D 251 to Saint-Martin-d' Arberoue (total 30 km.).

The three tiers of caves carved by the river Arberoue through the Massif de Gastelu over many millennia were favoured by Magdalenian hunter-gatherers of the Upper Palaeolithic period (from 20,000 BC), who decorated them with vivid representations of animals, human beings, and religious symbols.

The lowest level, the Grotte d'Erberua, cannot be visited, whilst the rock paintings and engravings in the middle level, the Grotte d'Oxocelhaya, are not on display, although visitors have access to the superb natural forms. In the Grotte d'Isturitz there is a fine collection of rock paintings showing ibex†, bison, horses, bears, and large felines, as well as several representations of men and women. Of special interest are the representations of two deer or ibex, a reindeer, a mammoth, a bear, and two horses engraved deeply into the north face of a large stalagmite in the Grande-Salle. Some of the remarkable collection of objects discovered during excavations are on display in the small site museum, but the majority are in the Musée des Antiquités Nationales at Saint-Germain-en-Laye, near Paris.

GB Aquitaine 143; Rigaud 129; PBSAF 300–1.

Midi-Pyrénées

7 Aventignan: Grotte de Gargas Prehistoric painted caves
Hautes Pyrénées (65)
Michelin 85/20. Take D 938 Montréjeau/La Barthe to Saint-Laurent, then D 26 to Aventignan; the caves are 1 km. SE of the village.

These two caves set into a promontory in the foothills of the Pyrenees were occupied and decorated by hunter-gatherer groups of the Perigordian, Chatelperronian, Aurignacian, and Gravettian cultures (*c.*25,000–20,000 BC). On the lower level, where traces of occupation (animal bones, stone tools) were found on excavation in the large chamber, the walls bear paintings and shallow engravings of animals, including cattle, bison, horses, mammoths, ibex†, and various types of deer.

The caves are, however, especially noteworthy for the vast number of hands outlined in red, yellow, and in one case white paint. For the most part left hands, they have been demonstrated to have been made by no more than a score of individuals, in the earlier rather than later phases of the human occupation. Some of the hands lack one or more fingers; the generally accepted theory nowadays is that the missing fingers were doubled over rather than amputated, as was once assumed.

GB Midi-Pyrénées 663–4; Rigaud 133; PBSAF 306.

Les Bariols *see* SAINT-BEAUZÉLY.

8 Bédeilhac-et-Aynat: La Grotte de Bédeilhac
Prehistoric cave paintings *Ariège (09)*   ★
Michelin 86/5. N 20 S from Foix 9 km. to Tarascon-sur-Ariège, then D 618 NW 3 km. (direction Massat); the cave is reached by a path.

The prehistoric paintings in this cave system in the slopes of the Montagne du Saudour, near Tarascon-sur-Ariège, were first recognized in 1906. There is a series of groups of paintings, all dating from the Late Palaeolithic Magdalenian period (15,000–10,000 BC).

The first main concentration, containing several unusually large (2.40 m. long) black and polychrome paintings, occurs in the Galérie Vidal, 150 m. from the entrance. Further on there is a group of smaller sections of cave containing painted figures, others delineated by finger impressions in the soft clay, and small plastic representations of animals in clay. There are further groups of representations, both two- and three-dimensional, in the main cave right to the end, 700 m. from the entrance.

The interest of this cave lies in the diversity of representational techniques used, and also in the rich artefactual material resulting from successive campaigns of excavation.

GB Midi-Pyrénées 698–9; Rigaud 142–4; PBSAF 306.

9 Biran Roman funerary monument *Gers (32)*

Michelin 82/4. Leave Agen by N 24 travelling W; at Saint-Jean-Poutge take D 939 S, then E after 3 km. to Biran. The monument is shown as 'Tour Gallo-Romaine'.

The remains of a number of massive constructions dating from the Gallo-Roman period are to be found in the countryside of south-western France. One of the best preserved is to be found between Biran and Le Mas close to the D 374 road. Rectangular in section (3.7 × 5 m.) and built of mortared undressed stones, it still stands to a height of over 11 m.; there is a large arched niche on the south side, which would have served to house a statue. It was probably originally sur-mounted by a pyramidal cap, like that on the monument at Saint-Roman-de-Benet (Charente-Maritime). Excavation has revealed that the Biran example, like others that have been investigated, was origin-ally surrounded by a walled enclosure, with which Gallo-Roman tombs were found. The function of these structures appears to have been to serve as funerary monuments, probably for rich land-owning families, and so they have been given the name *piles funéraires* by French archaeologists.

Other examples are to be found some 7 km. to the east of Biran between Boutat and Saint-Lary.

PBSAF 306.

10 Cabrerets: Grotte du Pech-Merle Prehistoric cave paintings *Lot (46)* ★

Michelin 79/9. Leave Cahors on D 653, then take D 662 after 12 km.; after 10 km., turn left at Cahors for Cabrerets.

The lower part of the vast cave system known as the Grotte du Pech-Merle, which dominates the village of Cabrerets, was favoured by people of the Solutrean and Magdalenian cultures of the Upper Palaeolithic period in three distinct episodes between 25,000 and 17,000 BC. The subject matter of the paintings with which they ornamented it com-prises most of the motifs used by Palaeolithic man—animals, human beings, outlines of human hands, and geometric figures—as well as virtually every technique. About 50 m. to the east of the entrance the gallery known as Le Combel has a cave lion and a number of horses, whilst at about the same distance to the west there is a series of decorated panels. In an alcove measuring 7 × 3 m. is to be found the famous 'Black Frieze', which depicts twenty-five animals, among them eleven mammoths, as well as horses, bison, and aurochs†. The sole

Hunters and gatherers

Early human groups followed a nomadic way of life, primarily in search of food. Thus they would follow the great herds of wild cattle and horses, deer, and other sources of meat in their quest for grazing. They would also move around in search of ripening vegetable foods, such as edible fruits, roots, and seeds, which they would harvest and consume. Anthropologists have given societies of this kind the title of 'hunter-gatherers'.

This way of life is still practised at the present time. Aboriginal peoples move in groups across the apparently inhospitable deserts of central and northern Australia, in search of their varied and highly nutritious diet, known colloquially as 'bush tucker'. They have developed sophisticated techniques of ensuring the renewal of their food supplies by means of controlled burning of tracts of bush, so as to encourage regeneration of the flora and maintenance of a varied fauna, both animal and insect. There is evidence that this form of landscape management was being practised as early as the Upper Palaeolithic, and possibly earlier.

The end of the last Ice Age around 10,000 years ago marked a gradual change in human existence. With a more settled climate constant movement became less important, and more permanent settlements developed, which would have been occupied seasonally, for several months at a time. With less pressure to seek food, the people of the Mesolithic (Middle Stone Age) had time to experiment with more sophisticated and diversified forms of tool and weapon manufacture: it is thought that the bow originated at this stage. It is possible that they also began to experiment with the domestication of the more amenable forms of wild life, leading to the introduction of farming and stock-rearing and the advent of the Neolithic.

representation of a fish in the cave is a little further along. Of especial interest are the eight stylized female figures, known as the 'Bison Women'.

Close to the entrance to the cave is the Musée de Préhistoire Amédée-Lémozi, which contains excellent displays and interpretative material relating to early rock art in the region in general and the Grotte du Pech-Merle in particular. A visit to the museum constitutes an admirable prelude to the visit of the cave itself.

GB Midi-Pyrénées 303–4; Rigaud 109–10; PBSAF 307.

11 Cahors   Roman street plan and remains *Lot (46)*

Michelin 79/8.

The territory of the Gaulish *Cadurci* in the difficult hilly country through which the river Lot flows was one of the last parts of Gaul to fall to Caesar's legions. Its capital was where modern Cahors stands, in a

▲ Horses and stencilled hands at the Grotte du Pech-Merle, Cabrerets

sharp meander of the river dominated by steep hills. Its site was easily defensible, but it also possessed a feature of great spiritual significance to the Gallic tribes, a spring, which was dedicated to the goddess Divona. When the town came under Roman rule, the goddess's name and that of the tribe were combined, as so often the case, in the Roman name *Divona Cadurcorum.*

The regular street pattern of the Roman town that grew up is still clearly discernible in the present-day urban plan, but little else can be seen, since the site has been continuously occupied for two thousand years. All that is visible is a small part of the public baths, including the so-called Arch of Diana and some wall footings, incorporated into later buildings situated near the Place de Thiers.

GB Midi-Pyrénées 248–55; PBSAF 310.

Cougnac, Grottes de *see* PAYRIGNAC.

12 Cras: Murcens   Iron Age ramparts   Lot (46)

Michelin 79/9. D 653 10 km. E from Cahors, turn left on D 7.

The massive ramparts that run for nearly 2 km. across part of this plateau of the Causse de Gramat, on the south-eastern edge of the Massif Central, defended this *oppidum*† of the Iron Age *Cadurci* tribe who inhabited this region in the latter part of the first millennium BC. The ramparts can be up to 15 m. thick, and in places still stand to a

Roman baths

Bathing was a very important feature of Roman private and public life, with both hygienic and social functions. Large town houses and country villas and the residences of military and civil administrators and officials were invariably equipped with a suite of baths, whilst every town of any size had a public bathing establishment, and often several. As a result of the rapid adoption of the Roman way of life following the absorption of Gaul into the Roman Empire, baths were essential components of the new urban settlements and country estates.

The layout of Roman baths follows a regular sequence (see p. 23), beginning with a changing room (*apodyterium*), equipped with niches for discarded clothes, benches, etc. The bather passed from here to the cold room (*frigidarium*), where surface dirt was washed off in a cold plunge bath. Suitably prepared, the bather then passed to the cool room (*tepidarium*), heated by hot air that passed through ducts under the floor and was exhausted through hollow tiles (*tubuli*) set into the walls. In this room the bather would remove more deeply ingrained dirt by rubbing himself (or being rubbed) with olive oil, which was then removed by means of a curved bronze scraper (*strigil*). Finally, he moved into the hottest room (*caldarium*), next to the furnace (*praefurnium*) that supplied the hot air. This was usually equipped with a heated plunge bath containing very hot water. In the more elaborate bath houses there was a further room (*sudatorium*) that was heated to even higher temperatures, designed for sweating and similar to a Scandinavian sauna. Having completed his toilet, the bather then returned by the same route, the temperature reducing at each stage.

The public baths were elaborate monumental complexes, ornately decorated with mosaics and mural paintings and often with the facilities duplicated (as in the Baths of Caracalla in Rome) to permit segregation of the sexes. In other cases (e.g. Herculanaeum) there were separate establishments for men and women. They served as meeting places for business and politics, and there is evidence from finds associated with them that wine and food (and other more disreputable services) were available to the bathers. The larger establishments also had large exercise areas (*palaestrae*)—large open colonnaded courtyards.

height of 4 m. When they were excavated in the 1860s evidence was found that the earth and stones were built round a stout timber framework, held together with large iron nails. This was the first certain identification of the *murus gallicus*† described by Caesar in his *Gallic Wars*, many examples of which have been found since that time. Excavations in the interior of the *oppidum* indicate that there was only scattered permanent occupation, which has been dated to the late C2 and early C1 BC.

GB Midi-Pyrénées 411; PBSAF 312.

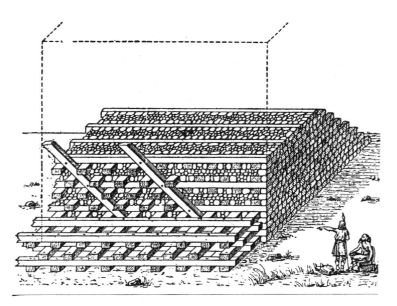

▲ The construction of a *murus gallicus* (from Joseph Déchelette, *Manuel d'archéologie*, vol. iv, Fig. 412; 2nd edn., Paris: 1927).

The murus gallicus

'All Gallic walls are built to the following pattern. Wooden beams are laid on the ground at two-foot intervals along the entire length of the wall, at right-angles to it. These are fastened to one another transversely [by long beams] and are covered with a great deal of rubble; the outer faces of the gaps between the beams are packed with large stones. Once this first course has been laid down and fastened together, another course is laid on top, with the same spacing of two feet [two Roman feet = 56 cm.]. They are, however, not in direct contact with those of the first course, but separated by a course of stones of the same size, so that large stones lock them together. The whole wall is built up progressively in this way to the required height. A structure built up in this way is not lacking in order, being composed of alternate layers of timber and stone, each following straight lines. It provides an effective means of defending a town: the stonework provides protection against fire and the wood against battering rams, which cannot breach or destroy a structure reinforced internally by beams that are usually some forty feet long.'

Caesar: *Gallic Wars* 7. 23

Oppida and hillforts

As early as the Neolithic period, social and political pressures led to the fortification of strategic hilltops by means of deep ditches fronting high earthen banks for defensive reasons. These were generally little more than lookout posts which became refuges for the inhabitants of the surrounding area when an enemy was sighted. They contained few, if any, permanent structures, since sieges were unlikely to have lasted more than a few days.

As prehistoric societies became more complex and competition for territories increased, the defences became progressively more complex, with multiple sets of banks and ditches and elaborate defensive works outside the entrances. The most spectacular example of such a hillfort is probably Maiden Castle in Dorset, which covers some 20 ha. and has triple ramparts over more than half its enceinte.

In the 'Celtic' lands on the continent of Europe these hillforts developed further in the C2 and C1 BC, to which Caesar in his *Gallic Wars* applied the Latin word *oppidum*. These were often much larger than their earlier counterparts, covering as much as 200 ha., and enclosed well-laid-out streets and houses that were permanently occupied. The presence of larger structures indicates that they were administrative and religious centres; they often also contained extensive industrial and craft areas, for the production of manufactured goods of various kinds. Their siting overlooking commercially important rivers and mountain passes shows that they were also important mercantile centres (something confirmed by extensive finds of imported materials during excavations). They were in effect proto-towns, and in some cases became Romanized. In the majority of cases, however, they were abandoned and replaced by new Roman settlements laid out according to classical town-planning precepts with a grid pattern of streets at sites on lower-lying land nearby that were less easily defensible but more closely linked with the main trade routes.

The protohistoric hillforts or *oppida* of Southern France are not as large as those in northern France or Germany, though their functions and layout were largely the same. The *oppida* of L'Impernal (Luzech) or Nages are small by comparison with Alésia or Bibracte, but they are nonetheless defended proto-towns.

Gargas, Grotte de *see* AVENTIGNAN.
La Graufesenque *see* MILLAU.
L'Impernal *see* LUZECH.

13 Laissac: Montmerlhe Pre-Roman earthworks *Aveyron (12)*

Michelin 80/3. 30 km. E of Rodez on N 88, then S on D 95.

The Plateau de Montmerlhe, east of Rodez, is located at an altitude of 920 m. at the edge of the Massif des Palanges, on the left bank of the river Aveyron. There are two prehistoric enclosures on it, the first at the summit and the second on the steep western slopes; the total area enclosed is nearly 150 ha. This was the *oppidum* of the Gaulish *Ruteni* tribe between the late C2 and the mid-C1 BC.

The massive earthworks, 15 m. thick, still stand to a height of 3 m. and are pierced by three original entrances. No trace was found during the excavations in 1985–8 of any internal timber interlacing. The site is accessible by means of a narrow path on the southern side.

GB Midi-Pyrénées 316–17; PBSAF 314.

14 Luzech: L'Impernal   Pre-Roman hillfort *Lot (46)*

Michelin 79/7. D 911 W from Cahors, then S at Labastide-du-Vert, or follow D 8 S of river.

A long-running debate among French archaeologists relates to the identification of *Uxellodunum*, where in 51 BC Julius Caesar fought the last decisive battle of his campaigns in Gaul. This site, in one of the meanders of the river Lot below CAHORS, was fortified with a massive *murus gallicus* (see CRAS above) during the early C1 BC and was largely abandoned in mid-century. Along with the Cras *oppidum†* and another at Vayrac, the L'Impernal site is still in contention as the site of *Uxellodunum*, but the jury is still out.

The material from the C19 excavations is on display in the small museum in Luzech.

GB Midi-Pyrénées 259–60; Bromwich 44 (as Aubenas); PBSAF 315.

15 Marsoulas   Prehistoric cave paintings *Haute-Garonne (31)*

Michelin 86/2. N 117 SW from Toulouse, then D 117 (direction Saint-Girons) to Salies-du-Salat, D 69 to Marsoulas.

The archaeological material in the Grotte de Marsoulas, which is over 60 km. long, is from the Magdalenian phase of the Upper Palaeolithic (13,000–10,000 BC). The rock paintings are largely of bison and horses, plus some deer and ibex†; the representations of human beings are exceptional for this period. The cave is of historical importance, since it was here that the great French prehistorian, the Abbé Henri Breuil, evolved the method of dating cave paintings based on their superposition that has become standard.

Visits to the caves, which are located 1 km. from the village, can be organized by arrangement in Marsoulas.

GB Midi-Pyrénées 675; PBSAF 315.

▲ Le Mas d'Azil

16 Le Mas d'Azil Prehistoric cave paintings *Ariège (09)*   ★★

Michelin 86/4. D 919 NW from Foix, D 119 at Pailhès (20 km.) to Le Mas-d'Azil.

The Mas d'Azil is one of the most spectacular cave systems in the region, as well as a very important archaeological site. The river Arize runs through this great cavern, 420 m. long and an average 50 m. wide, rising in places to a height of 140 m.

Its archaeological significance was first recognized in 1887, when excavations revealed the existence of a cultural group that began around 10,000 BC which provided the bridge between the Late Palaeolithic Magdalenian and the early Neolithic. It was given the name of the Azilian Culture, after the site of Le Mas d'Azil.

The prehistoric rock art was not recognized until the early years of the C20. In terms of the artistic style of the paintings, it dates essentially from the end of the Magdalenian Period and is difficult of access. It consists largely of painted and engraved representations of horses, bison, deer, and felines, along with various symbols and signs. There are also some representations of fish and human masks.

Of greater interest and significance is the remarkable collection of artefactual material resulting from the many excavation campaigns since 1887 on both sides of the river as it flows through the cave and in some of the most remote side passages on the right bank, the latter excavated by Saint-Just and Marthe Péquart in 1937–42. These include hundreds of hunting spears, arrowheads, awls, gravers†, spear-throwers†, 'spear straighteners', and other tools and weapons in stone, bone, and antler, many of them elaborately carved and engraved. This material is to be seen in the **Musée du Mas-d'Azil**, in the heart of the picturesque Ariègeois village.

GB Midi-Pyrénées 516–18; Rigaud 126–8; PBSAF 318–19.

17 Millau: La Graufesenque Roman pottery kilns Aveyron (12) ★

Michelin 80/14. On southern outskirts of Millau, on D 991.

The production of 'Samian ware' (*terra sigillata*†) began at this site at the confluence of the Tarn and Dourbie rivers, near modern Millau, around the end of the first millennium BC. Between 10 BC and *c.* AD 150, more than 500 potters were working here, producing decorated and plain moulded pottery, mostly in the unmistakable red slipware. At first the potters were local craftsmen, producing coarse wares and relatively crude imitations of the Italian ware, but within thirty years of the foundation of the new settlement (known as *Condatomagus*, 'the market at the confluence') the quality of the product soared, presumably with the arrival of Italian master potters.

La Graufesenque and its satellites in the region, such as Le Rozier, Aspiran, and Banassac, dominated the market in red slipware until around 120, when the main production area moved to around Lezoux in the Puy-de-Dôme region of central France. Ceramic production continued at La Graufesenque until the mid-C3, but it became confined to less exotic forms and fabrics, aimed at a local market rather than the Empire-wide market of the industry's heyday.

Extensive excavations took place at La Graufesenque between 1973 and 1981 and the results are on display to the public. The extent of the settlement has not been established, but it is estimated to cover several tens of hectares. The excavated area comprises a group of pottery sites and habitations alongside the junction of two paved streets, which enclose a simple Gallo-Roman temple (*fanum*) of characteristic form, with a square sanctuary (*cella*) enclosed by a portico or ambulatory. There are two phases of the temple, the earlier dating from the first half of the C1 AD and demolished around AD 60, to be replaced by another, similar in form but slightly larger, which survived until the end of the C3.

The houses are simple, with the exception of one with a channel hypocaust†. The workshops consist of large structures for preparing the clay alongside the kiln buildings. The main kiln, which is estimated to have been capable of firing between ten and forty thousand vessels, was a massive structure some 6 m. square and over 8 m. high. The discovery of the debris from a furnace that was fired at well over the operating temperature of 950–1050 °C, causing the carefully stacked pots to fuse together, revealed that the furnaces were used by groups of potters, who entrusted the firing of their products to specialists known as *casidani.*

There is a small display at the site, but those interested in Roman pottery should not miss the excellent **Musée de Millau et des Causses**

*Samian ware (*terra sigillata*)*

The Early Roman Empire in the western provinces is characterized by the red slipware† pottery known as Samian ware† or *terra sigillata*†, which occurs in profusion on sites from the humblest north British farmstead to the great towns and villas of Provence, the Iberian peninsula, and the North African provinces. This type of pottery was particularly favoured by the soldiers of the Roman army, whose forts produce immense quantities of potsherds.

Potters in the Arezzo region of Italy had discovered the technique of producing a fine glossy surface on moulded pottery in the C1 BC, and their products, both plain and ornamented with mythical scenes and other motifs, became the standard tableware of late Republican Italy. The technique was brought, probably by master potters from Arezzo in central Italy (whence the name for their product, 'Arretine ware'), towards the end of C1 BC. They worked first at Lyons and then moved to the Massif Central, where suitable clays and abundant supplies of timber for fuel were available. The most influential of these new pottery centres, which quickly drove the potters of Arezzo out of business, were LA GRAUFESENQUE in southern Gaul and Lezoux, near Clermont Ferrand, in central Gaul. Both were in full production in the early C1 AD, and a measure of their commercial success is given by the unopened crate of La Graufesenque pottery found at Pompeii after the eruption of AD 79.

The central Gaulish industry was eclipsed by that of southern Gaul until the early C2, when competition for the Mediterranean markets from potteries in Spain and North Africa drove La Graufesenque out of business. The Lezoux group of potteries were thus able to dominate the northern market, until they in their turn were superseded by potteries in eastern Gaul, around Trier and Rheinzabern, in the C3. By the end of that century, however, Roman taste had changed and red slipware finally lost its hold on the market.

This type of pottery acquired the name 'Samian ware' from an alleged resemblance to that produced on the island of Samos during the Hellenistic period. That appellation has now largely given way to the name *terra sigillata* (ware with stamped decoration), but that, too, is misleading, since much of the pottery was plain and undecorated. It is now more common to see it described as 'Gaulish red slipware'.

in Millau, which has a magnificent display of the wares of the potters of La Graufesenque.

GB Midi-Pyrénées 541; PBSAF 320.

18 Montmaurin Roman villa *Haute-Garonne (31)*   ★

Michelin 82/15. D 632 75 km. W from Toulouse to Boulogne-sur-Gesse, then 10 km. S on D 633.

During the Late Iron Age a farm was set up in this hilly region. With the advent of the Romans in 121 BC it became the centre of a large estate and a large villa complex was constructed in the mid-C1 AD. This comprised a large but simply decorated residence, with a central courtyard, and an immense rectangular open farmyard round which a number of relatively plain buildings with agricultural functions were disposed.

This establishment was severely damaged by flooding at the end of the C2 and rebuilt in much the same form, only to be slighted during the barbarian incursions of AD 276. In its final form, dating from around AD 350, the residential part of the villa was rebuilt in a very lavish style. The existing rooms were renovated and new wings were added, to create a luxury establishment that must have housed a rich and important proprietor. With nearly 200 rooms, it covered some 4 ha., whilst the entire estate, which comprised more than thirty large agricultural buildings, extended over 1,500 ha. Montmaurin is an outstanding example of the palatial residences that are a striking feature of the Roman economy in the C4 and C5. Its subsequent history is unclear, but it was in all probability looted and burned by the Vandals on their way to Spain and North Africa in the early C5.

The remains of the villa that are now visible date from its final, palatial, rebuilding in the mid-C4. It is organized round three successive courtyards. The spacious D-shaped entrance court has a semi-circular colonnade; there is a small Gaulish sanctuary with a hexagonal *cella†* within one of the segments. From here access is gained to the main building, consisting of a series of richly decorated rooms round a large peristyle†. There is an extensive suite of baths adjoining the rooms to the north-west. The final element is a smaller, apsidal, peristyle in the form of a *nymphaeum†*. Remains of some of the working buildings—stables, forge, carpenter's shop, etc—are set round a farmyard beyond the baths.

Although the buildings have suffered from vandalism and decay over many centuries, they retain abundant evidence of the richness of their decoration in the final stage of the life of the villa, in the form of walls and floors decorated with mosaics, paintings, or marble veneer.

Material from the site is displayed in the small museum, located in the *mairie* of the village.

GB Midi-Pyrénées 579–81; PBSAF 324.

Montmerlhe *see* LAISSAC.

▲ The Montmaurin villa: general view

Roman villas

The Latin word *villa* basically means a rural building, as opposed to one in a town (*aedes*). In modern academic usage it is applied to residential and production establishments in the countryside. These may vary in size and splendour from a simple pre-Roman farm that has been reconstructed using Roman construction techniques, perhaps with the addition of a small bath house, to monumental complexes such as the palatial villas of Tiberius on Capri, Hadrian at Tivoli, near Rome, or Maximian at Piazza Armerina in Sicily.

The phenomenon of the spacious and architecturally developed rural establishment appeared first in the late Republican period in the C2 BC. It quickly spread throughout Italy, and was eagerly seized upon as a model by the upper classes of conquered regions in western Europe as they were absorbed into the Roman Empire. Initially they were associated primarily with agriculture, but regions such as eastern France and Spain have produced examples of villas whose economic basis was mining and metal production. It was not until the C3 AD that the palatial country house, built for the rich citizens of nearby urban communities and with no direct involvement with the local economy, began to appear.

The classic villa consisted of two parts, the *villa rustica* and the *villa urbana*. The former was the working section, with granaries, presses for oil and wine, stables and animal sheds, and accommodation for workers, servants, and slaves. The *villa urbana* was the residential part, with fine rooms ranged round a central colonnaded *atrium*†, and invariably a suite of baths, the symbol of good living. The focal point was the elaborately decorated reception room (*triclinium*), often with a fine view over the surrounding countryside.

Within these basic parameters there was a wide spectrum of designs and layouts. In the more modest establishments the separation between the *villa urbana* and the *villa rustica* was indistinct, the two components being grouped round a single open courtyard. In others the *villa urbana* was almost non-existent, represented by no more than a few better-quality rooms for the use of a manager. In the C5, with the breakdown of the economic structure of the Roman provinces under barbarian pressure, changes in the way of life are graphically illustrated by the abandonment of the more sumptuous rooms and their reuse for more mundane purposes.

19 Montréal: Séviac Roman villa *Gers (32)*

Michelin 79/13. D 15 W from Condom to Montréal; the villa site is 1 km. to the SW.

The Gallo-Roman villa at Séviac is less palatial than that at MONT-MAURIN, covering less than 3 ha. Its layout is simpler, consisting of two courtyards surrounded by rooms with different functions and a sizeable baths suite. It is particularly noteworthy for the fine polychrome mosaic floors, dating from the C3 and C4; the motifs are principally geometric and vegetal, with some rare animal elements.

GB Midi-Pyrénées 324; PBSAF 324.

Murcens *see* CRAS.

20 Niaux: La Grotte de Niaux Prehistoric cave paintings
Ardèche (09)   ★★

Michelin 86/4. S from Foix to Tarascon-sur-Ariège on N 20, then 1 km. SW on D 608.

At Niaux, to the south of Tarascon-sur-Ariège, there is an enormous underground cave network extending for some 14 km. The first 2 km. of this is the Grotte de la Calbière, better known as the Grotte de Niaux, which is generally recognized to be one of the most important and best-conserved prehistoric cave sites in Europe, comparable with the more famous Lascaux group. The cave system had been visited regularly since the C17, but it was not until 1906 that its wealth of prehistoric art was recognized. Since that time it has been studied intensively.

A short way in from the vast entrance, at an elevation of 678 m., there is the first of a number of groups of prehistoric paintings, in this

▼ Painting of an ibex in the Grotte de Niaux

case various symbols leading to two bisons. A little further on the main gallery branches. The right-hand gallery, known as the *Salon Noir*, contains an elaborate composition of bison, horses, and ibex†, together with a salmon, a deer, and a possible rhinoceros. All the designs are in black outline, and they are accompanied by symbols and signs of various kinds, in black, red, and brown. The figures are in groups, occupying concavities in the walls of the cave.

After passing through the *Galerie Profonde*, with its representations mainly of bison, the visitor reaches the *Galerie Cartailhac*, lavishly decorated with aurochs†, bison, and ibex†, and a unique representation of a mustelid (beaver or otter). In a side-passage of the Galerie Profonde there are some forty footprints made by two children. The Galerie Cartailhac is followed by the *Galerie des Marbres*, where the decoration is confined to horses and ibex, and finally the *Grand Dôme* is reached, where horses predominate.

The 1.2 km. long *Réseau René-Clastres*, which was not discovered until 1970, only became accessible after several small underground lakes had been drained. It was in all probability accessible by another route, now blocked, in antiquity. It is of particular interest partly because of the exceptionally good state of preservation of the paintings (bisons, a horse, and a weasel) and partly because of the extraordinary concentrations of footprints of prehistoric adults and children on a long sandbank.

The materials used for producing the prehistoric art of the Grotte de Niaux have been the subject of scientific study. Black and red pigments were produced from charcoal or manganese oxide and red ochre (iron oxide) respectively, with a mineral binder. It was possible from the analysis of the binders used to distinguish two successive periods of occupation of the cave, despite the fact that the stylistic features showed no apparent evolution. It is generally accepted that this art dates from the Middle Magdalenian Period (14,000–10,000 BC).

GB Midi-Pyrénées 592–3; Rigaud 128–9; PBSAF 326–7.

21 Payrignac: Grottes de Cougnac Prehistoric cave

paintings *Lot (46)*

Michelin 79/8. 25 km. N from Cahors on N 20 to Saint-Chamarand, then 14 km. NW through Gourdon.

This cave system is of special importance, since excavations have revealed that its outer part was inhabited by Neanderthal Man during the Middle Palaeolithic period (before 100,000 BC), who left behind some of their characteristic stone tools. However, it was during the Magdalenian period, around 20,000 BC, that part of the interior was richly decorated with representations of animals such as ibex†, deer, mammoths, and horses, as well as many geometrical motifs whose symbolism is not understood. The technique used for the animal paintings

The rock art of the Old Stone Age

With the end of the last Ice Age around 20,000 BC, human groups moved progressively northwards, in pursuit of the herds of wild animals which provided their main source of food, along with wild plants and seeds. These are known to archaeologists and anthropologists as 'hunter-gatherer societies'. At the end of this long segment of human cultural evolution the Magdalenian Culture, the final phase of the Upper Palaeolithic (Old Stone Age) period, produced an astonishing flowering of representational art, now only to be found in caves and rock shelters.

For the most part Upper Palaeolithic art depicts the prey of the hunters—various forms of cattle such as the aurochs†, horses, bison, ibex (wild goats), deer, reindeer, bears, and mammoths, with occasional felines and fish. Representations of human beings are rare, and usually in hunting scenes, although some have been interpreted as depictions of rituals, including burial practices, or armed conflict. Geometric and other non-representational motifs are also known, along with stencilled outlines of hands, often mutilated.

The most common medium is paint, using natural pigments such as charcoal (black) and yellow and red ochre. Techniques vary from simple outlines to detailed naturalistic representations, and there is a vast range of sizes, from very small figures to some which are life-size. Natural differences in the surface of the rock are often utilized so as to give three-dimensional effects.

The other main technique was that of engraving. In its earliest forms, the engraving was crude and deeply incised, but it developed progressively into a delicate art-form. The two techniques can be found side by side in certain caves, and there are rare examples of the two being used together.

There has been much debate about the significance and purpose of Palaeolithic rock art. The ritual message of some paintings and groups is beyond doubt: they depict group activities without any direct relationship with hunting, whilst certain fantastic human figures have been interpreted as shamans or deities in human form. Hunting scenes and wounded animals may represent propitiatory activities designed to achieve success in the chase.

With gradual climatic improvement and the introduction of a settled farming way of life in the Neolithic period, rock art declined and ceased, but it had a revival in the Bronze Age around 2000 BC, when there was a relatively sudden colder episode. The caves of the Vallée des Merveilles and the Vallée de Fontalba in the MONT BÉGO region contain many thousands of engravings from this period, which illustrate a dramatically different society from that of the Upper Palaeolithic.

was a striking one, the main features of the animals being outlined with bold red or black strokes. The four human figures, executed in black, are of interest, since two of them suggest that their subjects had been wounded. The Cougnac material is from the same general culture as that in the GROTTE DU PECH-MERLE.

GB Midi-Pyrénées 409; Rigaud 117; PBSAF 329.

Pech-Merle, Grotte du *see* CABRERETS.

22 Saint-Beauzély: Les Bariols Roman sanctuary *Aveyron (12)*

Michelin 80/14. 10 km. NW from Millau on D 911, then 5 km. on D 30.

This Roman sanctuary was discovered on the Plateau de Lévézou, 20 km. north-east of Millau, during forestry operations. It is an almost square enclosure (22.50 × 20.60 m.), the corners of which are aligned on the cardinal points of the compass. Eight small shrines have been identified; the two oldest, each 2.80 m. square, were destroyed when the later ones were built.

The somewhat sparse finds from the excavations show that this cult centre was in use between the beginning of the C1 and the C4 AD. The material now on display in the Musée de Millau et des Causses gives no indication of the deities to which they were dedicated.

PBSAF 331.

23 Saint-Bertrand-de-Comminges Roman town *Haute-Garonne (31)* ★★

Michelin 86/1. 30 km. N from Bagnères de Luchon on D 125/N 125, then D 22 and D 26.

The territory of the *Convenae* occupied a key area for ancient trade, commanding the navigable rivers flowing northwards and the land routes running east–west. The name of its main town, *Lugdunum Convenarum*, first appears in the *Geography* of Strabo, who interpreted the name of the tribe as meaning 'gang', a derivation that is given some credence by the fact that the town seems to have been founded around 72 BC by Pompey the Great after his campaign in Spain in order to bring some of the more unruly tribesmen in the foothills of the Pyrenees under Roman surveillance. Later, Caesar rewarded the town for not having become embroiled in his campaigns in Gaul and for having taken his side in the Civil War against Pompey by granting Latin citizenship rights to its people.

Under Augustus the town grew rapidly, with the construction of a number of major public buildings, such as a theatre, a temple to the Imperial Cult, and the forum† baths. The commercial importance of *Lugdunum* was emphasized by the construction of a large market hall

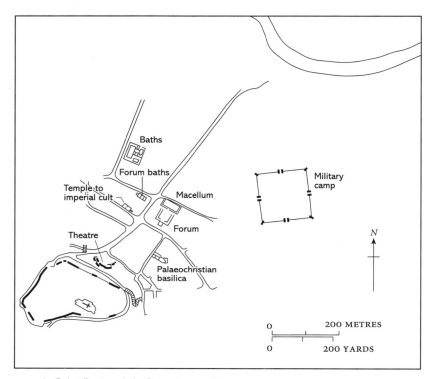

▲ Saint-Bertrand-de-Comminges: plan

(*macellum*†). Legend has it that Herod Antipas, along with his wife Herodias and his daughter Salome, spent their last years in exile in *Lugdunum*.

By the C2 the town had been elevated to the status of a *colonia*† and had spread over more than 100 ha. The number of inhabitants probably exceeded 20,000, their economy being based on mining, agriculture, and forestry in the surrounding territory and on the provision of services for travellers and the collection of customs duties. Its prosperity is witnessed by the frequent reconstruction on more lavish lines of the public buildings during this and the subsequent century. In the C4 its status was further raised when it became the capital of the new province of *Novempopulania*, as well as the seat of a bishopric.

For some reason it escaped the attentions of the marauding Vandals in the early C5. It was to come under a benign Visigothic rule a few years later, but suffered grievously during the internal struggles of the Frankish rulers in the C6. Despite being totally destroyed by fire after a siege in 585, part of the site was quickly reoccupied, to survive through to the present day.

The modern town is on a rocky outcrop overlooking the Garonne valley, where there was in all probability a Gallic *oppidum*† and where the first Roman settlement was founded. The Augustan† planned town lies beneath this hill, in an area that has not been built up and where it has been possible to carry out major excavations since the 1920s.

The centre of the Roman town is denoted by a circular monument, where two ancient routes crossed. It is flanked by the ruins of the **Macellum**†, the commercial heart of the town; this was a large open structure (54.50 × 26.60 m.), with two rows of covered shops around a rectangular central courtyard, the floor of which is covered with a black-and-white mosaic pavement.

To the south of the *macellum* there is a broad open space, surrounded on three sides by a portico, which is believed to have been the **Forum**†. Facing this on the west are the fragmentary remains of the **Temple to the Imperial Cult**. The temple proper, measuring 28 × 15 m., consists of a square *cella*† and a hexastyle *pronaos*† formed of Corinthian† columns on a high podium†; it is surrounded by a precinct wall which encloses an area 40 m. square. Remains of statuary excavated earlier in the present century suggest that a large trophy†, comparable with the intact example at LA TURBIE, stood here, commemorating the victory of the future Emperor Augustus over Mark Antony in 31 BC.

Two large sets of **Public Baths** have been excavated. The Forum Baths, which adjoin the temple precinct, are largely traditional in layout, comprising a cold room (*frigidarium*†) and two hot rooms (*sudatorium*†, *caldarium*†), plus an open-air pool with a sunbathing facility (*solarium*). They were reconstructed and modified several times subsequent to being built in the C1 BC. A second set of baths, built about a century later, lies to the north of the Forum Baths. This is a simpler complex, believed to have been used for some form of sacred therapeutic activity.

The remains of a conventional square **Military Camp**, dated to the C3 AD, have been discovered to the east of the Roman town, but at the time of writing this well-preserved site, with its defensive walls standing in places to 4 m. high, was not open to visitors. The **Theatre** is situated at the foot of the hill on which the modern town is located, and so was within the enceinte of the Roman town, serving to link the earlier upper town with the Augustan† 'new town'. The remains are very fragmentary, since it served as a quarry for building materials for many centuries.

Not far from the theatre are the remains of the C5 **Palaeochristian Basilica**†. In its earliest form this was a modest structure adapted from a private house, consisting of a 20 m. long nave with a short chancel. It was progressively extended to the east and the west, so that in its final phase it was 45 m. long by 13.60 m. wide, with a number of ancillary buildings to north and south. It fell into ruins in the early medieval period, being replaced by the Romanesque† cathedral that dominates the landscape.

GAF 33; GB Midi-Pyrénées 654–63; PBSAF 332.

Barbarians in Southern France

Following the pacification of Gaul at the end of the C1 BC, its citizens enjoyed more than two centuries of peace and prosperity. However, the end of the Severan dynasty in AD 235 marked the beginning of a half-century of chaos. Imperial pretenders followed in rapid succession, taking troops away from Gaul to fight their rivals and leaving it open to raids by both barbarians from outside and dissident groups within. GLANUM never recovered from a brutal sack by Germanic raiders in the 270s.

During the C4 increasingly intense pressure from the barbarian tribes outside the frontiers of the Western Empire resulted in the progressive decay of effective government. The climax came when the Rhine froze in the winter of 406 and hordes of barbarians swept into Gaul. Vandals, Suebi, and Alans spent the years that followed in an orgy of pillage and destruction, before crossing the Pyrenees into Spain.

The Visigoths, originally from Dacia (modern Romania), had moved across the Danube and through the Balkans to northern Italy. They came into Gaul in 412 to turn the balance in a conflict between rival candidates for the Imperial purple. After a short spell in northern Spain they were invited back into Gaul and given the province of Aquitania with its capital at TOULOUSE. Although they were nominally there as allies of the Romans, their autonomy was total, marking the end of the Roman Empire in the west. The Visigoths remained there in Southern France until 507, when the Franks under Theodoric the Great drove them out and laid the foundations of the great Frankish empire of Charlemagne.

24 Saint-Lizier Roman town walls *Ariège (09)*
Michelin 86/3. 40 km. W of Foix on D 117.

The *civitas†* capital of the Gallic *Consaranni* tribe in the Roman period has received very little attention from archaeologists. At the end of the Early Empire the walls of this town perched on a 460 m. high hill that dominated the mineral-rich valleys of this region of the Pyrenees enclosed an area of 3 ha. Today a stretch of *c.*750 m. of massive walls is still visible, defining a roughly oval enceinte; there are twelve bastions surviving, six square ones on the north side and six semi-circular ones on the south. Whilst the upper levels are of medieval date, the lower courses are Roman, in the style of the C4, with courses of brick binding the regular stone courses.

GB Midi-Pyrénées 680–1; PBSAF 333.

Séviac *see* MONTRÉAL.

25 Toulouse Roman and medieval town *Haute-Garonne (31)* ★

Michelin 82/7–8. Musée Saint-Raymond: Place Saint-Sernin.

The region around Toulouse (ancient *Tolosa*) was occupied by the *Volcae Tectosages* some time in the C2 BC. When the Romans established the province of *Gallia Transalpina* towards the end of the century, the *Volcae* entered into a treaty with them and even allowed them to install a garrison in their main settlement, *Tolosa*. However, they broke the treaty during the invasion of the Germanic tribes, the *Cimbri* and *Teutones*, and captured the Roman garrison. This was an unwise move, since their Germanic allies abandoned them to the wrath of the Romans, who quickly incorporated their territory into the province.

By virtue of its situation on the Garonne, Toulouse developed rapidly as one of the most important trading ports in Gaul, handling wine (a major trading material before the Roman occupation, as demonstrated by the enormous numbers of *amphorae*† found in excavations at the *oppidum*† of Vieille-Toulouse) and metals, in which the surrounding

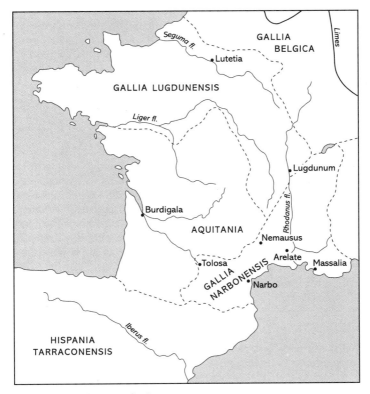

▲ The provinces of Roman Gaul

area is very rich. Its inhabitants were granted the status of Latin citizenship, whilst its strategic and commercial importance resulted in its receiving a 3 km. defensive wall, enclosing 90 ha., one of the earliest in Gaul. The town was to retain its administrative and commercial significance throughout the Roman period, and it survived the barbarian invasions to become one of the most influential cities in medieval and modern France.

The provinces of Roman Gaul

Victory over Carthage in the Second Punic War (218–201 BC) established Rome as the dominant power in the western Mediterranean. At the same time the influence of *Massalia* was significantly weakened, and it became exposed to increasing attacks from its more warlike neighbours. It called upon Rome, with whom it had long had good relations, on several occasions in the C2 BC, and Roman armies were sent to help defeat the attackers, withdrawing afterwards to Italy. In 125 BC, however, when it came under attack from the *Salyes*, the Roman armies under the command of Caius Sextius Calvinus stayed on. He was succeeded in 122 BC by Cnaeus Domitius Ahenobarbus, who finished the successful campaign against the *Salyes* and their allies, the *Allobroges*. Roman colonies were established at AIX-EN-PROVENCE and NARBONNE and the region became known as *Provincia Gallia Transalpina* (Province of Transalpine Gaul).

With the subjugation of the rest of Gaul by Julius Caesar in his campaigns of 58–51 BC, new administrative divisions were established. *Gallia Transalpina* was renamed **Gallia Narbonensis** (after its main town, NARBONNE), the westernmost part being designated an independent province, *Alpes Maritimae*. The rest of the territory was divided into three provinces, corresponding to the 'Three Gauls' defined by Caesar in his *Gallic War*: *Aquitania*, **Gallia Lugdunensis**, and **Gallia Belgica**. There was a significant difference between the Gallic provinces: *Narbonensis* was a senatorial province, in which no legions were stationed, under a civilian governor nominated by the Senate in Rome, whereas the Three Gauls were Imperial provinces with permanent military garrisons and administered by a governor nominated by the Emperor.

During the reigns of Diocletian (284–305) and Constantine (306–37) the whole Roman administrative system was radically changed. *Narbonensis* was divided into three new provinces: **Narbonensis Prima** (the western part), **Narbonensis Secunda** (the eastern part), and **Viennensis** (central Provence and the lower Rhône). Together with *Alpes Maritimae* and three new provinces created from *Aquitania* (**Aquitania Prima**, **Aquitania Secunda**, and **Novempopulana**), they formed part of the new diocese of **Viennensis** or **Septem Provinciae** (The Seven Provinces).

Intensive continuous occupation since prehistory has meant that there is very little of the city's origins to be seen today. The only substantial Roman remains are those of the **Amphitheatre** (*Les Arènes*) in the Saint-Michel-du-Touch-Purpan quarter on the left bank of the Garonne. It is interesting in that it was constructed in brick, the dominant building material in the region right up to the present day.

However, the museums of Toulouse contain excellent collections of prehistoric and Roman material. The **Musée Saint-Raymond**, near the superb **Basilique Saint-Sernin**, one of the greatest examples of Romanesque† architecture in France (begun in 1080), contains an important collection of archaeological material from Toulouse and the surrounding region.

GB Midi-Pyrénées 713–46; PBSAF 334–5.

Languedoc-Roussillon

26 Agde Museums with important classical finds *Hérault (34)*

Michelin 83/15,16. N 112 from Béziers/Sète. Musée Agathois: Rue de la Fraternité; Musée d'Archéologie Sous-Marine et Subaquatique: Mas de la Clape, Cap d'Agde, 4 km. to S, reached by D 32.

Agde contains little evidence of its ancient past, but it is well worth visiting for its museums.

A settlement known as *Agatha* was founded by local merchants as early as the C7 BC to handle trade with Greeks, Etruscans, and Phoenicians on the river *Auraris* (Hérault), on a high point that would be clearly visible to shipping. In its first phase it was no more than a trading station, which most likely provided the base for a colony of foreign merchants. There are indications that it became a dependency of Massalia (MARSEILLES) early in the C4, when the town was given a standard Hellenistic† chequer-board street pattern over some 4 ha. and invested by strong ramparts.

The town lost its important trading role after the Roman conquest, with the development of major commercial centres at NÎMES, NARBONNE, and BÉZIERS. Occupation continued, however, without interruption right through to the present day.

All that is to be seen of ancient Agde in the modern town is the street pattern in the centre, which closely follows that laid out in the C4. However, the Musée d'Archéologie Sous-Marine et Subaquatique at Cap d'Agde contains a fine collection of material, including ships' gear and trade goods, from the region, and in particular the Bassin du Thau. Material from excavations in and around the town are housed in the Musée Agathois.

GB Languedoc-Roussillon 144–9; Bromwich 51–4; PBSAF 340–1.

Ambrussum *see* VILLETELLE.

27 Amélie-les-Bains Roman spa town *Pyrénées-Orientales (66)*

Michelin 86/18. On D 115, 14 km. SW of Le Boulou.

This modern spa town is built over a Roman establishment (possibly called *Aquae Calidae*), of which two elements survive intact, albeit adapted to modern uses. The changing rooms for visitors to the contemporary thermal establishment, known as *Les Thermes romains*, have been inserted into the spacious room (24 m. long, 12 m. wide, and 12 m. high) that has survived intact from the Gallo-Roman period, still retaining its brick barrel-vaulted† roof. Adjoining it is the original swimming pool (*piscina*), heavily restored but still in use, supplied from the hot spring reputed to be sovereign in the treatment of chest complaints and rheumatism.

GB Languedoc-Roussillon 628–9; Bromwich 120.

28 Argelliers: Boussargues Neolithic village *Hérault (34)* ★

Michelin 83/6. N 109/E 11 W from Montpellier, then right on D 111/D 27 at Bel-Air to Montarnaud, N on D 111 to Argelliers.

This small late Neolithic (Chalcolithic) village site lies about 20 km. north-west of Montpellier on a small plateau overlooking a deep ravine. It belongs to the same period and culture as VIOLS-EN-LAVAL. The village is enclosed by a drystone wall in the form of an irregular hexagon, with a circular structure at each corner. In the interior the remains of five houses were discovered, built up against the interior of the rampart. Excavations have shown the circular structures to have been constructed first and then joined together by the walls; the houses were built later. In the centre of the enclosure there is a shaft 1.5 m. deep which opens out into a small room that gives access to a system of passages.

The settlement is believed to have been occupied by no more than two families, and for a short period, since there is no evidence of any rebuilding or repairs. The staple food appears to have been bread made from acorn flour.

Rigaud 107; PBSAF 341.

29 Balaruc-les-Bains Roman spa buildings *Hérault (34)*

Michelin 83/16. N 300 from A 9 to Sète or D 2 from Poussan to Sète.

The little town of Balaruc-les-Bains, as its name implies, possesses hot mineral springs. The Roman love of such springs is well attested and it was no surprise when in 1984 a C2–C3 AD building, tentatively identified as a basilica, was found when work was in progress on the erection of a new school in the town centre. The ornately decorated main room, measuring 12.60 × 14.70 m., had an octagonal basin in it, and there was another rectangular example on the west side in the gallery through which the main room was entered. The remains, consisting of the bases of walls and columns, are well preserved and displayed in a garden.

GB Languedoc-Roussillon 609; Bromwich 82; PBSAF 341.

30 Beaucaire Roman and medieval town *Gard (30)*

Michelin 80/20. Musée de la Vignasse: Rue Roquecourbe.

Where the main Roman road built in the late C2 BC between Italy and Spain, the *Via Domitia*, crossed the Rhône, a settlement grew up on the right bank at Ugernum (modern Beaucaire), close to an earlier *oppidum*† that was flourishing as early as the C7 BC. By virtue of its strategic military and commercial location, this developed into a thriving town, along with its twin town on the opposite bank of the river, *Tarusco* (Tarascon). Its existence as an urban centre continued uninterrupted into the medieval period, when Beaucaire became the site of one of the most important commercial fairs in the region in 1217.

Because of the unbroken evolution of the town over more than two millennia, little is known of the exact form of the protohistoric and Roman towns. Excavations on La Redoute, the hill that dominates the town from the north, have shown this to be the site of the early *oppidum*. This was the site of the former medieval castle, of which only the massive keep known as the *Tour Polygonale* survives. There are substantial remains of Roman buttresses on the southern side of the hill, still standing to a height of 4 m. in places; they were built to resist the pressure exerted from above by a large building, which may have been a fort or a temple.

Archaeological finds from Beaucaire and the surrounding area are displayed in the **Musée de la Vignasse**.

Several Roman milestones on the *Via Domitia* survive *in situ*—near the Marroniers cemetery and on the minor roads leading to the modern D 999 at Redessan.

GB Languedoc-Roussillon 188–95; Bromwich 58–60.

The Via Domitia

When southern Gaul was conquered by the Romans in 121 BC, one of the first acts of the new rulers was to build a road on the alignment of the prehistoric route, the so-called *Via Herculaea*, to enable military units to be moved swiftly into the more unruly regions lying to the west of the new province and beyond, into the Iberian peninsula. The road was named the *Via Domitia* after the first *proconsul* (governor) of the new province of *Gallia Narbonensis*, Cnaeus Domitius Ahenobarbus. It runs from Tarascon (on the left bank of the Rhône opposite BEAUCAIRE) through ARLES, NÎMES, BÉZIERS, and NARBONNE- to LE PERTHUS on the border with the province of Hispania, established eighty years earlier than *Narbonensis*, a distance of nearly 400 km.

---

31 Béziers Museum with important Roman collections *Hérault (34)*

Michelin 83/15. Musée du Biterrois-Saint-Jacques: Caserne Saint-Jacques, Avenue de la Marne.

A settlement was created by Iberians on a hill overlooking the river Orb in the C5 BC to trade with the Greek ports further to the east, but for reasons that are not understood it was abandoned at the end of the C4. The site was not to be occupied for another hundred years, when it was adopted by the local tribe, the *Longostaletes*, as their capital and port.

Some time in the second half of the C2 BC veterans of the VIIth Legion were settled here in what received the resounding title of *Colonia Urbs Iulia Baeterrae Septimanorum*. It became one of the main Roman towns in southern Gaul, and has continued as an urban centre without interruption to the present day.

As a result there are no visible Roman remains, although something of the original street pattern is preserved in the existing plan. It does, however, possess an outstanding collection of material, with a series of striking Imperial portrait busts, in its **Musée Biterrois-Saint-Jacques**.

GB Languedoc-Roussillon 200–16; Bromwich 60–3; PBSAF 342.

Boussargues *see* ARGELLIERS.

Cambous *see* VIOLS-EN-LAVAL.

32 Carcassonne Medieval town with Roman walls *Aude (11)* ★★
Michelin 8/11.

Carcassonne is best known nowadays as the archetype of the medieval fortified hill town (although much of its present-day appearance is due to the restoration work of the great French conservation architect Eugène Emmanuel Viollet-le-Duc in the mid-C19). However, its site on a hilltop dominating the river Aude where it approaches the gap between the two mountain massifs of the Montagne Noire and the Corbières is one that has attracted human settlement from pre-Roman times.

Excavations at Carsac, 2 km. south of Carcassonne (not visitable), have shown that an unusual structure was erected there during the third millennium BC. This consisted of a double fortified enclosure, which has been interpreted as a cult centre. It was reoccupied in the Late Bronze Age, when a hillfort† enclosing some 20 ha. was constructed. It was extended to cover 25 ha., making it the largest example of its type in southern Gaul, and given complex entrances in the second half of the C7 BC. The Etruscan, Massaliote, mainland Greek (Phocaean and Attic), and Phoenician finds demonstrate that this important trade route along the Aude and the Garonne between the Mediterranean and western Gaul was fully operational at this time.

The Carsac *oppidum†* was abandoned in the early C6 and a new hillfort† was built, most probably by the Gaulish *Volcae Tectosages* tribe, at the site of modern Carcassonne. Little is known of its subsequent history until it appears in Pliny's list of Latin *oppida* under the name *Carcaso Volcarum Tectosagum*, although it has been suggested that it served for a time as a fortified Roman encampment. Some inscriptions from the vicinity show that it was elevated in status as *Colonia Iulia Carcasonis* by Augustus as part of his policy of developing the trade between Narbonne and Aquitaine, and thereafter it continued to have an

▼ Carcassonne: plan

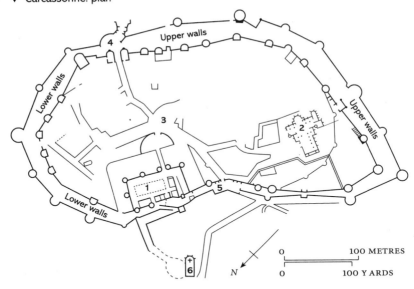

important commercial function. There are indications, however, that it declined in the late C3 or early C4 and lost its privileged *colonia*† status.

The Roman town was taken by the Visigoths in 436 and it served as the base for their conquest of the region, becoming the capital of the Kingdom of Toulouse (later *Septimania*). With the conversion of the Visigoths to Christianity it became an episcopal see. Carcassonne fell to the Franks in the C8, to become the prosperous capital of a county, and later a viscounty, under the suzerainty of the powerful Counts of Toulouse.

Little of Roman *Carcaso* remains visible at the present time. Excavations have revealed a number of buildings, the most notable of which was a large town house with mosaic floors, discovered in 1923 but covered by a later building. The main Roman feature in Carcassonne is the **defences**, whose late Roman origins were first recognized by Viollet-le-Duc.

An area of a little over 7 ha. is enclosed by 1,070 m. of walls. The classic Roman technique for building large walls using courses of small dressed stone blocks with bonding courses of brick and a rubble core, erected on foundations of large undressed stone, can be seen at a number of points. These walls had a rampart walk level at 6–7 m. and were strengthened by the addition of semicircular projecting bastions at intervals. It is in the northern section of wall between the Tour du Moulin de Connétable to the Tour du Moulin d'Avar that the most extensive Roman work is to be seen. Original Roman windows at rampart-walk height can be discerned on the Tour de Saint-Sernin and the Tour de la Marquière. The postern gate alongside the Tour du Moulin d'Avar is the best preserved of several that can be confidently dated to the Roman period.

In addition to the magnificent fortifications with their monumental gates, such as the *Porte Narbonnaise* (4) and the *Porte d'Aude* (5), Carcassonne has much to offer the visitor. The *Château Comtal* (1), built at the end of the C12, is an outstanding example of the military architecture of the period. The *Cathedral of Saint-Nazaire-et-Saint-Blaise* (2) is similar in quality; it consists of a Romanesque† nave that is flanked by aisles and crossed by a transept in early Gothic style.

The historic walled city of Carcassonne was inscribed on the World Heritage List by the UNESCO World Heritage Committee in 1997.

GB Languedoc-Roussillon 248–59; Bromwich 63–7; PBSAF 343–4.

Castellas *see* MURVIEL-LÈS-MONTPELLIER.

Les Castels *see* NAGES-ET-SOLORGUES.

La Caune d'Arago *see* TAUTAVEL.

Le Cayla *see* MAILHAC.

33 Le Cham des Bondons Neolithic standing stones and dolmens *Lozère (48)*

Michelin 80/6–7. The area lies to the north of D 998 between Florac and Pont-de-Montvert, at the foot of Mont-Lozère. Details of the precise locations of monuments can be obtained at the Écomusée du Mont-Lozère at Pont-de-Montvert.

The limestone plateau known as Le Cham des Bondons, lying between the Grands Causses and the granite massif of Mont Lozère, is interrupted by a series of outcrops, known locally as *puechs*. It was settled towards the end of the Neolithic period, and a number of occupation sites have been identified from flint and pottery scatters. The bleak landscape of the present day contains striking evidence of this period of settlement in the form of more than 150 standing stones, some over 5 m. high. The significance of these stones, which are common features over much of Bronze Age Europe, has long been the subject of debate among prehistorians. They are generally considered to have been erected for ritual purposes, and may represent deities or totem figures. The remains of several Neolithic passage graves† (dolmens†) and over thirty Iron Age burial mounds can also be seen.

PBSAF 343.

34 Château-Roussillon (Castel-Rossello) Forum of Roman town *Pyrénées-Orientales (66)*

Michelin 86/19. Take D 617 E out of Perpignan (direction Canet), then right on C 7, follow signs to Château-Roussillon Centre Commercial, fork right under D 617.

The hierarchy of Roman towns

Latin authors use a number of words to describe urban settlements. Whilst some of these, such as the generic word *urbs* (from which the adjective 'urban' derives), have no administrative significance, others are specific in their application.

The highest grade of town in the provinces during the first four centuries of the Roman Empire was the **colonia**. This was applied to a provincial town with a charter (*lex coloniae*) whose citizens enjoyed full citizenship, which was itself divided into two grades. Roman citizenship was originally exclusive to those born in the city or to Roman citizens, but was extended to citizens of the Latin states that it absorbed during the early years of the Republic, while Latin citizenship was granted to other groups in Italy. These conferred voting rights, obligations for military service, and eligibility in varying degrees. With the expansion into Gaul Latin rights were conferred on the citizens of the new *coloniae* that were established, giving them the rank of *coloniae latinae*. In exceptional cases they would be given full Roman citizenship, becoming *coloniae romanae*. Many of the *coloniae* were in fact pre-existing communities upon which this distinction was conferred, whilst others were new creations in which to settle time-expired legionary veterans; because legionaries acquired Roman citizenship automatically on retirement, these were invariably *coloniae romanae*.

The **municipium**, like the *colonia*, was a self-governing community with a charter. Initially it was an Italian town whose citizens had Latin citizenship, but many later received full Roman rights. In the Gallic provinces this rank was accorded to a number of pre-Roman communities, such as MARSEILLES and ANTIBES; Verulamium (St Albans) is the sole example known in Britain. Some sought and were successful in eventual promotion to the rank of *colonia*. Both *coloniae* and *municipia* had an extensive area around them (the *territorium*) which was an integral part of the town, and in which the more affluent citizens owned farmland with country houses (*villae*).

Civitas, the basic meaning of which is 'citizenship', is a word used to denote an urban community without Roman or Latin rights (native or *peregrini*), of which there were many thousands in the provinces. Some of them, however, had special functions as the administrative centres of a former tribal territory—the so-called *civitas capitals*.

There was a hillfort† of the powerful Iberian *Sordi* tribe on a low plateau overlooking the Tet river as early as the C6 BC (and possibly earlier): local tribes assembled there, when the settlement was known as *Ruscino*, in 218 BC in a vain attempt to block Hannibal's army on its way to Italy. The tribal capital was elevated to high status as *Colonia Iulia Ruscino* soon after the region came under Roman rule, since it occupied a key point on the *Via Domitia*. During the Early Empire, it flourished, being embellished with public buildings—forum†, baths, basilica†, etc. However, for reasons that remain obscure, the town fell into decline in the later C2 and was progressively abandoned.

The excavated area open to the public covers the forum†, dated to the Augustan period (20–25 BC). It is typical of the urban public spaces in the towns created at this period in its relatively small size. There are porticoes on three sides, the fourth being closed by a three-aisled basilica†, with a three-roomed annex (possibly a *curia*†) adjoining it. Within the open space there are three statue bases; small shops open into the portico. More than forty inscribed stones were found during the excavations. Recent excavations have revealed the remains of some elegant houses from the same period, and also the remains of pre-Roman dwellings of the C6–C3 BC.

GB Languedoc-Roussillon 543; Bromwich 68–71; PBSAF 360.

La Clape *see* LAROQUE-DE-FA.

Les Cluses *see* LE PERTHUS.

Col des Panissars *see* LE PERTHUS.

Les Courtinals *see* MOURÈZE.

Hannibal and the Second Punic War

Following the defeat in the First Punic War (264–241 BC), which resulted in the loss of Sardinia and Sicily to Rome, Carthage sought revenge. To pre-empt a Roman assault on its possessions in Spain, a large army (variously estimated at 35,000 and 100,000 men) under the command of the brilliant general Hannibal crossed into Southern France in 218 BC. By April he had reached the Rhône, brushing aside any resistance from the native inhabitants or the Greek colonies of *Massalia* (whose influence in the region declined significantly, to the eventual advantage of Rome). To avoid a pitched battle with a small Roman force of two legions (some 10,000 men) commanded by the consul Cornelius Scipio, he then turned northwards up the Rhône valley seeking another route into Italy.

He decided to take his army across the Alps in one of the epic marches of history, though by the time he reached Italy his forces had been reduced to no more than 25,000 men. There followed a series of victories over the armies sent against him, culminating in the crushing defeat of the Romans at Cannae (216). However, despite his success in attracting the support of enemies of Rome such as Capua and Tarentum, Hannibal was unable to exploit his advantages against stubborn Roman resistance. His army was driven to Calabria, on the toe of Italy, and eventually forced to retire, albeit undefeated in battle, to North Africa in 203, where the Carthaginian forces under his command were to be overcome at the final battle of the Second Punic War at Zama in the following year.

Ensérune *see* NISSAN-LEZ-ENSÉRUNE.

Les Fades *see* PÉPIEUX.

35 Gailhan: Plan-de-la-Tour   Iron Age settlement *Gard (30)*

Michelin 83/7. W from Nîmes on D 40 to Sommières, then N 10 km. on D 35.

In the late C6 BC a small settlement of wooden houses was established on a limestone outcrop in the present-day commune of Gailhan. Some time in the succeeding half-century the crest was encircled by a retaining wall and the interior was levelled up so that a new, more permanent settlement could be constructed in the form of a courtyard house covering some 100 sq. m. It was built in local stone mortared with clay and roofed in clay mixed with straw.

The excavated building has been reconstructed so as to give an impression of life in Languedoc in the Early Iron Age.

GB Languedoc-Roussillon 614; PBSAF 346.

36 Javols   Remains of Roman town *Lozère (48)*

Michelin 76/15. NW 25 km. from Mende on N 106 to Saint-Amans, then D 3 and D 50 to Javols; the ruins are just to the north of the village.

Little is known about *Anderitum*, the central settlement of the Gaulish *Gabali* tribe in the region lying to the north of the Cevennes. Like many other tribal centres, it was quickly Romanized after the conquest. Excavations over many decades have revealed that this was a flourishing town, with baths, an aqueduct†, and at least one temple. It was destroyed by a disastrous fire at the end of the C2 AD and abandoned by the surviving inhabitants, to be occupied again only for a short time in the early C5.

The remains of a number of modest houses and shops, with a small square and streets, are on display near the cemetery in the present-day village of Javols, which covers much of the Gallo-Roman town.

GB Provence 623; PBSAF 346.

Lamalou, Dolmen de *see* ROUET.

37 Lanuéjols   Roman mausoleum *Lozère (48)*

Michelin 80/6. Take D 25 from Mende to Langlade (8 km.), then D 21 (4 km.) to Lanuéjols.

The region around Mont Lozère was rich in iron and copper ores, and also contained some areas of fertile land suitable for intensive agriculture. It appears to have been divided up into a number of large villa estates. The rich proprietors of one of these were responsible for the erection of the exceptionally well-preserved mausoleum† dating from the C4 AD on the outskirts of the present-day village of Lanuéjols. It is

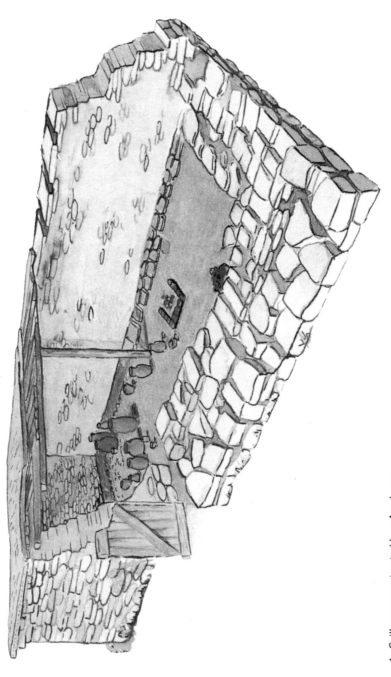

▲ Gailhan: reconstructed Iron Age house

▲ Lanuéjols: the mausoleum

cruciform in plan, constructed of large dressed stones (*grand appareil*); the central chamber (*cella*) is flanked by three rectangular niches. It still stands to a height of 7 m., and is estimated to have been at least 5 m. higher in antiquity. There is a dedicatory inscription on the massive lintel over the large entrance, commemorating the two sons of L. Julius

Bassianus and his wife, Pomponia Regula. Nearby there is the plinth of a second mausoleum† of similar proportions.

GB Languedoc-Roussillon 414; PBSAF 347.

38 Laroque-de-Fa: La Clape   Megalithic cemetery *Aude (11)*

Michelin 86/8. D 611 SW from Lézignan-Corbières to D 613, turn right and continue about 25 km. to Laroque.

This cemetery, which dates to the later Neolithic period (early third millennium BC), consists of eight tombs located on a prominent hill. Several types of grave are included in the group—corridor tomb, rectangular cist grave†, polygonal chamber—and all contained multiple burials.

Rigaud 112–13.

39 Lattes   Roman town *Hérault (34)*

Michelin 83/7. 5 km. S of the centre of Montpellier, from D 996.

There has been human settlement on the site of Lattes since the Middle Neolithic (fourth millennium BC), since this was a favourable habitat on the chain of lagoons along the Mediterranean coast of Languedoc, providing abundant food from the sea. By the C6 BC it had been transformed into a trading settlement, since Greek, Etruscan, and Carthaginian shallow-draught seagoing vessels could utilize channels through the sand-bars. Occupation spread more than 400 m. along the left bank of a branch of the Lez river (now dried up), and the limestone ramparts that were built around this time enclosed some 4 ha.

The town, known in antiquity as *Lattara*, flourished during the early Gallo-Roman period, but changes in the coastline led to its being replaced as a commercial centre by neighbouring Maguelone (*Magalona*).

Within the Iron Age enceinte, a formal chequer-board plan was laid out, based on two wide streets at right-angles to one another. This became more elaborate as contact with the rest of the Mediterranean world developed, with cross-streets forming *insulae*†. The houses, built of clay with only the foundations and lowest courses of stone, varied considerably in size, though only one room was used as living space, the others being for storage or craft activities. The site contains no spectacular remains, although it does give an interesting picture of what was essentially a working port. The remarkable range of imported materials found during excavations in Lattes are displayed in the **Musée Archéologique** in Lattes.

GB Languedoc-Roussillon 526; Bromwich 74–6; PBSAF 347–8.

Roman town planning

When the Romans added Gaul to their growing empire, they found a country in which, apart from the Greek colonies on the coast, the concept of urban living was in its infancy. The only human settlements of any size were to be found on the fortified hilltops (*oppida*), in which there was little more than a rudimentary attempt at deliberate spatial planning. All this changed when the Romans introduced the classical Mediterranean town layout, which is to be found over much of the Western Empire.

This is the grid pattern of streets intersecting at right-angles, generally attributed to the Greek, Hippodamus of Miletus (Asia Minor), who lived in the first half of the C5 BC; his best-known work was the town plan of Piraeus, the port of Athens. The Hippodamian model was taken to Italy by the Greek colonists and adopted by the Romans when they extended their rule over the entire peninsula, and eventually to most of western Europe.

The foundation of the grid is provided by two main streets intersecting at right-angles, the *cardo* and the *decumanus*; they connected with the main roads linking the town with its neighbours. The forum, where the main administrative, religious, and commercial buildings of the town were located, was generally situated at the intersection of the two main streets. Other streets were laid out parallel to the *cardo* and *decumanus* at set intervals, which ranged widely from 50 m. to as much as 200 m. Their intersections created blocks of land, known as *insulae* ('islands'), on which houses, shops, and other public buildings (baths, minor temples, etc.) were built. Some *insulae* were sometimes occupied by a single luxurious urban villa, built by one of the wealthier citizens, but most were divided up into smaller plots.

If the town boasted a theatre, this was usually located within the street grid, but amphitheatres were always outside the main urban area, outside the walls that were built round most of the Gaulish towns following the barbarian incursions in the late C3 AD. The more offensive trades and crafts, such as tanning and smithing, were also usually banished to areas removed from the residential area.

40 Loupian: Villa des Près-Bas   Roman villa *Hérault (34)*   ★

Michelin 83/16. On N 113 30 km. SW from Montpellier

The prosperity of the Roman province of *Gallia Narbonensis* is reflected not only in its towns, but also in the many villas to be found in some of the most desirable stretches of the coast and its hinterland. The Villa des Près-Bas, situated on the coast of the lagoon known as the Bassin de Thau, is one of the finest (and earliest) examples of the palatial villas that were built in imitation of those in Italy.

From its inception in the early C1 AD, Près-Bas was conceived on a grand scale, unlike contemporary establishments, which were often no

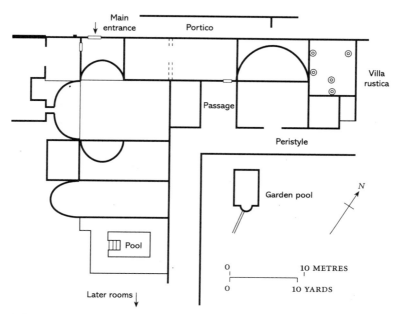

▲ Loupian: plan of the Villa des Près-Bas

more than Romanized versions of the Iron Age farms of the region. Even at this stage the living quarters of the proprietor and his family (the *villa urbana*†) were decorated with marble facings and mosaic floors, as well as a substantial bath suite. In the C4, like others in the region such as MONTMAURIN, it was comprehensively remodelled and extended. It was to be abandoned progressively in the C5, as Roman society in the region disintegrated under barbarian pressure.

In its final, palatial phase the *villa urbana*, which covered half of the complex, may have been as much as 100 m. square, although much of it is still unexcavated. In its remodelled form it was reorientated round a central peristyle† garden. Several of the rooms opening out on the garden have apses (in one case three, reminiscent of the contemporary Villa del Casale at Piazza Armerina in Sicily). However, the glory of the villa resides in its mosaic floors—more than 200 sq. m. of mosaics, with largely geometric or vegetal designs (although there are two sets of representations of personified seasons) in brilliant colour. Scholars have identified the motifs as deriving from more than one region of the Roman Empire, since there are echoes of designs from Antioch and Syria.

The *villa rustica*† section, which housed servants and estate workers, along with kitchens, store-rooms, and workshops of various kinds, adjoins the residential area, and parts of it have already been revealed,

▲ Loupian: detail of mosaic

including a room containing *dolia* (gigantic ceramic vessels) used for storing wine, oil, or grain. Near the edge of the Bassin de Thau the remains of a large structure have been found which has been tentatively identified as a warehouse connected with the villa's own harbour.

GB Languedoc-Roussillon 607–8; Bromwich 78–82; PBSAF 349.

41 Lunel-Viel Small Roman settlement *Hérault (34)*

Michelin 83/8. On N 113 between Nîmes and Montpellier.

The small Roman settlement (*vicus*) just to the south of the present-day hilltop village of Lunel-Viel lies on the route of the Via Domitia; it covered less than 3 ha. It was laid out on regular lines and the simple single-roomed houses were built of clay with beaten-earth floors. There was, nevertheless, some element of Roman urban life in the form of a set of public baths and a large buttressed building, which may have been a courthouse. Archaeological evidence suggests that this was a C1 AD foundation and that it continued to be occupied continuously into the Middle Ages, when the centre moved to the present village.

Finds from the site, and in particular from the cemeteries dating from the C1 to the medieval period that have been excavated, are in the **Musée Archéologique** in LATTES.

GB Languedoc-Roussillon 399; PBSAF 352.

42 Mailhac: Le Cayla Pre-Roman hillfort *Aude (11)*

Michelin 83/13. 30 km. W of Béziers on D 11/D 5 to Mirepeisset, then 3 km. NW on D 605.

Le Cayla, the isolated flat-topped hill at Mailhac, west of BÉZIERS, was continuously occupied from the Late Bronze Age until it was deliberately destroyed and its defences razed around 75 BC.

Successive excavations have identified at least six distinct phases of permanent settlement on this easily defensible site. The first, in the Late Bronze Age (C7 BC), saw the summit covered with small huts built in wattle-and-daub†, with a large cemetery at the base of the hill, where over four hundred graves have been excavated. A new settlement was created in the C6 BC, when a substantial stone defensive wall was raised. Finds from this phase include a considerable quantity of pottery imported from Etruria and Greece, indicating regular contacts with the Greek trading communities of southern Gaul.

This settlement was destroyed by fire: it has been suggested that this was a consequence of the Celtic migrations of the C5 BC. However, it was quickly rebuilt, this time in stone and unfired brick, and it continued to flourish right down to its destruction following the Roman conquest of the region. During this period the artefactual material reflects the volume and extent of trade between the Mediterranean and the Celtic lands to the north.

There is a good site museum.

GB Languedoc-Roussillon 418–19; PBSAF 352.

43 Montferrand Roman posting station *Aude (11)*

Michelin 82/19. On north side of N 113 Carcassonne–Toulouse, 12 km. NW of Castelnaudary.

One of the main migration and trade routes in antiquity went from the valley of the Aude to that of the Garonne through the so-called *Porte de Carcassonne*. The highest point on this route, the Seuil de Naurouze, is commanded by the village of Montferrand, which has been tentatively identified with the site of the ancient posting station of *Elesiodunum* on the Roman road from CARCASSONNE to NARBONNE. The remains of a bath house which probably belonged to a *mansio*† are visible beneath those of the palaeochristian† chapel near the church of Saint-Pierre-d'Alzone, 1 km. north-west of the present-day village.

GB Languedoc-Roussillon 382–3; Bromwich 121.

44 Mourèze: Les Courtinals Prehistoric settlement *Hérault (34)*

Michelin 83/5. 7 km. W of Clermont-l'Hérault on D 908 and D 8.

The landscape around the old village of Mourèze is a spectacular one of contorted rock formations. There was human settlement here at various

Roman roads

Roads were an essential component of the administration of the Roman Empire. They provided a carefully laid-out network of communications linking civil settlements and military establishments. They served primarily as means of rapid transit for military units in times of crisis and for Imperial dignitaries and civil servants in the course of their duties. However, they were also heavily used by ordinary citizens—by travellers from one town or region to another on business or pleasure and by merchants with their goods for sale in the urban centres or transhipment by river or sea to distant markets.

Posting stations (*mansiones*) were established, primarily for the Imperial officials and couriers, at intervals of roughly 40 km., the equivalent of a normal day's journey. These provided accommodation and food, along with changes of horses, at the expense of the towns through whose territories they passed. In the more populous areas these often developed into small towns.

Even the most cursory study of a map of Roman roads throws one salient feature into high relief, the long straight stretches of road, often many kilometres in length, and this is confirmed on the ground and, most particularly, from the air. The Romans were the great engineers of antiquity, and their surveyors were capable of laying out alignments of this kind using the simplest of equipment and often through thickly forested areas. Only in the most rugged uplands do Roman roads acknowledge the problems of terrain and adopt more sinuous courses, following the contours of the mountains (as, for example, where the *Via Domitia* crosses the Pyrenees).

The main roads were built and maintained by the Imperial administration. They were generally around 8 m. wide (though considerable variations can be observed), with ditches on either side, to ensure good drainage of the road surface. Where a road crossed unstable or swampy land, it was raised on a causeway (*agger*), often laid on brushwood or even wooden piles. The make-up of the roads themselves was carried out with great care: a base of large stones was overlaid by successive courses of gravel or small stones, depending on the materials available locally, and these were set in clay to bind them together and provide a firm surface.

As in modern Europe, there were several grades of road, ranging from the great Imperial highways down through local roads (often more winding and less elaborately prepared) to mere trackways with rudimentary surfacing.

times during prehistory, due to the security afforded by the natural enclosure of about 0.5 ha. known as Les Courtinals. Excavations have revealed that humans first came here in the Neolithic period. The site was occupied again during the Bronze Age, and then during the Iron

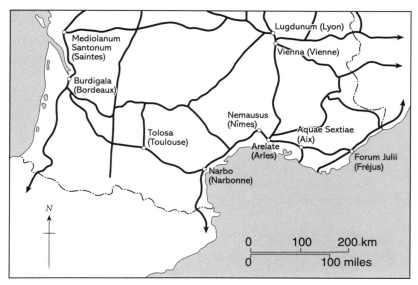

▲ Roman roads in Southern France

Age, around 450 BC. It was during this last period of occupation that a house, covering some 12 sq. m., was constructed using two natural stone walls, which were closed off by low stone walls. Inside there are the remains of a hearth, a bench made of stones and clay, and a structure that has been identified as having been used for drying grain.

GB Languedoc-Roussillon 316–17; PBSAF 353.

45 Murviel-lès-Montpellier: Castellas Iron Age hillfort

Hérault (34)

Michelin 83/6. 10 km. W of Montpellier on N 109 to Bel-Air, then 4 km. S on D 102.

The Castellas *oppidum*† is one of many founded in the C2 BC by the Iron Age peoples of this region, as the concept of urban culture slowly developed, influenced by the Greek settlements along the coastal strip. It served both as a central market and administrative centre and as a defended centre in a period of general unrest. It appears to have been abandoned towards the end of the C1 BC, as its functions were superseded by new Roman urban centres nearer the Mediterranean and on the major land routes.

When the settlement took on a more defined form and function, an area of 22 ha. was enclosed by a substantial rampart built of undressed limestone blocks. The main entrance was from the east, where the gate was protected by a massive stone tower; a smaller gate and two posterns gave access through the northern rampart.

Excavations over more than a century have revealed the remains of small houses in both native and Roman style. The main discovery was that of a large temple, built on the highest point of the promontory. It was built of dressed limestone from the region of Nîmes and decorated with various types of marble from the surrounding area. A considerable quantity of statuary and architectural fragments was found on the site and is on display in the **Musée Municipal** in the *mairie* of Murviel-lès-Montpellier.

GB Languedoc-Roussillon 470; PBSAF 353.

46 Nages-et-Solorgues: Les Castels Iron Age hillfort
Gard (30)   ★
Michelin 83/8. D 40 W from Nîmes to Langlade, then D 14/D 137.

Occupation of this commanding site on the hill of Castels dates from the later Iron Age (early C3 BC). Around the middle of the C3 the settlement was brought within the territory of the historically attested *Volcae Arecomici.* The initial rectangular enclosure defined by massive earthen ramparts was largely overlaid by the defences of the new *oppidum*†, with

▼ Nages-et-Solorgues: the ramparts of the *oppidum*

strong bastions and an ordered town plan inside. Imported materials found during excavations indicate that the *oppidum* played an important role in trade between Italy and central Gaul.

The town was greatly enlarged and given a new defensive wall in the later C2 BC, following substantial damage attributable to the Roman conquest of 121 BC, but it began to decline shortly afterwards: considerable sections within the new enclosure were not built upon and existing buildings gradually fell into decay. It appears to have been abandoned completely at the beginning of the C1 AD, when the square temple (*fanum*) built around 70 BC was destroyed by fire; according to the excavators, this was a deliberate act on the part of the departing occupants, to symbolize the end of the town decreed by the intensive Romanization of Augustus.

The *oppidum* of Les Castels is noteworthy for its massive surviving defences, which still stand in places to nearly 5 m. in height. They are constructed of parallel, irregularly coursed drystone† walls with rubble cores; in places the addition of internal reinforcements gives them an overall thickness of some 7 m. The semicircular towers and bastions are built using the same technique.

Within the enceinte the regular town plan can be discerned: it is based on elongated *insulae*† of classical type running downhill. In the earlier phase the dwellings were small single-roomed structures, extended considerably in the later period. It is noticeable that the layout in the latest quarter added to the town is less regular, with many vacant plots that often served as rubbish dumps.

The finds from the excavations are on display in the *mairie* of Nages.

GB Languedoc-Roussillon 516–17; Bromwich 109; PBSAF 354.

47 Narbonne   Roman remains and museum *Aude (11)*

Michelin 83/14. Musée Archéologique: Place de l'Hôtel de Ville; Musée Lapidaire: Place Lamourgier.

The area of modern Narbonne and its islands has been inhabited by humans since early prehistory. The first permanent settlements appeared during the Neolithic period, starting in the late fourth millennium BC, around the lagoons between the present-day city and the Mediterranean—at Armissan and Peyrac-sur-Mer, for example. Communities based on fishing were established in the Bronze Age in the islands: the village at Roc de Conilhac has been dated to 1300–850 BC.

The creation of trade links between southern Gaul and the Mediterranean in the later C7 BC, following the establishment of the Greek settlement at Massalia, resulted in the nucleation of these scattered rural communities into trading settlements. A hillfort† was constructed at Montlaurès, 4 km. to the north-east of the present city, and this has been identified as *Nar(b)o*, the capital of the Ligurian *Elisyces* tribe, whose influence spread over a large region (cf. Le Cayla de MAILHAC, BÉZIERS, and NISSAN-LEZ-ENSÉRUNE) and who were to be conquered in the late C3 BC by the *Volcae*. Excavations testify to the importance of Montlaurès as a trading centre: even British tin was reaching the Mediterranean on the Garonne–Aude route in this period.

Following the successful outcome of their war against the *Arverni* and the *Allobroges*, the Romans were attracted by the commercial power of Narbo, and it was chosen as the capital of the first Roman province to be established outside Italy, *Gallia Transalpina*, in 118 BC. The new town of *Colonia Narbo Martius* was set up below the earlier hillfort, with better access for shipping. It was populated by two thousand settlers from Umbria, Picenum, Latium, and Campania, who were allocated plots of land within the town; the indigenous inhabitants were not dispossessed completely, being allowed to retain their farmlands around the earlier *oppidum*†.

With the systematic reorganization and stabilization of the land routes in southern Gaul, Narbonne achieved a commercial and political pre-eminence that it was to retain until the collapse of the Western Empire. It played a key military role during the invasion by the *Cimbri* (104 BC), Pompey the Great's campaigns in Spain (77–76 and 74–73 BC), those of Crassus in Aquitaine (56 BC), and above all Caesar's campaign against the revolt of Vercingetorix (52 BC). The town's service was recognized by Caesar in 45 BC, when he refounded it as *Colonia Julia Paterna Narbo Martius Decumanorum* and settled the veterans of his favourite X Legion there (*Claudia* was added to the name later by the Emperor Claudius).

It was to Narbonne that Augustus summoned the whole of Gaul in a general assembly in 27 BC when he had assumed the Imperial purple, for the purpose of organizing the administration and census of the provinces. Five years later he further honoured the town by giving its name to the province, *Narbonensis*. The town prospered greatly during the Early Empire, favoured by successive Emperors, notably Antoninus Pius, who was responsible for a massive reconstruction programme following a disastrous fire in the 150s. It became the principal port for the whole of Gaul, trading in grain, wine, pottery, and many other commodities. During the C3 it began to lose some of its commercial importance as trade moved towards ARLES and the Rhône, and the situation was aggravated by the barbarian incursions of the late C3. Their impact can be judged by the fact that the walls built at that time enclosed no more than 16 ha. It was at this period that Diocletian reduced its administrative role by dividing Narbonensis in two, only the south-western part (*Narbonensis Prima*) being governed from Narbonne. Doubtless by reason of the many people from other parts of the Empire that its trade attracted, Narbonne adopted Christianity early, and it was accorded metropolitan rights in the C5.

The Visigothic invasion of 412 saw Narbonne seized the following year, but the occupation was short and, despite several sieges, it remained in Roman hands until 462, when it was yielded to Theodoric II. It did not lose its administrative importance, however: in 507 it became the capital of Septimania, which formed part of the Visigothic kingdom of Spain. It was taken by the Arabs in 721, but returned to Christian Frankish rule in 759. From then on its administrative role declined, but its religious importance grew, especially in the Carolingian period. A great deal of excavation has been carried out at Narbonne for more than a century, but very little of the Roman town is now visible.

Like most Roman towns, it has a chequer-board layout. A number of public buildings, such as the 14,000-seat amphitheatre, forum†, municipal baths, and a temple dedicated to the Imperial Cult, have been recorded and then built over. The only important site that can be visited

▼ Narbonne: map, showing museums and Roman remains

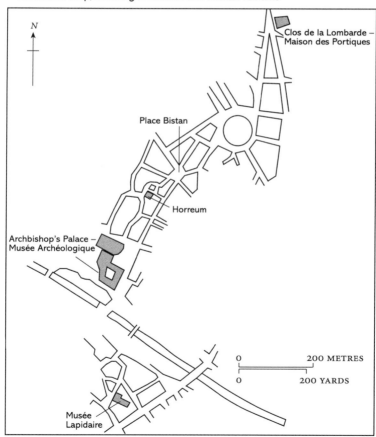

N

Clos de la Lombarde –
Maison des Portiques

Place Bistan

Horreum

Archbishop's Palace –
Musée Archéologique

Musée
Lapidaire

0   200 METRES

0   200 YARDS

▲ Narbonne: gallery in the *horreum*

is the **Horreum** (grain warehouse), now open as a museum. Two of the galleries around the rectangular courtyard, each divided into a series of individual rooms, give an indication of the scale of trade in the Roman period. The whole complex, which was set 3 m. below the original ground level, covers 51 × 38 m.

In the Place Bistan some fragments of columns from the forum have been set up against a modern wall painted with a scene illustrating Roman construction techniques. An urban area to the north-west known as the Clos de la Lombarde displays the foundations of a high-quality town house known as the **Maison des Portiques**. It is partly overlaid by the ruins of a palaeochristian basilica†. The crypt of the Romanesque-Gothic transitional Basilique Saint-Paul, which contains several Roman sarcophagi, is considered to have been the mausoleum† of a wealthy family.

There are several museums with archaeological collections in Narbonne. The **Musée Archéologique** is part of the medieval Archbishops' Palace and has prehistoric and Gallo-Roman finds from the town and its surroundings. There is a large collection of monumental stonework in the **Musée Lapidaire**, which is housed in the former church of Notre-Dame de Lamourgier.

GAF 8; GB Languedoc-Roussillon 479–88; Bromwich 83–93; PBSAF 354–5.

The Imperial Cult

During the closing years of the Roman Republic the state religion of Rome, dedicated to the worship of the Capitoline triad of Jupiter, Juno, and Minerva, fell into disrepute because of the corrupt and cynical way in which it had been misused for their own ends by Julius Caesar and others. It was for this reason that, on becoming Emperor in 27 BC, Augustus chose to identify himself and the Imperial family with the state religion and the old Roman values that it represented. By 12 BC this had developed into the Imperial Cult, worshipping together the divine embodiment (*genius*) of the city of Rome and the Emperor, and in due course other members of the Imperial family. By the mid-C1 AD Emperors were being deified in their lifetime. Some of them (notably Caligula, Commodus, and Elagabalus) demanded that they be accorded priority over all other deities, though most of the others recognized the cult for what it was, a valuable adjunct to civil government in the provinces. The cult was not to lose its impact until the formal adoption of Christianity by Constantine I (the Great) in 325.

The Imperial Cult was especially strong in Gaul. In 12 BC Drusus dedicated a temple to Rome and Augustus at *Lugdunum* (Lyons) that had been built by sixty tribes from all three Gaulish provinces. Ceremonies attended by delegates from the three provinces were held there annually for many years afterwards.

48 Nîmes Roman public buildings *Gard (30)* ★★

Michelin 80/19 and 83/9. Musée Archéologique: Boulevard Amiral Courbet.

As with so many important Roman towns in the Midi, human occupation at Nîmes began in the Late Bronze Age on the hill known as Mont Cavalier. It expanded substantially during the Iron Age, owing to its trading links with the Greek centres around Massalia (MARSEILLES), taking its Celtic name, *Nemausus*, from the deity of a local spring. It became the centre of the tribal group known as the *Volcae Arecomici*, who dominated the region from the mid-C2 BC.

Following the Roman conquest in 121 BC and the construction of the *Via Domitia*, a strong Roman military post was set up, since an important ancient north–south road crossed the new road at this point. This fortunate location led to the rapid growth of a major mercantile and administrative centre, which was given the status of a *colonia latina* in the mid-C1 BC, possibly by Julius Caesar. Although *Narbo* (NARBONNE) remained the official capital of the province of *Gallia Narbonensis*, Nîmes eclipsed it in commercial and cultural importance from the beginning of the Empire. When he disbanded many redundant military units after his victory at Actium in 31 BC, Augustus settled a large contingent of Egyptian and other African veterans in *Nemausus*, at

the same time endowing the town with a number of major public buildings, as well as its fortifications.

The new town, covering more than 220 ha., was enclosed by over 6
km. of walls in 15 BC. Its population is estimated to have risen to more
than 30,000 in the century that followed. During the C2 AD it benefited
further from the favour of the Emperors Hadrian and Antoninus Pius.
Its important role in the economy and polity of the region seems to have
declined when Roman rule yielded to that of the Visigoths and their
successors (unlike its neighbour, ARLES), although this period of the
history of the town is not well known.

Nîmes has preserved a number of outstanding monuments testifying
to its ancient glory. The circuit of the Roman **walls** has been traced with
some measure of certainty over more than half its course. The ramparts,
which survive to a considerable height at several points (Carrière de
Canteduc, Colline de Montaury), were 2.10 m. thick, built of small,
regularly coursed, dressed stones facing a mortared rubble core. They are
adapted to the irregular contours of the terrain. Semicircular solid
bastions were spaced at regular intervals along the ramparts.

The most imposing monument is the **Tour Magne**, which survives

▼ Nîmes: map, showing the principal monuments

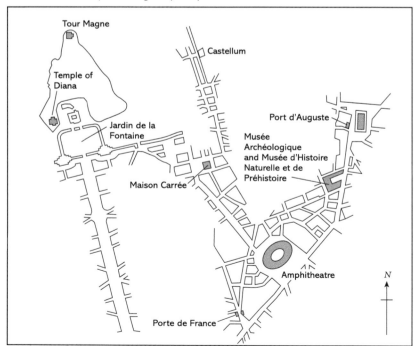

to a height of 33 m. at the summit of Mont Cavalier in the beautiful C18 Jardin de la Fontaine. Its core was a massive watch-tower within the earlier *oppidum*†, which was totally enclosed by the Roman engineers; sadly, all trace of the pre-Roman structure was destroyed in the C17 and C19. The Roman structure consists of an irregular plinth surmounted by an octagonal tower, the topmost storey of which has disappeared. Access is gained to the top, from which there is a fine view, by means of a modern staircase. The tower is flanked by substantial remains of the fortifications, into which it was incorporated.

Two of the original four gates survive. The better preserved is the **Porte d'Auguste** (formerly known as the *Porte d'Arles*), on Boulevard Amiral-Courbet opposite the church of Saint-Baudile: it gives access to the *Via Domitia* in the direction of Arles and Beaucaire. The two large central entrances were intended for wheeled transport and the two smaller side entrances for pedestrians. Slots along their sides show that there were originally portcullises, whilst the sockets for the doors are still clearly visible. There was a strong semicircular tower on either side, the locations of which are marked in the pavement. Niches over the side

▼ Nîmes: the Maison Carrée

▲ Nîmes: the amphitheatre (*Les Arènes*)

entrances originally held statues, whilst the keystones of the two main arches are ornamented with bulls' heads, now badly eroded. The gate originally had an upper storey. An inscription refers to the gate having been constructed in 15 BC on the instructions of Augustus. The **Porte de France** (also known as the *Porte d'Espagne*) in the Place Montcalm, although the main access to the *Via Domitia* to the south-west, is only a single arched gate; like the Porte d'Auguste, it was originally flanked by towers, the partial remains of one of which are preserved in the wall of the adjacent house.

The most complete survival of Roman Nîmes is undoubtedly the so-called **Maison Carrée**. This centre of the Imperial Cult, dedicated to the memory of the two adopted sons of Augustus, Gaius and Lucius, is one of the best-preserved examples of a Roman temple. It originally formed part of the impressive public buildings surrounding the forum of the town. The high podium† is reached by a wide staircase of fifteen steps. The *cella* (cult centre) is located at the opposite end of the podium from the steps and surrounded by Corinthian† columns. Free-standing columns form a portico (*pronaos†*) in the front area, whilst the *cella* is enveloped in embedded columns. The capitals of the columns, entablature†, cornice, and pediment† are decorated with acanthus† leaves and bouquets and geometrical mouldings in high Corinthian† style. The temple has been in constant use ever since it was built, latterly as church,

stables, store, archives, and now museum; as a result, nothing of the original interior survives.

The Imperial Cult was also celebrated at the **Sanctuaire de la Fontaine**, located below the Tour Magne on Mont Cavalier. The spring here was the sacred site of pre-Roman *Nemausus*, from which the town gained its name, and was renowned for its healing properties. The area was laid out as a park in the early C18 by a military engineer, J.-P. Mareschal, but it preserves many of its original features. The spring itself, the pool into which it drains, and the *nymphaeum*† dedicated to the Imperial Cult are essentially as they were in the Roman period, though remodelled by Mareschal.

The so-called **Temple of Diana** formed part of the sacred complex (which also included a theatre, now covered over). It is thought to have been a library, built in the Augustan period† and modified in the C2 AD. The barrel-vaulted† interior with its niches around the walls is closely reminiscent of the Library of Celsus at Ephesus. It survived intact as a church until the Wars of Religion in the C16, when it was badly damaged and has been a ruin ever since.

The water-supply of Roman Nîmes was brought from near Uzès by an aqueduct†, part of which survives spectacularly as the PONT DU GARD. It has been calculated that more than 30,000 cu. m. of water would have been delivered daily in this way. It came though an underground channel into a basin, known as the **Castellum Divisorium** (Rue de la Lampèze), from which it was distributed to public buildings, fountains, and private citizens. This very rare survival of what must have been a common feature of Roman civic life consists of a 5.5 m. diameter circular basin, 1 m. deep. Water was distributed by means of ten large lead pipes opening out of the basin. There was also provision for disposal of overflow and for cleaning the system.

By far the largest Roman monument in Nîmes is the famous **Amphitheatre** (*Les Arènes*). It is now believed to have been built at the end of the C1 AD, and so is roughly contemporary with the Colosseum in Rome and with the amphitheatre at nearby Arles. It covers an area of 133.38 × 101.40 m. The façade, which rises to a height of 21 m., is formed of two equal storeys separated by a massive cornice and surmounted by an attic storey† in which the sockets for the masts of the fabric internal covering (*velum*) are still clearly visible. The structure is composed of radiating supporting walls and vaulted galleries. Access to the centre of the buildings is by means of staircases and corridors (*vomitoria†*) opening out from the galleries that encircle the entire building.

The interior is divided into numerous blocks, within which the seats are arranged in four sections (*maeniana*) separated by low parapets. The lowest of these, reserved for important citizens, consists of only four tiers, and the other three are each composed of ten tiers. It is estimated that there was seating for over 20,000 spectators. The bottom row of seats is separated from the arena proper, which measures 69.14 × 38.34 m., by a parapet 3 m. high; access to this was from entrances on the two axes, and also in all probability from below.

The **Musée Archéologique**, housed in the Ancien Collège des Jésuites, contains an outstanding collection of material, most of it from the classical period. Prehistoric finds are to be found in the same building, in the **Musée d'Histoire Naturelle et de Préhistoire**, notably several statue-menhirs† from the Chalcolithic period.

GAF 27; GB Languedoc-Roussillon 492–516; Bromwich 93–109; PBSAF 356–7.

49 Nissan-lez-Ensérune Pre-Roman settlement *Hérault (34)* ★★

Michelin 83/14. 10 km. W of Béziers on N 9 or D 11; take D 62E to reach site.

Settlement of the commanding hilltop site of Ensérune began in the mid-C6 BC, on what had been no more than a seasonal camp. This was one of the first of the new type of permanent settlement, known to archaeologists as *oppida†*, to be created by the early inhabitants of the region. In the earlier phases the single-room houses were simple structures of wattle-and-daub†, no more than 15 sq. m. and distributed randomly, conforming to the topography of the plateau and the upper slopes of the hill rather than with any notion of urban planning.

Roman amphitheatres

Although they adopted the theatre from the Greeks, the Romans can justly lay claim to the invention of the amphitheatre. It is essentially formed by putting two semi-circular theatres together, to create an elliptical enclosure with tiers of seats surrounding a central arena. The earliest known example is that at Pompeii, dated to around 80 BC. Interestingly, the area of this structure is below ground level, the seating being supported by a bank of earth held by retaining walls, suggesting an origin in the Greek theatres, which utilized natural slopes rather than being free-standing.

The Latin writer Pliny the Younger ascribes the introduction of this form of building to Gaius Scribonius Curio in the mid-C1 BC, and the first free-standing amphitheatre there was built (largely in wood) by Statilius Taurus in 28 BC. In the latter part of that century this type of public building became very popular and examples were built in many towns across the Empire. It was, however, in the second half of the C1 AD that the most spectacular examples were built in stone: the Colosseum in Rome (built in the 60s to replace that of Statilius, destroyed by fire in AD 64), and those in Verona (Italy), Pula (Croatia), NÎMES, and ARLES all date from this period. The magnificent example at *Thysdrus* (El Djem, Tunisia) is a little later.

Amphitheatres were used for staging spectacular shows of various kind. Gladiatorial contests were especially favoured, pitting these professional fighters against one another or wild beasts. Whilst bloody spectacles of this kind were the most common events in amphitheatres, however, there is some evidence that athletic performances and civic ceremonies sometimes took place in them.

The free-standing amphitheatres conform to a general pattern. Their external walls are composed of superimposed arcades of elegant arches, with minimal ornamentation. These enclose a second wall, with concentric barrel-vaulted† galleries between them. Spectators reached their seats by means of galleries in the space between the inner and outer walls, and thence through passages (*vomitoria*) opening into the interior. The public areas were spacious, in order to provide room for the movement of large numbers of spectators (the NÎMES amphitheatre has seating for at least 20,000 spectators).

The tiers of seats, divided into horizontal blocks known as *maeniana*, surround an elliptical central open space known as the *arena* (from the Latin word for 'sand' with which they were covered). Access to the *arena* for performers was effected through large entrances at each end of the long axis. In the larger amphitheatres there were cages and pens for animals beneath the *arena*, which led up through stairways in the centre of the *arena* and communicated by tunnels to the exterior.

Following the foundation of MARSEILLES by the Phocaeans around 600 BC, trade rapidly developed between Greek merchants and the hinterland, and this was to have a profound impact on Ensérune, like other *oppida* in the region. The favoured building material of the Greeks, stone, began progressively to replace wood and clay from the later C5 BC, and the settlement slowly expanded, whilst a stone rampart was constructed around the upper part of the hill. Order was introduced into the layout of houses, which were henceforward built in *insulae*† clearly defined by streets on a chequer-board pattern. The extent of commercial relations with the Mediterranean world is demonstrated by the wealth of imported Greek and Etruscan materials, found in particular in the extensive cemeteries that have been excavated.

The next major phase in the life of Ensérune came around the end of the C3 BC; this has been attributed variously (without much justification) to the passage of Hannibal's army on its way to Italy or to the first contact with the Celtic peoples coming down from the north. Whatever the cause, the result was spectacular: the town expanded over the entire hill, outside the earlier ramparts, where the hillside was terraced to allow houses to be built, and new, more impressive fortifications were constructed. In one of the new quarters, which developed on the site of an earlier cemetery, Graeco-Roman influence was clearly apparent in the size and style of the new houses, many of which were built round courtyards in the Italian style. Wall paintings, mosaic floors, and colonnades embellished some of the more elaborate houses. However, the adoption of classical Mediterranean town planning did not extend to the large-scale creation of major public buildings, none of which has been identified with certainty during many decades of excavations. It seems likely, therefore, that Ensérune preserved its indigenous appearance to a considerable extent (although a number of architectural elements, such as column bases and capitals, have been found in the lower part of the plateau).

The subsequent history of the town seems to have been one of slow decline. Its trading role disappeared, to be replaced by that of the centre of a major agricultural area. Gradually, the disadvantages of a hilltop site, with chronic problems of water supply, led to the abandonment of the urban complex in favour of more convenient villas in the midst of the vast agricultural estates of the surrounding plain. It seems likely that it was a ghost town by the end of the C5 AD.

Ensérune is built on a hill some 120 m. high, dominating the Béziers coastal plain; there is a magnificent view from the summit. Only part of its enceinte, measuring 600 m. east–west by 150 m. north–south has been excavated, and not all the excavated area is open to the public.

On entering the site from the east, the visitor first passes by some deep **grain silos** that were brought to light when this part of the hillside was terraced for cultivation. They are bottle-shaped cavities cut into the

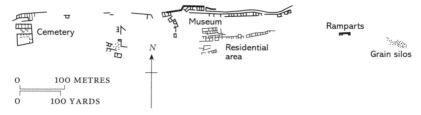

Cemetery
N
Museum
Residential area
Ramparts
Grain silos

0   100 METRES

0   100 YARDS

▲ Nissan-lez-Ensérune: plan of excavations

soft tuff rock† of the hillside, and are thought to date back to the C4 BC. Next comes a section of the first **Ramparts**, built before 400 BC of large dressed stone blocks, from which access is gained to the upper part of the plateau.

To the south of the Museum (see below) is the southern **Residential Area** (identified as *insulae* I–IV, using the numbering assigned during the excavations). The buildings, ranged along a street, are simple stone structures with only one room, but all equipped with silos or *dolia* (enormous storage jars) partly buried in their floors. These buildings are

La terrasse est et ses silos (insula XVII).

▲ Nissan-lez-Ensérune: grain silos

from the last phase of the site, from the C3 BC to the C1 AD. Part of the later rampart has been reconstructed in *insula* III. There is another residential quarter to the north of the Museum (*insulae* V and VI), stretching some 250 m., and here, too, there is an intact stretch of the ramparts. The buildings in *insula* VI are the best preserved on the site and well illustrate the relative simplicity of the Ensérune dwellings. In their present form they date from the last period of occupation, but excavation showed that they were constructed on the foundations of earlier buildings.

Moving eastwards, the visitor leaves the oldest part of the settlement and descends to *insulae* VIII and IX. Here the buildings are more substantial, and were supplied by a large water cistern. Water collection was originally thought to have been the main function of the group of structures further to the west (*insula* XII). The earliest intervention on this part of the settlement was the digging of more than forty deep silos which were interpreted as being for storing water, but recent research indicates that they were used for stocking grain. Later, a road was driven through the silos and what may have been a public building of Hellenistic† type was built (only a small portion of the building survives). To the south of the road one room of a building (8 × 3.40 m.) was found that had painted plaster on its walls and a simple black-and-white mosaic floor; this has been tentatively identified as the dining room (*triclinium*) of a C1 AD urban villa.

Finally, at the other end of the site, 400 m. from the museum, there is a further group of excavated buildings (*insulae* VII, X, and XI), constructed in the latest phase of the settlement and overlying an earlier cemetery, which went out of use in the C3 BC. To the north there is a section of the later rampart, built of ashlar-faced† rubble. Here the buildings are larger and more elaborate than those above. One of the houses is typical of those built in Italy around the same time, with a number of rooms ranged around a central courtyard, in the centre of which there was a shallow basin (*impluvium*) fed by rainwater from the roofs of the surrounding wings of the complex. They were linked by a colonnaded corridor or peristyle†. A large rectangular structure to the south of this complex has been identified tentatively as a market (*macellum*†) from the final phase of the settlement.

The site **Museum**, created by rehabilitating and extending a private house that stood in the centre of the ancient town, houses many of the important archaeological finds from the site, including a large amount of material imported from Rhodes and elsewhere in the Graeco-Roman world.

GAF 28; GB 217–18; Bromwich 71–4; PBSAF 358–9.

Le Palet-de-Roland *see* PÉPIEUX.

50 Pépieux: Les Fades/Le Palet-de-Roland Neolithic

passage grave *Aude (11)*

Michelin 83/13. 30 km. E of Carcassonne on N 113/D 610, then D 910 to Olonzac and D 115 W to Pépieux.

The Neolithic passage grave†, or *allée couverte*†, at Les Fades (also known as Le Palet-de-Roland), is at 24 m. the longest in Southern France; the mound that originally covered it was 36 m. long.

The passage is formed of alternating dressed slabs and drystone† sections; it leads to the higher central chamber, which is supported on pillars, and there is a smaller terminal cell. Access to the chamber is through a round opening formed by two hollowed slabs; there is a similar entrance to the terminal chamber.

Excavation has shown that this large collective tomb was in use from 3000 to 1500 BC, into the Early Bronze Age. It is the best example of this type of prehistoric monument in the region; it owes its present condition to a restoration in 1972. There is another well-restored example at Laure-Minervois known as the Dolmen de Saint-Eugène.

PBSAF 360.

51 Le Perthus: Les Cluses and Col de Panissars Roman

fort and monument *Pyrénées-Orientales (66)*

Michelin 86/19. On N 9 from Perpignan to Spanish frontier.

There are two Gallo-Roman monuments on the Col du Perthus (known to the Romans as the *Summum Pyrenaeum*), on the frontier between France and Spain, where the *Via Domitia* crossed the Pyrenees.

Just south of the small village of Les Cluses there are the remains of a Roman fort, mistakenly called in Catalan the *Castell dels Moros* ('Castle of the Moors'). There was what is considered to have been a small customs tax collection office here, only fragments of which survive alongside the track of the Roman road to the west of the little river Rome. The remains of the fort are at the top of the steep slope above. The walls, with three square towers, typical of later Roman defences, enclosed nearly 1 ha. The main entrance can be clearly seen, and there is also a postern gate in the west wall.

Closer to the present-day frontier in the section known as the Col de Panissars the ruins of the Romanesque† church have been shown by excavation to overlie the remains of an unusual Roman structure. It consists of two parallel rectangular elements through which the *Via Domitia* passed; they were erected on solid foundations constructed of massive sandstone blocks. The whole complex measures 31.8 × 16 m. It has tentatively been identified as the Trophy of Pompey, mentioned by the C1 AD geographer Strabo.

GB Languedoc-Roussillon 159–60; Bromwich 76–7; PBSAF 360.

Plan-de-la-Tour *see* GAILHAN.

52 Le Pont du Gard Roman aqueduct *Gard (30)*   ★★
Michelin 80/19. N 86 NE from Nîmes to Remoulins, then D 981.

Its aqueducts† are among the most spectacular monuments of Roman engineering. Rome itself was supplied with water from several aqueducts, visible to the traveller approaching the capital from different directions; the modern city of Segovia is dominated by the soaring arcades of its aqueduct; the graceful structure at Aspendos (Turkey), with its high pressure relieving towers, sweeps majestically across the valley of the Eurymedon. However, none of these has the dramatic impact of the Pont du Gard, part of the water-supply system more than 50 km. long built to supply the fountains and baths of *Colonia Augusta Nemausus* (NÎMES).

Before the establishment of the *colonia*† of Nîmes by Augustus (or perhaps earlier, during the First Triumvirate of Caesar, Crassus, and Pompey in the mid-C1 BC), the city's water supply came from a spring, which is still to be seen in the Jardins de la Fontaine. However, this was insufficient for the newly settled legionaries, accustomed to the abundance of water in their Italian home towns. Around 20 BC, therefore, work began on the construction of a substantial aqueduct. This is traditionally attributed to Marcus Agrippa, son-in-law of Augustus and senior magistrate (*aedile*†) in Rome, where he was responsible for improving the water supply by building aqueducts. However, some scholars put up a strong case for a date in the late C1 AD for the Nîmes aqueduct.

Whenever it was begun, it was an ambitious project, typical of the early Imperial period. Water was brought from the Fontaine d'Eure, near Uzès. Although this is only some 20 km. from Nîmes as the crow flies, the aqueduct itself followed a course of around 50 km., in order to ensure a steady gradient for the water on its way to the city. The difference in height between the source and the *castellum divisorium* (water distribution point) in Nîmes is less than 17 m., i.e. an average fall of 0.342 m. per km.

Like most Roman aqueducts, that of Nîmes consisted of a variety of different techniques of channelling the water over its length. Wherever possible it consisted of no more than a stone-lined channel cut into the ground, which meant that in places a very winding course had to be followed, to maintain the steady fall in height. Elsewhere (at Sernhac, for example) the water passed through tunnels cut into the rock, or was carried on low walls, some of them built with low arches, or bridges, in order to span small rivers and streams, as at Bornègre. It was only when confronted with the deep valley of the Gardon that the Roman engineers

▲ Le Pont du Gard: general view

▲ Le Pont du Gard: interior of the water conduit

had to have recourse to a monumental construction, in the shape of what is today known as the Pont du Gard.

It seems likely, judging from the sediments in the water channels, that the aqueduct went on supplying water to Nîmes until the early medieval period. Even after its original function had been lost, it retained its subsidiary function, as a passenger bridge across the Gardon valley. The right of levying tolls on users was granted by the King of France to the seigneurs of Uzès in the C13, passing to the Bishops of Uzès three centuries later; in return they were responsible for maintaining the bridge in good repair. When in 1704 the current bishop refused to pay the cost of restoring the bridge the toll system was abolished and responsibility for maintaining it passed to the Assemblée des États du Languedoc. That body was responsible for restoration work in the 1740s, as part of the strengthening of the road between Paris, Lyons, and Provence.

The Pont du Gard is built entirely of limestone from quarries some 600 m. distant, on the left bank of the Gardon. This coarse-textured stone gives the whole structure a warm coloration.

The structure is 48.77 m. high and divided in three stages, with six arches in the lowest stage, eleven in the second, and thirty-five at the top. These stages decrease in width as they ascend: 21.87 m. high by 6.36 m. wide in the lowest tier, 19.50 m. by 4.56 m. in the second, and 7.4 m. by 3.04 m. at the top. They also increase in length, to fit the widening out of the valley that they are crossing—142.35 m., 242.55 m., and 275 m. The arches also vary in size, care being taken to ensure that those in the two lower stages spring from the same upright alignments.

These dimensions, which are exceptional even among Roman structures, stem from the fact that the Pont du Gard is built on solid rock, so as to resist the often torrential floodwaters of the Gardon. This strength is reinforced by the slight curvature of the structure, by the cutwaters on the upstream side of the uprights, and by the wide span of the lower tiers of arches (especially the centre one).

▼ Le Pont du Gard: construction detail

It is built using the drystone technique (i.e. without mortar) of very large undressed stones, the largest of which measure more than 2 m. cubed and weigh around 6 tonnes. The only decoration consists of large mouldings at the points where the arches spring from the uprights. Larger stones protruding inside the arches served as supports for the wooden frames used in construction. The keystones of the arches bear inscriptions indicating their precise location within the structure.

Roman water supplies

One of the many aspects of engineering in which the Romans excelled was that of water management. The establishment of organized towns in Gaul after it became part of the Roman Empire, coupled with the more sophisticated life-style imported from metropolitan Italy, created an intensive requirement of water for a variety of purposes—drinking, cooking, bathing, crafts, sewage disposal—in densely populated communities. Existing resources from wells, springs, and rivers were often not adequate to meet these requirements, and so water supplies had to be obtained from distant sources.

When a source of abundant pure water was discovered, it was brought to the town by means of an aqueduct† (in the more general sense of the term, referring to any artificial channel for conveying water). Channels were dug into the ground, lined with waterproof clay, and capped with stone slabs, with settling tanks at intervals for the separation of silt where necessary. The Roman command of surveying and levelling techniques ensured that water would travel at a steady flow-rate at constant reductions in elevation, making use of natural gradients. Sometimes a solid obstacle that was difficult to circumvent would be traversed by means of short tunnels through the natural rock.

Occasionally it became necessary to span a river valley or a marshy area to reach the town. In such cases an aqueduct in the better-known sense of the term, an arched structure with the watercourse at the top, was built. Many of these, such as the PONT DU GARD or the aqueduct of Segovia (Spain), were masterpieces of functional architecture. Others covered long distances, such as the 9.5 km. of the Marcian aqueduct or the 16 km. of the Claudian aqueduct that supplied Rome. Where the angle of descent from the source was steep, the water pressure was reduced by means of uncapped humps in the line of the water channel (as at Aspendos in Turkey)

On arrival in the larger towns, where there was a multiplicity of users, the water was led into a receiving tank, known as a *castellum divisorium*. This had a number of outlet ducts, some leading to public works such as the fountains located at street intersections (there are good examples in Pompeii) or public baths, and others to private houses, the property of the wealthier citizens. In the latter case, provision was made for these to be closed if the property owner failed to pay his civic taxes.

The water channel at the top is 1.30 m. wide and is lined with waterproof concrete. Like the other known sections of the aqueduct system, it is covered with stone slabs, which would have served as a pathway for foot passengers. The interior is coated with a thick layer of calcareous sediment which has greatly reduced its interior volume.

The Pont du Gard was inscribed on the World Heritage List by the UNESCO World Heritage Committee in 1985.

GB Languedoc-Roussillon 562–4; Bromwich 110–20; PBSAF 367.

Près-Bas, Villa des *see* LOUPIAN.

Roque-de-Viou *see* SAINT-DIONIZY.

53 Rouet: Dolmen de Lamalou Prehistoric dolmen *Hérault (34)*

Michelin 83/7. 25 km. N of Montpellier on D 17 to Saint-Martin-de-Londres, then D 122E.

As many as thirty dolmens†, the remains of prehistoric chambered tombs, have been discovered on the wide Causse de l'Hortus north of Montpellier. Among these, the best preserved and most representative is undoubtedly the Lamalou dolmen, which dates to the third millennium BC. The tomb is covered by a circular mound of stone. The overall length is 10 m., the first 5 m. of which is the passage-way, roofed with large stone slabs; from here access is gained through a portal formed by two large upright dressed stones to the small antechamber. This in turn leads to the much larger trapezoidal burial chamber at a slightly higher level, which has survived with its capstone intact. Excavations revealed the remains of many individuals buried there over a long period.

Nearby is the Dolmen de Feuilles, which is comparable in size and structure. Other monuments of this type in the region are simpler, lacking the antechamber of the Lamalou and Feuilles examples.

PBSAF 362.

54 Saint-Dionizy: Roque-de-Viou Pre-Roman settlement *Gard (30)*

Michelin 83/8. D 40 W from Nîmes to Langlade, then D 14/D 137.

This settlement was the precursor of neighbouring LES CASTELS. Occupation began in the C8 BC during the Late Bronze Age, the inhabitants living in simple houses of wood and clay. In the C4 BC a stone rampart was erected, houses being built up against its inner surface. It appears to have been abandoned in favour of Les Castels in the early C3 BC. All that remains of the settlement are the lower courses and foundations of the defensive walls.

PBSAF 362.

La « fabrique » d'amphores de Sallèles d'Aude est un véritable complexe artisanal qui regroupe l'habitat des potiers, les carrières d'argile et le quartier réservé à la production. Le vin gaulois est présent du Ier au IIIe s. sur les grands marchés du monde romain. Les belles amphores dans lesquelles il est conditionné sont fabriquées dans les nombreux ateliers de poterie du midi de la Gaule.

▲ Sallèles-d' Aude: reconstruction of the pottery

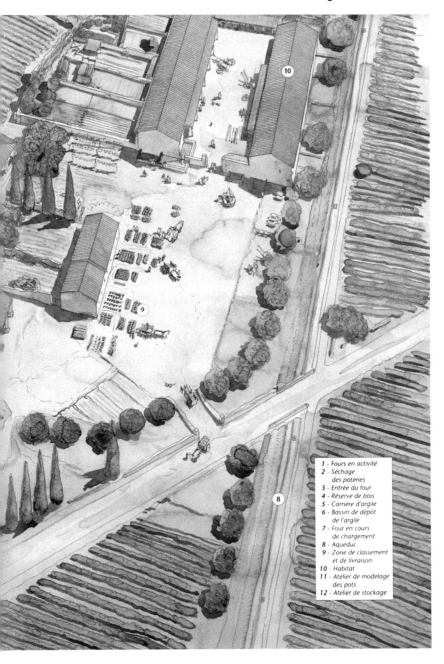

1 - Fours en activité
2 - Séchage
    des poteries
3 - Entrée du four
4 - Réserve de bois
5 - Carrière d'argile
6 - Bassin de dépôt
    de l'argile
7 - Four en cours
    de chargement
8 - Aqueduc
9 - Zone de classement
    et de livraison
10 - Habitat
11 - Atelier de modelage
    des pots
12 - Atelier de stockage

55 Sallèles-d'Aude Roman pottery factory *Aude (11)* ★
Michelin 83/14. D 607 NW from Narbonne, then D 1118.

The large pottery vessels known as *amphorae*† are among the most common finds from the Roman period in excavations, both on land and under the sea. They were used for the transportation of such commodities as wine, oil, and the Romans' favourite fish sauce, *garum*†. A large pottery producing large quantities of *amphorae*† has been excavated at Sallèles-d'Aude, near NARBONNE. This ceramic factory was set up at the end of the C1 BC, first producing mainly brick and tile and coarse pottery and then concentrating on large wine *amphorae*† from the mid-C1 AD until it closed at the end of the C3. The products were used for transporting Gaulish wine over a wide area of the Roman Empire: many examples have been found in Rome, on the great refuse heap known as the Monte Testaccio, whilst others have turned up on the Rhine frontier and in Britain.

The whole process can be studied on the site, both from the preserved remains and the site museum. The excellent local clay was exploited opencast and in shafts, and it then underwent treatment in large tile-lined tanks. This process was followed by the forming of the various products—bricks and tiles, storage jars, *amphorae*†—and firing. The kilns, fourteen of which have been conserved, first had a capacity of some 10 cu. m., but these were replaced during the C1 AD by enormous kilns, up to 100 cu. m. in capacity, for the production of wine

Garum

For the Roman gourmet, one indispensable element in his kitchen was the fermented fish sauce known as *garum* or *liquamen*. This delicacy was produced in many places around the Roman world and was transported widely in *amphorae*† by boat.

The method of manufacture is described by one ancient writer. The guts of small fishes such as red mullet, sprats, and anchovy were put into a pot and salted. After they had been left in the sun, and shaken from time to time, the sauce was extracted by straining it through a 'fine-weave basket'. Another method described by the writer involves putting the fish into strongly salted water, adding oregano, boiling it, and then straining the resulting liquid until it is clear. The best *garum* was apparently made from the guts, gills, blood, and juices of tuna, which were salted and left in a container for up to two months. The side of the container was then pierced, allowing the sauce to run out.

Several experiments have been made to reproduce this sauce by contemporary archaeologists and cooks alike, but it has proved to be totally unacceptable to modern palates!

amphorae†. The later kilns were capable of producing around a thousand *amphorae†* from each firing.

PBSAF 363.

56 Tautavel: La Caune d'Arago Prehistoric inhabited cave
Pyrénées-Orientales (66) ★★

Michelin 86/9. D 117 N from Perpignan, then D 59 to Tautavel; the cave is 2 km. N of the village, on D 9.

This cave is set in a limestone massif on the left bank of the river Verdouble. Occupation deposits 11 m. thick containing the bones of many different types of animal, some of them long extinct in Europe, have been excavated systematically over many years, revealing more than twenty occupation levels, the earliest dating back more than 500,000 years and continuing intermittently until around 100,000 BC. The occupants were *Homo erectus*, the ancestor of modern human beings: one of the oldest hominid skulls ever found is that of 'Tautavel Man', who died around 450,000 years ago. There is also evidence of the cave having been visited by Neanderthal Man (*Homo neanderthalensis*).

A visit to the cave must be complemented by a visit to the splendid **Musée de Préhistoire** in Tautavel, where the story of the earliest humans in the area is graphically illustrated by dioramas and interactive videos, as well as the rich harvest of finds from the cave.

GB Languedoc-Roussillon 340; Rigaud 130–3; PBSAF 366.

57 Villetelle: Ambrussum Pre-Roman and Roman settlement
Hérault (34)

Michelin 83/8. D 40 W from Nîmes, then D 249 and D 12 to Villetelle; the site lies 2 km. further south.

Like so many archaeological sites in the region, the slight eminence on which *Ambrussum* is situated was originally settled in the Neolithic period and became a fortified settlement (*oppidum†*) during the Iron Age (second half of the first millennium BC). It occupied a commanding position overlooking the important trade route down the river Vidourle. With the advent of the Romans, it became an important staging post on the strategically and commercially important Via Domitia, linking Italy with Spain. A stone bridge was constructed to carry the road across the Vidourle in the early C1.

During the early part of the C2, however, the occupied area was reduced to the lower part of the pre-Roman town, alongside the river. Its economic role continued to diminish, and by the end of the C3 it appears to have been abandoned completely (although it is likely that some form of staging post would have survived at the bridge itself).

The most notable feature is probably what remains of the **Roman**

Bridge, which was more than 100 m. in length. It appears to have been in use well into the medieval period, and two of its nine original arches were still standing in the early C20, but one of these was swept away during floods in 1933. It is constructed on massive foundations and lower courses, with cutwaters upstream, in typical Roman form. However, the small size of the apertures cut into the pillars was a source of weakness when flood waters hit the structure: the much larger holes in the *Pont Julien* at BONNIEUX bear witness to the need to reduce the impact in this way.

A road led from the bridge up the slope into the town, and a 40 m. stretch has been uncovered about 100 m. south of the bridge. It is carefully made of laid cobbles, and deep grooves have been cut by the wheels of carts. The road enters the town from the north through a gate, now disappeared, and winds sinuously through to the south gate with its hornworks†, of which traces survive. A long stretch of the **Ramparts** is

▼ Villetelle: the Roman bridge

still visible on the west side of the town. They were built using rectangular stone blocks, subsequently reinforced on the inside.

Several private **houses** within the town have been excavated. They represent a fusion between the indigenous house plans and those imported from Italy, nucleated around a small courtyard. Part of a much larger and imposing structure have been found near the south gate; its function is as yet unknown, but it was undoubtedly a public building of some kind, perhaps a market.

Bromwich 54–7; PBSAF 368.

58 Viols-en-Laval: Cambous Prehistoric village *Hérault (34)* ★
Michelin 83/6. D 986 19 km. NW from Montpellier, then D 113.

The poor soils of the uplands to the north of Montpellier have not been cultivated in recent times and are covered by a tough scrub vegetation (*garrigue*). As a result, there are substantial remains of early human settlement in this 'relict cultural landscape', as is the case in Dartmoor in England, which have yielded a great deal of information on excavation. Among them are a number of small settlements dating from the transition from the Late Neolithic to the Chalcolithic (2500–2800 BC). Part of one of these, at Cambous in Viols-en-Laval, is open to visitors.

The **village** consists of four groups of houses, each consisting of eight to ten buildings. The clusters are 50–100 m. apart from one another. Within each cluster the individual buildings, which are elongated with rounded ends, abut closely up against one another. A large

▼ Viols-en-Laval: reconstructed Iron Age house

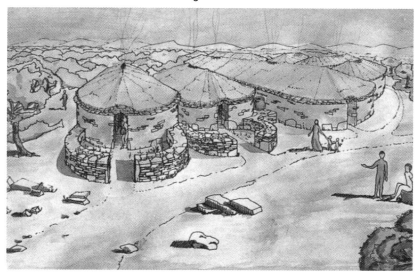

structure, up to 24 m. long, has four or more smaller ones adjoining it, to form what appears to have been a farming unit. The substantial walls, made of ashlar† facings and rubble cores, can be up to 2 m. thick, and in places they have survived to a height of more than 2 m. Lines of post-holes on the axis of each building held wooden posts supporting a pitched roof, most probably of thatch. The reconstruction of one of the buildings gives an impression of how they may have looked. The distribution of finds within the buildings suggests that the area furthest from the entrance, in one of the apsidal ends, was the living area, with a hearth in the middle separating it from the sleeping quarters. Natural cavities in the soft limestone of the area were used for storage purposes. The inhabitants practised mixed farming, raising cattle and pigs and cultivating wheat and barley.

Near the village there is a **passage grave**† (dolmen†) in a circular mound characteristic of the Chalcolithic culture of the region which probably served the villagers of Cambous. The material excavated from the settlement is displayed in the **Musée Préhistorique** at nearby Viols-le-Fort.

GB Languedoc-Roussillon 476; PBSAF 369.

Provence-Alpes-Côte d'Azur

59 Aix-en-Provence Town walls, museum *Bouches-du-Rhône (13)*
Michelin 84/3. Musée Granet: Place Saint-Jean-de-Malte.

Following usual Roman practice (cf. Maiden Castle and Dorchester), a garrison was installed close to the fortified hilltop *oppidum*† of the *Salyes* or *Salluvii* (ENTREMONT) by Caius Sextus Calvinus after he had defeated its occupants and founded the province of *Gallia Transalpina* in the late 120s BC. The site he selected, 2.5 km. from Entremont, was strategically and commercially well sited, since it is where the route running north from *Massalia* (MARSEILLES) and the main east–west highway along the coastal strip cross. The strategic value of the site was confirmed in 102 BC, when Marius led the Roman army to victory over the invading *Teutones* close by Aix.

It was also endowed with natural hot springs, which always attracted the Romans. When peace had been restored to the province and the need for a fort had disappeared, an urban settlement replaced it, taking its name from the springs and the name of the victorious general, *Aquae Sextiae*. The exact date of the formal creation of the civil town is not known, though it seems likely that Julius Caesar gave it the status of a *colonia latina*, to be upgraded to that of a full *colonia romana* by Augustus (see p. 66).

Although its commercial significance declined to some extent with the gradual transfer of the centre of trade from Marseilles to ARLES, which reached its apogee in the late C3 AD, *Aquae Sextiae* remained a prosperous town and administrative centre throughout the Early Empire. Its importance was confirmed in the late C3 when the province of *Narbonensis* was divided and it became the administrative and episcopal capital of the new province of *Narbonensis Secunda*.

The town retained some measure of status and prosperity following the barbarian conquest of the early C5, but it was not to achieve anything like its former eminence again until the late C12, under the Angevin Counts of Provence.

Virtually no evidence survives of the glorious Roman past of Aix. Excavations and chance discoveries have given some idea of the layout of the Roman town. The fine Romanesque and Gothic Cathedral of Saint-Sauveur was built on the site of the forum†, with its imposing basilica†, and the circuit of the walls (which were probably Augustan† in date) can be traced from early prints and fragments preserved in later buildings.

Despite its lack of visible remains, however, Aix-en-Provence is a town that should not be overlooked by the archaeologically minded visitor. In addition to being a medieval and C18 town of great charm, it

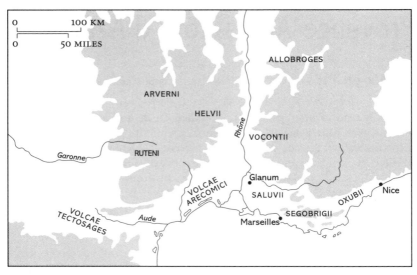

▲ The Gallic tribes of Southern France

The tribes of Southern France

When the Romans began to infiltrate into Southern France the Mediterranean hinterland was occupied by a number of indigenous tribes. It is difficult to be specific about their ethnic origins, since this had been a region of migration and settlement for many centuries and they had cultural affinities with the surrounding regions—Spain, the Massif Central, the upper Rhône valley, the Alpine massif, and the north Italian plain. They are generally treated as a mixed group known as Celto-Ligurians.

In the west the dominant tribe was that of the *Volcae Tectosages*, who occupied the area between the Aude and the Pyrenees with the *Tolosates* to the north of them. Further to the west were the *Tarusates* in the foothills of the Pyrenees, the *Sotiates* and the *Elusates* south of the Garonne, and the *Petrucorii* and the *Nitiobriges* to the north. The *Volcae Arecomici* occupied a wide strip of the coastal plain between the Aude and the Rhône, with the *Ruteni* in the rugged Cevennes region. The powerful *Arverni* and *Helvii* dominated the Massif Central.

East of the Rhône were the *Salyes* (or *Saluvii*) and the *Segobrigii*, in the lower-lying lands, and the *Cavares* in the mountains of Vaucluse. The *Vocontii* were in the lower Rhône valley, with the *Allobroges* on the left bank in the region of Vienne. The mountainous region of the Alpes Maritimes was occupied by the warlike *Ligurii* and the *Oxubii* nearer the coast.

possesses in the **Musée Granet** one of the finest collections of Roman material in France; it also serves as an excellent starting point for visiting Entremont.

GB Provence 154–72; Bromwich 127–36; Musée Granet: Place Saint-Jean-de-Malte.

60 Antibes   Fortified town on Greek and Roman foundations *Alpes-Maritimes (06)*

Michelin 84/9. On N 98, 5 km. E of Cannes. Musée d'Histoire et d'Archéologie: Bastion Saint-André.

Following the establishment of their main trading settlement at *Massalia* (MARSEILLES) around 600 BC, the Phocaean Greek colonists established a chain of trading posts or 'factories' along the Mediterranean coast to trade with the local Ligurian tribes and, through them, with the wider hinterland of Gaul. Among these was *Antipolis*, with its excellent natural

▼ Antibes: map showing the early remains

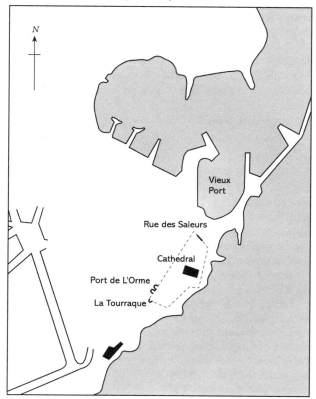

harbour and access to the interior. It is likely that there was a 'native' settlement here from as early as the C10 BC.

A permanent town soon developed and spread around the harbour, a process that continued after the arrival of the Romans. The inhabitants prudently declared for Caesar, with the result that the town was immediately granted the status of an Italiote city (*oppidum Latinum*), later to be upgraded to *municipium*. It was famed for its own version of the fermented fish sauce known as *garum*† that was so essential for the Roman cuisine; other known exports were olive oil and pine resin.

The commercial and military value of its excellent harbour ensured the continued survival of Antibes in the centuries that followed, though it often changed hands. It was noted for its fortifications (of which only the Fort Carré survives); these achieved their final form at the hands of the great military architect, Vauban.

The Massaliote Greek town was small, but it expanded considerably during the Roman period. Little remains to be seen of the ancient town, however, apart from some fragments of the Roman fortifications. These include the corner tower known as La Tourraque (Rue Barque-en-Cannes), the Porte de l'Orme and the base of the fortifications visible in the Rue des Saleurs over the Vieux Port. Excavated remains are on view in the Chapelle Saint-Esprit and under the cathedral.

A temple complex was excavated at Vaugrenier, 4.5 km. to the north of Antibes (N 7, direction Nice), in the 1970s, and some remains are on display in a public park. Built in the C1 AD around the end of the C1 BC, it went out of use a century later. All that is now visible is the south wall of the precinct.

The substantial remains of the aqueducts† that supplied *Antipolis* can still be seen. The Aqueduc de la Bouillide lies 13 km. to the north of

Vauban

Sébastien le Prestre de Vauban (1633–1707) was one of the great masters of fortifications and siege warfare, which he elevated into a science. The widespread adoption of artillery necessitated a radical new approach to fortifications. The sheer masonry walls of Roman and medieval fortresses were replaced by low earthwork ramparts surrounded by a ditch, with a gently sloping approach (*glacis*) that could be swept by the fire of the defenders. Elaborate bastions provided all-round fields of fire. The system of siege warfare that he developed involved pushing forward zigzag approach trenches that permitted siege guns to be brought forward under cover to concentrate their fire on a selected point in the defences, while at the same time galleries were driven under the walls in which mines could be exploded, thereby creating a breach for storming parties.

Antibes, taking its waters from the Bouillide brook along a sinuous course partly excavated into the calcareous rock and partly on arched aqueducts, which can be seen at La Valmasque. Other sections of channel and aqueduct are to be seen near the Chapelle de Saint-Claude and on the left bank of the Laval valley.

GB Provence 184–90; Bromwich 247–52; PBSAF 375.

61 Arles Roman town with theatre and amphitheatre Bouches-du-Rhône
(13) ★★

Michelin 83/10. Musée Lapidaire d'Art Païen: Place de la République.

A visit to Arles is one of the highlights of any tour of the archaeology of Southern France. Its role during the Roman period was paramount, and so it was embellished with many fine public buildings, a number of which, such as the amphitheatre, survive in a remarkably intact condition.

Documentary sources, supported by finds of Greek material in excavations, indicate that the settlement here on a hill that commands the Rhône delta, the marshy expanses of the Camargue, and the waste of stones and garrigue† known as the Crau, was created by Phocaean merchants from MARSEILLES as a trading centre (*emporion*) in the C6 BC. Its original name, according to the C4 AD historian Avienius, was *Theline*.

It clearly flourished in this role: in the mid-C1 BC Caesar had no difficulty in finding facilities and craftsmen capable of building twelve warships for him in a very short time in order to fight against the Massaliotes ('Caesar resolved . . . to build twelve ships at Arelate, which were completed and rigged in thirty days from the time the timber was cut': *Civil War* 1. 36). This link with shipbuilding and navigation continued after Romanization: inscriptions found in the town refer to guilds of shipwrights (*fabri navales, fabres tignarii*), river boatmen (*utricularii*), and sea captains (*navicularii marini*).

The town remained part of the Massaliote territory until that city was defeated by Caesar in 49 BC. Three years later he awarded the distinction of *colonia romana* (see p. 66) to this dependency, in which he settled veterans of his VI Legion, and gave it most of the lands of *Massalia* as its *territorium*, ensuring a sound basis for its future growth. The new colony was eventually to become known as *Colonia Julia Paterna Arelate Sextanorum*, a name accorded to it by Augustus in honour of his uncle.

Because of its situation *Arelate* prospered during the Early Empire, along with other towns such as AIX-EN-PROVENCE. It was laid out according to the best principles of ancient town-planning and embellished by Augustus and his successors with splendid public buildings. The town fortified under Augustus expanded greatly in the Flavian period (late C1 AD), doubling in size, with a quarter of especially opulent town houses developed in the Trinquetaille suburb across the river.

However, even before this expansion the town was described as *urbs opulentissime* ('most opulent of cities') by Pomponius Mela, writing in the 40s AD.

The town underwent a setback, like so many other Gallo-Roman towns, during the troubled period when much of Gaul was devastated during the incursions by savage barbarian hordes in the later C3 AD, demonstrated by destruction and abandonment layers found in excavations of the extra-mural quarters. This was to be a relatively short episode: under Constantine (who built an Imperial palace there) it assumed an even more important role than hitherto as an administrative and political centre, as barbarian pressure on northern Gaul mounted.

During the C4 and C5 Arles was frequently honoured by Imperial visits and it hosted important events, such as the important ecclesiastical Council of Arles (314) and the regular meetings of representatives of the Seven Provinces that began in the early C5. In 313 the Imperial mint was transferred there from Ostia, and in 428 Honorius made it the seat of the Prefecture of the Gauls in place of Trier (*Augusta Treverorum*). It became the seat of the Christian primacy of Gaul in 417, a role that was usurped from Lyons. In a lyrical eulogy of the town the Gallic poet Ausonius called it 'the Gallic Rome', through which passed 'the merchandise of the entire Roman world'.

In the 480s *Arelate* came under the rule of the Visigoths, and in 508 it passed to the Ostrogoths, who were in their turn supplanted by the Franks in 536. The anarchy of much of the early Middle Ages saw the town lose its administrative and commercial supremacy and shrink within its defences. Older structures were converted into strongpoints: the amphitheatre, for example, became a fortress, known as the *Château*

▼ Arles: plan of the principal monuments

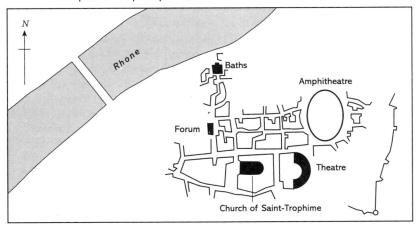

des Arènes. It was not to recover its commercial and religious eminence until the late C11.

The Roman urban layout survives strongly in the contemporary town plan and at its heart was the **Forum**†. Little survives of this very large area, although its extent has been established by excavation. The central open space, which lies beneath the modern Rue Baize and the Plan de la Cour, was surrounded on three sides by a portico. It was entered through a monumental gateway, fragments of which survive in the walls of the Hôtel du Nord.

Since the Forum is sited on sloping ground, it was necessary to build up the downhill side in order to achieve a flat interior. Unusually, this was done by means of a U-shaped cellar or **Cryptoporticus**†, which survives to the present day. The long sides are 90 m. in length and the shorter side 60 m.; two vaulted corridors are separated by a row of massive rectangular pillars. The function of this remarkable structure is obvious: it supports the main forum buildings. However, controversy surrounds their daily use: storage of foodstuffs, slave quarters, or covered promenades have all been suggested.

The **Theatre** also dates from the early years of the town (*c.*26 BC). It served as a quarry for later buildings (especially churches) and was converted into a fort in the C9. Subsequent building activities meant that it was completely submerged and was not cleared until the mid-C19. It is a standard Roman theatre in form; with a diameter of 102 m. it is almost exactly the same size as the much better-preserved example at ORANGE. Unlike the Orange theatre, it does not make use of a natural slope, and so it was built free-standing, the tiers of seats being supported on twenty-eight radiating walls. It is estimated that the building would have been able to seat around 11,000 spectators. Little remains of the *scenae frons*†, apart from two splendid columns in African breccia† and Italian marble.

The finest Roman monument in Arles is the **Amphitheatre**, dating from the late C1 AD. Its survival is attributable to its reuse as a fortress in the Middle Ages, and then as a small town of some 200 houses and two churches. The clearance of these later accretions began in 1825, and all that remains of them are three of the four medieval watch towers.

The structure is very similar to that at NÎMES, consisting of two storeys, each of sixty arcades, surviving to a height of 21 m. (but originally higher, with the addition of an attic storey†). Inside there are thirty-four rows of seats which would have accommodated over 20,000 spectators. The arena is oval, measuring 60 × 40 m., and it is separated from the seating by a protective wall, which still retains much of its marble cladding. The amphitheatre retains its original role as a place for public spectacles and entertainments to the present day: it is the venue for bull-fights, Provençal races, and folk festivals every year.

All that remains visible of Constantine's Imperial palace is part of

▲ Arles: the Roman theatre

▲ Arles: the amphitheatre

the enormous **Baths.** These are dominated by the apse, still surmounted by its cupola, which once contained the hot plunge bath. The *caldarium* (hot room) and *tepidarium* (warm room) can be visited: both were exceptionally large, the former measuring 10 × 20 m. and preserving its hypocaust† (hot-air heating system).

Roman cemeteries were always located along the roads leading to the towns that they served: the best-known example is probably that on the Via Appia outside Rome. *Arelate* had a cemetery that compared favourably in the quality of its funerary monuments with the Appian Way. Known as *Les Alyscamps*, it runs along the Via Aurelia, coming up from Italy. Its renown grew from the C3, when the remains of the martyr St Genesius were interred there (it was also reputed that the body of St Trophimus, first bishop of Arles in the early C3, was buried there). Thousands of sarcophagi of pious Christians accumulated in the cemetery in the succeeding centuries, and numerous chapels were built for the use of pilgrims.

With the advent of the Renaissance the sanctity of Les Alyscamps declined and sarcophagi were removed, either as gifts to visiting notables or, more mundanely, for building purposes. Only one of the many

▼ The general layout of Roman theatres

original rows has been preserved, lined with noble trees and leading to the C12 church of Saint-Honoratus.

No visit to Arles should omit the late Romanesque† **Church of Saint-Trophime** and its superb portal and cloister, which was built

---

Roman theatres

The Romans acquired a passion for drama from the Greeks, who had evolved a specialized form of structure in which to present plays. This was a series of rising tiers of seats arranged in an arc slightly greater than a semicircle which faced a circular open space (*orchestra*–C) in front of a raised stage (*proskenion*–E), backed by a row of columns (*skene*). The tiers of seats were built into a hillside, so as to obviate the need for supporting structures. The main dramatic action took place on the *proskenion*, the *orchestra* being used by the chorus and for dancing.

When the drama became part of Roman culture the form of the theatre underwent certain modifications which make it relatively easy to differentiate between Greek and Roman buildings. Roman engineering skills made it simple to build free-standing structures, the tiers of seats being supported on massive radiating masonry supports. The plan was changed so that the seating area (*cavea*–A) became a true semicircle, as did the *orchestra*. The simple *skene* was replaced by an impressive architectural façade (*scenae frons*–F), with ornate entrances and several tiers of windows and balconies, which served as a permanent backdrop to dramatic performances. Above the stage there was a wooden roof that sloped backwards towards the *scenae frons*, to protect performers from the weather and to act as a sounding board.

The audience was similarly protected by a large awning (*velum* or *velarium*) suspended from masts mounted on the rear wall. As in the amphitheatres, access to the auditorium was by means of porticoes formed by the outer, arcaded wall, which in the more elaborate examples rose to two or three storeys, and the inner wall. These communicated in turn with the *cavea* through passages (*vomitoria*–G). The seats on the *cavea* were divided by horizontal cross-aisles (*praecinctiones*–D) and further into wedges (*cunei*–B).

The best preserved and most complete examples of the large Roman theatre are undoubtedly those of ORANGE and Aspendos (Turkey). However, it should be noted that theatres of this type are for the most part only to be found in the larger towns, such as ARLES. In the smaller towns rising ground was often used for locating theatres, in order to reduce the need for elaborate masonry structures.

Theatres were used for the presentation of plays and mimes, but it is known that gladiatorial contests were sometimes staged in them. More intimate or refined presentations—of music, poetry readings, lectures, etc.—took place in a smaller version of the full-sized theatre, known as an *odeon*, which had seats for no more than a thousand spectators, compared with the 12,000 and more of the theatres proper.

close to the Roman forum on what was most likely a temple precinct. It is one of the masterpieces of the influential Provençal Romanesque art. The original church, built in the early C5, was reconstructed at the turn of the C10. However, Saint-Trophime owes its present appearance to further reconstructions in the late C11 (the transept) and the early C12 (the nave). The proportions of the interior are magnificent, emphasized by an almost total absence of decoration. This is concentrated on the late C12 portal, depicting the Last Judgement.

The Roman and Romanesque monuments of Arles were inscribed on the World Heritage List by the UNESCO World Heritage Committee in 1981.

GAF 17; GB Provence 203–19; Bromwich 138–52; PBSAF 376–80.

62 Avignon Medieval town on Greek and Roman foundations *Vaucluse (84)* ★

Michelin 81 / 12. Musée Lapidaire: Rue de la République.

Human settlement on the Rocher des Doms, the hill directly overlooking the Rhône, is attested from at least as early as the Neolithic period in the fourth millennium BC. There was a large settlement here in the Bronze Age, and in the Iron Age it became the central *oppidum*† of the Cavares tribe, known as *Avenio*. As might be expected, a commercially significant strategic site such as this attracted the Greeks from MARSEILLES in the late C6 BC and it became a major trading centre, handling the goods travelling down the Rhône from central Gaul and beyond to the Mediterranean. With the advent of the Romans after the fall of *Massalia* it quickly and smoothly evolved into a flourishing Gallo-Roman town; some measure of its importance in the economy of *Gallia Narbonensis* is indicated by the fact that it was raised to the status of a *colonia latina*† in the C1 BC, and then promoted to the highest grade, that of Roman colony, by Hadrian at the beginning of the C2 AD.

Its later history remains obscure, although it is known to have been occupied by the Moorish invaders in the C8. They were driven out by Charles Martel in 737, when the town suffered severe destruction. It does not emerge as a significant power again until the C12, but its most glorious time was when the Papacy installed itself there in the early years of the C14.

Visitors to Avignon are attracted primarily by its superb monuments from the Papal period in the C14. The Roman town was razed to the ground in the C8, whilst what survived of its early defences was levelled in 1226 as a result of the citizens' espousal of the Albigensian heresy.

There are, however, some fragments of the forum† visible around the **Place de l'Horloge**, which is known from excavation to have been the centre of the Roman town. At the end of the Rue Saint-Étienne a number of architectural elements (fragments of capitals and sculpture from the pediments† of buildings that lined the forum) are visible, and there is a double arcade at the junction with the Rue de la Petite-Fusterie. Three sections of walling near the church of Saint-Agricol are thought to have formed part of the basilica† that marked the southern limit of the forum. There is also arcading in the Place de la Mirande, which may have formed part of the town's Roman theatre.

The great glory of Avignon is, of course, the magnificent complex of buildings around its medieval **Palais des Papes**. In the early C14 Pope Clement V abandoned Rome, which was riven by feuds between its noble families, for Provence. His successor, John XXII, installed himself in the episcopal palace at Avignon, of which he was also Bishop, and it was his successor, Benedict XII, who undertook the task of reconstructing a relatively modest episcopal residence in a style worthy of its Papal occupant. The Great Schism (1378–1417) saw rival Popes in Avignon and Rome. The exile in Avignon left behind a magnificent fortified palace in the mature Gothic style of the period, decorated by the Sienese master Simone Martini and his school. The cathedral retains its masterly Romanesque† form and appearance, but it, too, benefited from Papal patronage in the form of frescoes by Simone Martini.

The historic centre of Avignon was inscribed on the World Heritage List by the UNESCO World Heritage Committee in 1995.

GB Provence 231–64; Bromwich 152–5; PBSAF 380.

63 Barbégal Roman flour mills *Bouches-du-Rhône (13)* ★

Michelin 83/10. Take D 17 Abbaye de Montmajour/Les Baux, then at Fontvieille S on D 33 for 2 km. and turn left on D 82.

The flour mills at Barbégal, 3.5 km. south-east of Fontvieille, are among the most impressive monuments to Roman engineering anywhere in the ancient world. The original establishment has been shown by recent research to have been built in the C2 AD, when the water supply to ARLES was considerably augmented with the construction of a new aqueduct†, but this was reconstructed and much enlarged in the early C4 AD to meet the greatly increased requirements of the inhabitants of Arles, which was the most important city in southern Gaul at that time. The fact that the mills were powered by one of the two aqueducts that provided a public supply of fresh water for that city suggests that this was a municipal enterprise. It should be borne in mind that there was no free distribution of bread in Narbonensis, as there was in Rome, and so sale of the output of this establishment would have made a significant contribution to the municipal coffers.

The remains of two aqueducts can be seen at Barbégal, both easily visible on either side of the D 82. The **Eygalières aqueduct** was probably constructed at the end of the C2 AD, to increase the water supply of the earlier Caperon water source. Its course has been traced for at least 50

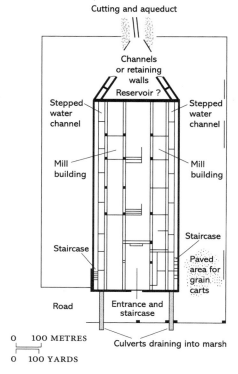

Cutting and aqueduct

Channels
or retaining
walls

Reservoir ?

Stepped
water
channel

Stepped
water
channel

Mill
building

Mill
building

Staircase

Staircase

Paved
area for
grain
carts

Road

Entrance and
staircase

0   100 METRES

0   100 YARDS

Culverts draining into marsh

▲ Barbégal: plan of the site

km. It crosses the Vallon des Arcs close to the mills on an arched structure of classical form, built in stone with bonding courses of brick. After having crossed the valley it swings abruptly westwards to Arles. For part of its course it runs parallel to the **Caperon aqueduct**, constructed in the late C1 BC, which comes from a source some 10 km. due east of the mills. This crosses the valley on a solid structure, built of dressed stone facing a rubble core. On the other side it continues straight ahead through a deep channel cut into the rock, to power the **mills**, which are ranged down the steep slope, with a fall of 1 : 3, on the other side.

Two parallel stepped rows, each of eight wheel-pits, can be identified. There appears to have been no holding reservoir at the top of the slope (although the interpretation of the triangular structure below the cutting is still a matter of debate as to whether it was a reservoir or merely the supporting structure for an elevated reservoir), and so the wheels were most likely driven by the direct flow from the aqueduct. Each powered a heavy basalt millstone used for grinding the grain, which would have been removed through the central aisle between the two rows of mills. The whole complex, which covers over 1,200 sq. m., is solidly constructed in dressed stone.

Estimates of the production from this complex vary substantially. The maximum water flow has been calculated to be 2000 litres/second, with an average of around 500 litres/second, given that the summer flow would be very low. This has been calculated to permit an optimum production of 9 tonnes in a twenty-four-hour day; however, a more realistic level, based on C19 mill outputs, would be no more than 3 tonnes per day. This would have been sufficient to feed at least 10,000 people.

GB Provence 291; Bromwich 156–60.

64 Bonnieux: Le Pont Julien   Roman bridge *Vaucluse (84)*

Michelin 84/2. N 100 W from Apt, then left on D 149 after 7 km.

The *Via Domitia*, the main east–west route across *Gallia Narbonensis*, had to cross the many rivers running down to the Mediterranean from the mountains of the hinterland. These were crossed by fords, ferries,

▼ Le Pont Julien

and in places by bridges, of pontoons or stone construction. One of the finest surviving bridges is to be seen spanning the Coulon (or Calavon) river 8 km. west of the important town of Apt (*Apta Iulia*) in Bonnieux commune.

The 68 m. long bridge is composed of three semicircular arches, unequal in size, so as to make use of different levels of bedrock for their foundations. The remains of buttresses can be seen on the upstream side and the two central pillars are pierced with holes to relieve pressure during periods of high water in the spring. The original humped parapet is still in place. The building technique using massive stone blocks suggests a mid-C1 BC construction date (this technique was replaced by the use of smaller dressed stones from the C1 AD onwards).

Bromwich 167–8; PBSAF 381.

65 Carpentras Roman triumphal arch *Vaucluse (84)*

Michelin 81/12. 20 km. NE of Avignon by D 942. Musée Comtadin-Duplessis (and access to Musée Lapidaire): Boulevard Albin-Durand.

With the consolidation of Roman rule in the region, the *Memini* were obliged to abandon their tribal *oppidum*†. The site of this is disputed: some authorities favour La Lègue, 2 km. to the east of the present town of Carpentras, which is known to have been founded in the C6 BC, whilst others prefer Venasque (*Vindasca*), 10 km. further away, in the foothills of the Vaucluse range. The new town, dominating the vital route along the Rhône valley, appears to have been founded around 46 BC and was given the name *Forum Neronis*, which suggests that it may originally have been created by Ti. Claudius Nero as a settlement for veterans of Caesar's legion, whilst the link with Caesar is strengthened by a later appellation, *Colonia Iulia Meminorum*; it later reverted to its native name, *Carpentoracte Meminorum*, from which its modern name derives. Little is known of its subsequent history, although it was to become the seat of a bishopric in the later Empire and was an important religious centre in the Middle Ages.

There is evidence of a Roman origin in the street pattern, but the only surviving monument is the **Triumphal Arch**. This impressive monumental structure, dated to the C1 AD, was in all probability originally located on one of the main streets of the Roman town. It owes its survival to having been dismantled and re-erected by a medieval bishop as the entrance to his palace, now used as the Palais de Justice.

The arch is in a somewhat mutilated condition, lacking its upper parts. However, the reliefs on the lower part have been preserved, especially on the west, where two prisoners are depicted chained to a pillar or tree, on which are draped their weapons. One is dressed in a cloak and is interpreted as a German tribesman, whilst the other, wearing a Phrygian cap†, trousers or leggings, and a short cloak, is believed to be a Parthian,

▲ Carpentras: the monumental arch

from the eastern boundaries of the Empire. The reliefs on the east, showing a similar scene, are heavily eroded; both prisoners seem to be in Greek dress and are thought to be from Asia Minor.

GB Provence 355–62; Bromwich 160–2; PBSAF 382.

Triumphal arches

The arch considered as a feature of the urban landscape began as a town gate, with a functional use, spanning the entrance from a main communications artery. These became increasingly ornate, decorated with symbolic reliefs and inscriptions, as towns grew in importance and wealth. They were also erected at the ends of major bridges, as at SAINT-CHAMAS, and on provincial frontiers, as boundary markers.

It was the Roman custom to grant their successful generals the honour of a triumph—that is to say, a lavish parade of his troops, his prisoners, and his booty. Soon, victorious commanders demanded more permanent witnesses to their military genius, and the symbol of the arch, which already testified to civic pride and dominated a major highway, was adopted for this purpose.

The earliest recorded examples date back to the early C2 BC, in Rome, but the oldest surviving examples are from the Augustan period (late C1 BC): they consist of massive rectangular structures with a single archway framed by pilasters and a plain entablature†. They were often surmounted by a low attic storey†, on which was mounted a chariot group.

Subsequently they became elaborately ornamented, with representations of soldiers, battle scenes, and trophies of arms†, as at CARPENTRAS and ORANGE. In some cases, such as the C2 Arch of Septimius Severus and the C3 Arch of Constantine in Rome, two additional side arches were added. In every case, however, they were sited at prominent points, either spanning the main streets of important towns or at prominent features on major roads.

The common term 'triumphal arch' is in some ways misleading, since not all the examples that have survived were erected to commemorate successful military operations. Some authorities prefer the more general term 'monumental arch'.

66 Cavaillon Roman triumphal arch *Vaucluse (84)*

Michelin 81/12. D 783, 20 km. SE of Avignon. Musée Archéologique: Cours Gambetta.

The Celto-Ligurian *oppidum*† of *Cabellio* was situated on what is now known as the Colline Saint-Jacques, where excavation has revealed traces of occupation from Neolithic times. It dominated the crossing of the Durance river, on the important east–west trade route. The local tribe of the *Cavares* came early under the rule of *Massalia* (MARSEILLES), which resulted in an urbanization on Hellenistic† lines that eased the transition into a Roman town. This spread down from the hill as a riverine port and the site of a ferry across the broad Durance. Its later history is obscure, though occupation was continuous up to the present day.

As with CARPENTRAS, urban continuity has masked the exact layout of the Roman town, the extent of which is perceptible to some extent in the contemporary street pattern. Rescue excavations in recent decades have revealed domestic dwellings and shops. The intersection of the two main streets, the *cardo*† and the *decumanus*†, is believed to have been where the Cathedral of Notre-Dame-et-Saint-Véran now stands, and it is here that a monumental arch was erected at the beginning of the C1 AD.

This structure, all that is now visible of ancient *Cabellio*, was originally incorporated in the medieval bishop's palace and was moved to its present site, in the Place François Tourel, in 1880. It was originally a tetrapylon (four-sided structure with arches between the massive corner pillars), but the linking vaults have disappeared and so it now consists of two separate arched structures that are sadly degraded. Sufficient of the decoration (notably the pilasters with their floral motifs) survives to demonstrate the high quality of the workmanship, and also to link the ornamentation with the Maison Carrée in NÎMES, where the same motifs are to be found.

GB Provence 369–74; Bromwich 163–4; PBSAF 382.

Château-Bas *see* VERNÈGUES.

67 Constantine Iron Age hillfort *Bouches-du-Rhône (13)*

Michelin 84/2. D 10 25 km. W of Aix-en-Provence, 1 km. N at Calissanne.

This is an Iron Age *oppidum*† with a well-preserved stone wall 350 m. long and the remains of ten towers. It was occupied from the C6 to the mid-C1 BC. Located 1 km. north-west of Château-Calissanne, it has a commanding view over the Étang de Berre from the north.

Bromwich 239.

68 La Couronne Roman stone quarries *Bouches-du-Rhône (13)*

Michelin 84/12. D 9 S from Marignane or D 5, then D 49 from Martigues.

The Iron Age settlement at this point on the Mediterranean coast of the Chaîne des Estaques that closes the Étang de Berre was one of the early Phocaean trading posts. However, nothing is to be seen at the present time. It seems likely to have lost this function with the growth of nearby *Massalia* (MARSEILLES), but settlement continued there in another role. The excellent building stone of Cap Couronne was exploited for use in the burgeoning Massaliote and Roman towns: it was used extensively, for example, in the Hellenistic† port of Marseilles. The ancient quarry workings are to be found on the eastern side of the small promontory.

GB Languedoc-Roussillon 364; Bromwich 166–7.

69 Entremont Pre-Roman *oppidum* *Bouches-du-Rhône (13)* ★★

Michelin 84/3. 3 km. N of Aix-en-Provence on D 14.

The *oppidum*† of Entremont, on its dramatic site commanding the plain in which AIX is situated, the Chaîne de l'Étoile, and the distant Montagne Sainte-Victoire so beloved of Cézanne, is unusual by virtue of the fact that it was occupied for a very short period, no more than a century, from *c*.190 to 90 BC. It was the capital of the Celto-Ligurian

▼ Entremont: plan of the excavations

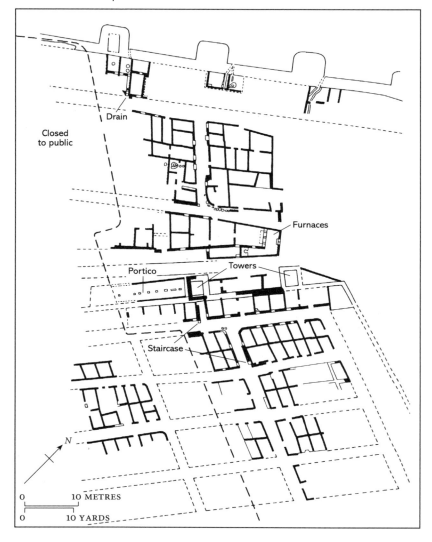

Closed to public

Drain

Furnaces

Portico

Towers

Staircase

N

0   10 METRES

0   10 YARDS

tribe of the *Salyes* or *Salluvii*, and has been variously interpreted. The original excavator saw the two distinct parts of the hillfort† as representing the fusion of two ethnically separate classes, a Celtic aristocracy who dominated a Ligurian plebeian group. However, later research sees in the two parts of the settlement an expansion resulting from an influx of Massaliote refugees, based on more precise dating of the finds.

The currently generally accepted view is that this settlement was founded by the *Salyes*, a culturally homogeneous group by this time, around 190 BC. It was continuously occupied, perhaps withstanding a siege in 124 or 125 BC, until 90 BC, when it was abandoned following an unsuccessful revolt against Roman rule. The Salyens had been involved in several unsuccessful risings by indigenous groups in the Massaliote region in the mid-C2, and it was after one of these was crushed around 150 BC that the Entremont *oppidum* offered sanctuary to refugees, necessitating an enlargement of the defended area.

The entire area of the archaeological site is open to visitors. The outline of the *oppidum* is triangular in plan, with steep slopes to the south; the gentler northern slope is cut off by a very substantial buttressed wall 380 m. in length. Access is from the north, through the outer defensive wall into the later Lower Town (*Ville Basse*), also known as Settlement (*Habitat*) 2. Over 150 m. of this wall is still visible. It is made of roughly coursed undressed rectangular stone facings with a rubble core, the whole some 3 m. thick. There are rectangular towers with rounded corners along the wall at 20 m. intervals. Both wall and towers still stand to a height of 4.5 m.; it is calculated that they were originally about 2 m. higher. Inside the area is laid out with rectangular streets with houses of two or more rooms opening on to them. Some of these contain metal-working furnaces and equipment associated with olive-oil production. The roads in this section of the *oppidum* were surfaced with small stones and crushed pottery and had gutters for removing rainwater.

One building on *insula* XI, at the junction between the two *habitats*, is set back from the street and had a pillared portico: this has been tentatively interpreted as a meeting place associated with the Celtic 'severed head' cult attested by the many carved heads and the fragments of human skulls found at Entremont. The building was constructed using stones from an earlier structure that formed part of the Settlement 1, some of which also carry the 'severed head' motif.

The addition of the Lower Town tripled the area of the settlement. The older part, known variously as the 'Upper Town' (*Ville Haute*) or Settlement 1, covers 1 ha. and was delineated by a defensive wall similar to that outside the Lower Town, of which several sections survive (including two towers). Its interior is divided on a rectangular grid pattern into *insulae*, with single-roomed houses aligned back to back. The walls of the houses are made of thin slabs of stone and the floors are of

The 'severed head' cult

A special characteristic of the pre-Roman sculpture of Southern France is the frequent occurrence of what are indisputably human heads that have been severed from their bodies. This is shown unambiguously in several examples from ENTREMONT, where heads are clearly being held in realistically carved hands. Certain statues of warriors are also shown wearing pectorals fastened with pins bearing severed heads.

The Greek philosopher and historian Posidonius, who visited Gaul around 100 BC, recorded that the Gauls cut off the heads of their defeated enemies and nailed them on the walls of their houses; the most important of them were pickled in a pungent oil and carefully stored in boxes. Strabo, writing at the end of the C1, reported that one Gallic warrior would not give up one of his trophy heads in exchange for its weight in gold. These observations are confirmed by the discovery in excavations at the *oppidum* of La Cloche (Bouches-du-Rhône), where human skulls were found that appear to have been mounted over the main gate.

This phenomenon is not confined to Southern France. There are numerous recorded examples of similar practices from Ireland, northern England, and Wales in the Late Iron Age. Whether it was in fact a cult is debatable: some scholars prefer to see it as a somewhat gruesome form of demonstrating warlike skills.

▼ Severed head from Entremont

beaten earth; each has a hearth in the corner. The streets were paved, but less elaborately than those in the Lower Town.

The finds from Entremont are on display at the Musée Granet in AIX-EN-PROVENCE.

GB Provence 172; Bromwich 130–1; PBSAF 372–3.

Fontalba, Vallée de *see* MONT-BÉGO.

Fontbrégoua, Grotte de *see* SALERNES.

70 Fréjus Roman defences, aqueduct, and public buildings *Var (83)*★★
Michelin 84/8.

There was probably a settlement on this site in the Early Iron Age, but the town known to the Romans as *Forum Iulii* owes its origins in the mid-C1 BC, as its name implies, to Julius Caesar, who either founded the settlement or, more likely, reorganized an existing native port and market. However, it was no more than a staging post until Augustus settled veterans of the VIII Legion and his fleet here in a *colonia*† after his victory at Actium in 31 BC. A large area was enclosed by a defensive wall with bastions and monumental gates, and the natural sheltered harbour was extended and deepened. Its role as a major Roman naval base declined rapidly with the consolidation of the Empire by Augustus, its role being taken over by Misenum, although there was a fleet presence here until the latter part of the C1 AD. However, this did not inhibit the growth of the civil town, which developed to become one of the important towns in southern Gaul, as a major outlet for the wines and other products of the region. However, this failed to occupy the entire area defined by the walls: excavations have shown that extensive intramural quarters were used for market gardens and craft workshops, normally located outside the walls of Roman towns. Its status is illustrated by the fact that it was not adopted as the capital of the province of *Narbonensis Secunda* created in the late C3 AD.

One famous citizen of *Forum Iulii* was Cn. Julius Agricola, Governor of Britain in the latter part of the C1 AD, whose biography was written by his son-in-law, C. Cornelius Tacitus, one of the greatest Roman historians.

Occupation has been continuous on this site since the C1 BC, despite its having suffered destruction at the hands of Saracen marauders, the fate of a number of the towns on this coast, in the C10.

Substantial remains of the **Ramparts** of the Early Empire are visible, especially on the eastern side of the town, to the north of Avenue du XVème Corps d'Armée. The impressive remains of the **Aqueduct**† entered the town here, at the site of the now vanished eastern gate, the Porte de Rome. The massive pillars were constructed using different types of local sandstone and faced with brick. Other sections of the aqueduct,

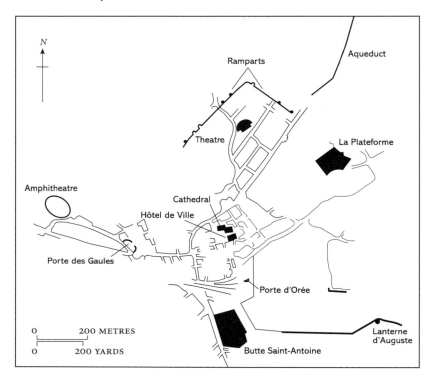

▲ Fréjus: map showing major monuments

brought water to the town from the river Siagnole, some 30 km. to the
north through channels and tunnels cut through the rock and artificial
raised channels. The **Porte des Gaules**, at the other end of the main
east–west street (*decumanus maximus*) from the Porte de Rome (access
from the Rue Henri Vadon) is, like its vanished counterpart, in the form
of a half-moon in plan; one of its two flanking towers survives, though
in the form of a C19 reconstruction that bears little resemblance to the
original.

To the south-east of the Porte de Rome (approached from the Rue
des Marsouins) is **La Plateforme**, a massive Roman defensive work
created by building walls round a natural hillock and then filling the
intervening spaces, so as to form a level surface. It has been interpreted
as the residence of an important military or civil official. Excavations
have brought to light a complex round a central garden or courtyard
with a massive cistern beneath. There is a small baths complex in one
corner of the ensemble.

A similar artificial mound is to be found to the south, on the western
side of the harbour. The **Butte Saint-Antoine** (on the Boulevard

▲ Fréjus: the aqueduct

Séverin-Decuers) duplicates La Plateforme and doubtless served a like purpose. Little now survives beyond the well-built retaining walls, reinforced by a series of semicircular niches, and three towers, one of which is considered to have been a lighthouse. Between the two official residences and overlooking the harbour is the so-called **Porte d'Orée**, which is not a gate but an arched section of the *frigidarium*† of the public baths that stood here.

The modern port conforms to a considerable extent with the Roman harbour, and was defended originally by walls, only small sections of which survive. One of the most impressive remaining features is the **Lanterne d'Auguste**, a massive tower surmounted by a hexagonal structure; this is interpreted as the marker for the harbour entrance, and is believed to have been supported by a similar building on the other side of the canal, 30 m. wide and 500 m. long, leading into the harbour.

Few of the public monuments and buildings of *Forum Iulii* are visible. The forum†, with its group of official religious and administrative buildings, is thought to lie beneath the present-day Early Gothic cathedral and its surroundings. The vestiges of the much-decayed **Theatre** are in the northern corner of the town (Rue du Théâtre Romain); to visit it application should be made to the Hôtel de Ville (Services Culturels).

The **Amphitheatre** (entrance Rue Henri Vadon) has fared better than the theatre. It is smaller than the amphitheatres at ARLES and NÎMES, measuring 114 × 82 m., and is more austere in design, probably because it was built for the use of naval personnel and army veterans, probably in the mid-C1 AD. The exterior façade no longer exists *in situ*, having been removed, it is believed, by the citizens in the C10 to prevent it from being turned into a strongpoint by Saracen marauders. Its use for various forms of spectacle in the present century has resulted in some reconstruction having been carried out that is not in keeping with an ancient monument, but the overall effect is still one of strength and power.

In addition to its interesting Early Gothic cathedral, the fortified episcopal complex in the centre of modern Fréjus contains an outstanding work of C5 art in its **Baptistery**†, the upper part of which has been reconstructed somewhat speculatively, but which preserves its fine late Roman baptismal pool.

There is a small archaeological museum in the cloisters of the cathedral.

GB Provence 476–83; Bromwich 252–67; PBSAF 387.

The Roman fleets

The Romans did not consider their navy as an independent service, unlike today: it was treated as part of the army, and its role was mainly in support of the legions. Thus, naval units were recruited to supply and transport armies by sea and along rivers during major campaigns such as Caesar's conquest of Gaul, when Fréjus was established as the main base.

In 37 BC Marcus Vipsanius Agrippa assembled an enormous fleet for Octavian (the future Emperor Augustus), which defeated first Sextus Pompeius, son of Pompey the Great, at Naulochus in 36 BC and then the combined fleets of Cleopatra and Marcus Antonius at Actium in 31 BC, bringing the civil wars to a final conclusion. During these battles the ships served primarily as fighting platforms for soldiers, rather than engaging in true naval battles in the way the Athenian triremes had in the C4 BC.

With the advent of peace, the Roman fleet was reorganized with what was essentially a supply and transportation function. The two main bases of the Imperial fleet were in the Mediterranean, at *Misenum* on the Bay of Naples and Ravenna, on the Adriatic coast of Italy. One of the most important roles of the Misene fleet was to protect the slow merchant vessels that brought grain to Rome from North Africa against pirates. In addition, auxiliary fleets were formed to provide sea-borne backup services in sensitive areas, such as the Black Sea, the Danube, the Rhine, and around the coasts of Britain.

71 Gap Roman defences *Hautes Alpes (05)*

Michelin 77/16. Musée Départemental: in Pépinière public garden.

The Colline Saint-Mens, 1 km. to the south-east of the modern town, was the site of a Gaulish hillfort†, probably of the Caturiges, one of the tribes swept aside by Caesar when he began his conquest of Gaul. *Vapincum*, the Roman town built on the route linking SISTERON with northern Italy, seems to have been settled by people of the Avantici tribe, brought here by Galba in AD 69.

Because of its strategic position, Gap has been destroyed on several occasions. All that remains visible of its Roman heritage is a stretch of the C3 wall and one of the towers. The **Musée Départemental** contains many rich finds from the surrounding area.

Bromwich 291; PBSAF 387.

Glanum *see* SAINT-RÉMY-DE-PROVENCE.

Grand-Loou, Villa du *see* LA ROQUEBRUSSANE.

72 Hyères: Olbia Remains of Greek town *Var (83)*

Michelin 84/16–17. On D 559 E of Toulon. Musée Municipal: Place Théodore-Lefèbvre.

Olbia was one of the latest colonies to be created by the Phocaean merchants in *Massalia* (MARSEILLES), *c.*330–300 BC, both as a trading centre and as a defensive outpost to provide protection against attacks from local Celto-Ligurian tribes. The settlement prospered, expanding to become an important farming centre. It continued in existence throughout the Roman period, but the lack of impressive public buildings suggests that it did not play an important role in the administrative life of the province. It seems to have been abandoned in the C6 AD, when its inhabitants relocated to a less vulnerable site, that of modern Hyères on a hill overlooking the coast.

▼ Hyères: plan of Olbia

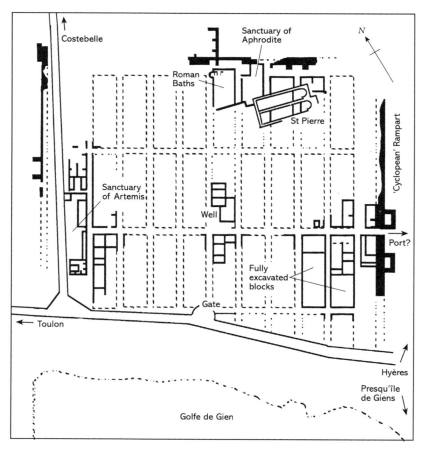

The Greek town was built on the coast, on the stretch now known as L'Almanarre. Erosion of this sandy coast by the sea has removed much of the ancient town.

The town founded by the Massaliotes covered an area 165 m. square, with a regular grid of streets, in characteristic Greek form. The two main axial streets created four quarters, each of which was in turn subdivided by alleys into ten rectangular *insulae*. The substantial walls, with a square bastion at each corner and others on the north and west stretches, were pierced by several gates. The massive nature of the defences and the character of the internal layout suggest that this settlement began life with its predominant role that of a fortress: the buildings on the *insulae* have an air of barrack-blocks about them.

With the coming of the *Pax Romana*† the military function disappeared, and the later buildings are wholly domestic in character. Modest public buildings such as the baths and the sanctuaries of Aphrodite and Artemis gave an indication of the status of the Roman town. There was some extra-mural development to the east, but none to the west, where the cemeteries were located.

The surviving remains include parts of the main gate, on the east, and some excavated areas within the walls containing the foundations of domestic buildings, a small bath suite, and a sanctuary.

The **Musée Municipal** contains finds from underwater excavations of Roman merchant vessels off the neighbouring Îles d'Hyères.

GB Provence 523–9; Bromwich 267–70; PBSAF 388–9.

7 3 Île Sainte-Marguerite (Îles de Lérins) Greek and Roman remains *Alpes-Maritimes (06)*

Michelin 84/9. The islands can be reached by boat from Cannes.

The two islands off the Mediterranean coast near Cannes were both occupied in antiquity. The more important was *Lero* (Île Sainte-Marguerite), reported by both Strabo, who describes a Greek sanctuary, and Pliny, who refers to an earlier *oppidum*† or town (*Bercona*).

The open excavated remains within the C17 Fort Royal to the west of the modern port date back in their earlier phase to the C4 BC. Roman influence can be seen from the C1 BC, especially in the mosaic floors. The sturdy rampart with its buttresses have been interpreted as a Roman reconstruction of the precinct wall of the Greek sanctuary in the C1 BC. A long esplanade was created in the early C1 AD by means of a series of *cryptoportici*†. There are also several substantial Roman water cisterns in other parts of the Fort.

There are vestigial remains of a Roman harbour on the western part of the island, and a number of wrecks of Roman vessels have been located in the waters nearby.

Although it is known that the other island, known in antiquity as

Lerina, was inhabited from an early period, there is nothing to see there relating to Honoratus, the C4 saint from whom it derives its modern name. It became a place of pilgrimage during the saint's lifetime and he founded a monastery there. The C11 fortified monastery, however, is known to have been constructed on Gallo-Roman foundations, and the restored Chapelle de la Trinité is laid out on a Byzantine trefoil plan, with a dome suspended on pendentives†. There is a small museum on the Île Saint-Honorat.

GB Provence 536–42; Bromwich 275–6; PBSAF 382.

74 Istres Pre-Roman *oppidum* *Bouches-du-Rhône (13)*

Michelin 84/1.

The Celto-Ligurian *oppidum†* of Le Castellan to the north of the town, overlooking the Étang de l'Olivier, is one of several in this area around the Étang de Berre (cf. CONSTANTINE, MARTIGUES). Walls of some of the houses are visible as are the rock-cut steps linking the terraces on which the houses were built. Finds are displayed in the **Musée du Vieil-Istres**, which has a fine collection of material from underwater excavations in the Golfe de Fos, and from the Roman port of *Fossae Marianae*, destroyed during the C20 development of the modern Port de Fos.

GB Provence 622–3; Bromwich 164–6.

Lecques, Villa des *see* SAINT-CYR-SUR-MER.

75 Marseilles Graeco-Roman remains *Bouches-du-Rhône (13)* ★

Michelin 84/13. Musée d'Histoire de Marseille: Rue Henri-Barbusse; Musée des Docks Romains: Place Vivaux; Musée d'Archéologie Méditerranéenne: Rue de la Charité.

Tin from the British Isles was one of the most important trade goods coming into the Mediterranean in the Bronze Age. One route brought it down the Atlantic coasts of Europe to southern Spain, the other came overland, using the great rivers of Gaul, and in particular the Rhône. Greek traders had already established contacts in Ligurian settlements around the mouth of the Rhône such as SAINT-BLAISE and LA COURONNE in the later C7. However, it was the foundation of *Massalia* by Phocaeans from Asia Minor, traditionally in 600 BC, that saw the opening up of southern Gaul and the expansion of the traditional trade routes between northern Europe and the Mediterranean. Marseilles became the commercial centre of this trade, and Massaliote daughter colonies were set up first at Ampurias (Catalonia) and later at ANTIBES, NICE, and HYÈRES (*Olbia*) to develop trade with indigenous groups (and also to provide protection for merchants against their not infrequent armed insurrections).

Little is known of the early settlement, round the protected

The coming of metals

The first metals to be worked by man were those which occur in a pure state ('native metals'), namely gold, silver, and copper. Of these copper was the only one which possessed the requisite physical properties that would make it suitable for the manufacture of tools and weapons. The great technological breakthrough came in the seventh millennium BC, when it was recognized that this material could be produced by the application of heat in controlled conditions to certain minerals (smelting of ores). Not long after, the copper workers discovered that the properties of copper—its hardness and ductility—could be improved by the judicious addition of a white metal produced by a similar process of smelting other minerals, namely tin.

The earliest recorded copper objects—mostly small blades—reached Southern France in the first half of the fourth millennium BC. However, these were no more than trade objects: it was not for several centuries that the technology was imported that would permit the local inhabitants to produce these high-value goods from their own natural resources. The discovery of rich deposits of tin ore in Brittany and Cornwall, which were traded down the Garonne into the Mediterranean, resulted in high-quality bronze tools and weapons becoming widely available in Southern France.

Iron was to come later, in the C8 BC, because its production required greater technological skills than that of copper. Knowledge of iron smelting penetrated Southern France both from Etruria, as part of the extensive trade with the Greek colonies on the Mediterranean coast, and from Germany and northern France down the trade artery of the Rhône valley. Iron ore is widely available in Europe—the immense deposits of the Montagne Noire in Languedoc were exploited on an industrial scale during the Roman period—and so it was much cheaper to produce than bronze. Once techniques for improving its physical properties, by hardening and tempering, became widely understood, iron replaced bronze for all but ceremonial and decorative purposes.

anchorage provided by this deep inlet (*calanque*†) overlooked by a narrow promontory—the classic site for a Greek trading settlement. Tradition has it that the local tribe, the *Segobrigi*, were persuaded to make the land available when Gyptis, daughter of the king of the tribe, chose Protis, one of the founding Phocaeans, as her husband.

It is clear that the new settlement rapidly prospered, since a treasury had been set up by the Massaliotes at the sanctuary of Apollo in Delphi as early as 525 BC. The main trade competition to Massalia came from the Etruscan cities of northern and central Italy. The establishment of a Massaliote colony at Alalia (Corsica) in the mid-C6 constituted a major threat to the Etruscans, who entered into a long struggle, supported by their Phoenician allies, that ended ultimately in victory for Massalia.

From that time, Massalia was unchallenged as the commercial and cultural centre of the region.

The protracted contest between Rome and Carthage that began in the C3, however, had an adverse effect on the development of Massalia, since it lay on the direct land route between Italy and the Carthaginian lands in the Iberian peninsula. In the Second Punic War the city was loyal to the Roman cause, providing valuable naval support. In return, Roman military aid was always available, as in 125 BC, when Massalia was attacked by the *Salyes*. This saw the beginning of Roman involvement in the region, leading to the creation of the Roman province of *Gallia Transalpina*.

Massalia and its dependent territory enjoyed a privileged status within the province as an independent republic allied to Rome with territories extending along the Mediterranean littoral. This status was not wholly forfeited when the Massaliotes opted for Pompey rather than Caesar during the Civil War. It was taken by Caesar's forces after a six-months siege in 49 BC, and much of its wealth was confiscated, but it was granted the status of a *civitas foederata*, although its dependent territory was much reduced in area.

The events of this period had an impact on the city's commercial role, which was henceforth shared with the ports of ARLES and NARBONNE, although it was to remain a centre of Greek culture in the Roman world. However, the traditional view that Massalia (or *Massilia*, as it was more generally known in the Roman period) declined greatly has been shown to be fallacious by recent excavations, which have shown that major new port installations were built in the late C1 BC that remained in use well into the C3 AD.

Loss of its autonomy in the later C3 AD was to some extent compensated by a new role as a centre of Christianity in the region. Its location ensured that it continued to play an important commercial role after the barbarian invasions of the C5, to such an extent that it was the object of bitter struggles between barbarian rulers. However, the Saracen raids that began in the C7 marked the end of this phase of the city's life; it was not to resume its leading role again until the C11.

There is little to be seen nowadays of the distinguished early history of Marseilles. The deliberate destruction of much of the old town above the Vieux Port (site of the *calanque*† that served as the original Greek harbour) by the German occupying army in 1943 and the effect of air raids in 1940 and 1944 provided the opportunity for considerable excavation starting in 1967, which has thrown much light on the development of the city.

The **Jardin des Vestiges** is an archaeological park on the Rue Henri-Barbusse, adjacent to the modern building housing the **Musée d'Histoire de Marseille**. It is an area to the west of the Phocaean settlement that was originally marshy, but which was progressively

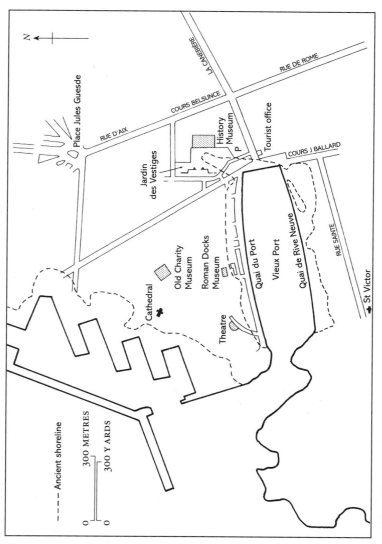

▲ Marseilles: map showing monuments and museums

N

300 METRES
0
300 YARDS
0

- - - - Ancient shoreline

Place Jules Guesde

RUE D'AIX

COURS BELSUNCE

LA CANEBIÈRE

RUE DE ROME

Jardin
des Vestiges

History
Museum

Tourist office

P

COURS J BALLARD

Cathedral

Old Charity
Museum

Roman Docks
Museum

Quai du Port

Vieux Port

Quai de Rive Neuve

RUE SAINTE

Theatre

St Victor

drained over the succeeding years. The small creek was widened and deepened to form a harbour. Most of the remains date from the Hellenistic† and Roman periods.

A section of the 3 m. thick Hellenistic city wall, built of large blocks of dressed stone, with some late Roman modifications, is on display; its course has been traced over a considerable part of its alignment. A section of road, which replaced an earlier causeway, is preserved, running up to the city gate.

The quays of the Flavian period (late C1 AD) harbour or 'horn' were built of stone blocks up to a height of 4.5 m. A stone basin, sealed with pitch, was added later, to combat the problem of silting, and this provided drinking water for ships; it also powered a small waterwheel used to raise water from the basin.

Although the visible monumental remains are slight, Marseilles has several fine museums. The **Musée des Docks Romains**, to the north of the Vieux-Port, covers part of a Roman warehouse; its main importance, however, lies in the material that it contains from several underwater excavations of shipwrecks in the area. The remains of a Roman merchant ship discovered just outside the horn in 1974, plus a

▼ Marseilles: interior of the Musée des Docks romains, showing excavated areas

full-scale replica, can be seen in the **Musée d'Histoire de Marseille**, along with much other archaeological material from the city; there is also a fine view over the archaeological remains in the Jardin de Vestiges. The restored C17 Centre de la Vieille Charité contains the **Musée d'Archéologie Méditerranéenne**, where the material from ROQUEPERTUSE is on display in the Celto-Ligurian Gallery.

GB Provence 565 ff.; Bromwich 168–76; PBSAF 391–2.

The Greeks in Southern France

The important trade in tin, essential for making bronze, was originally down the west coasts of France and the Iberian peninsula into the Mediterranean through the Pillars of Hercules (Straits of Gibraltar). This was dominated by the Phoenicians, from Carthage and their ports in North Africa and Spain. The Greeks from Phocaea in Asia Minor, who were great seafarers, began the Greek colonization of the western Mediterranean, setting up trading colonies along the coast of southern Italy in what became known as *Magna Graecia* (Greater Greece) during the C7 BC. In order to circumvent the Phoenicians, they began to explore the overland route across south-western France, from the Garonne across to the Hérault and the Mediterranean.

Phocaean traders had established contact with native settlements such as SAINT-BLAISE and LA COURONNE at the mouth of the Rhône in the later C7, thus gaining access to the heartlands of Gaul by river. *Massalia* (MARSEILLES), the site selected for the first Phocaean colony around 600 BC, was some 50 km. to the west, on a good natural harbour well sited to trade both up the Rhône and with the commercial overland Garonne–Hérault route. It prospered rapidly and soon set up daughter colonies all along the coast—*Nicaea* (NICE), *Tauroentium* (Le Brusc, near Toulon), *Olbia* (HYÈRES), *Antipolis* (ANTIBES), and *Agatha* (AGDE) in the west.

The main competition came from Etruria, on the western coast of central Italy, which had been trading actively in southern Gaul for many years. The Etruscans formed an alliance with Carthage, but were decisively beaten at Alalia (Corsica) by the Massaliotes in 537 BC. Thereafter *Massalia* and its daughter towns enjoyed virtual hegemony over trade between Southern France and the rest of the Mediterranean world until the advent of the Romans in the C2 BC.

---

76 Martigues Iron Age settlement *Bouches-du-Rhône (13)* ★

Michelin 84/12. On N 568 30 km. W of Marseilles. Musée Ziem: Boulevard du 14 Juillet.

In the C5 BC a small settlement was established on an islet in the channel linking the Étang de Berre with the Mediterranean by the *Avatici*, a

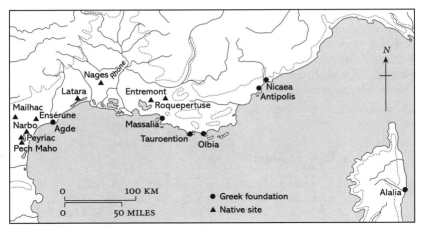

▲ Greek colonization of Southern France (from Barry Cunliffe, *Greeks, Romans and Barbarians: Spheres of Interaction*, Fig. 7; 1988: Batsford, London)

member of the confederation of Celto-Ligurian tribes dominated by the *Salyes*, whose capital was at ENTREMONT. It continued in occupation until at least the end of the C2. It appears to have come under Roman influence and it is identified with the *Maritima* in Pliny's list of tribal settlements. Nothing is known of its subsequent history in antiquity.

The Iron Age settlement was brought to light during rescue excavations in 1978–89. It was surrounded by a high stone wall with bastions, enclosing a roughly oval habitation area. Inside the layout was rectilinear, with small single-room square houses lining the ramparts and a series of straight streets. There was no public open space nor were any larger public buildings discovered; this layout is characteristic of the small indigenous settlements associated with the Greek colony at MARSEILLES.

The houses themselves, built mainly in unfired brick and tile, were small, each with a hearth near the door. There was clearly marked division of the interior space for specialized activities, such as sleeping, eating, cooking, and the storage of grain. The houses point to a communal way of life that took place largely in the streets, which were carefully made up of sand and pebbles.

Some of the houses have been reconstructed and conserved and can be seen in the museum in the northern part of this attractive little town.

GB Provence 616–18; Bromwich 240; PBSAF 393.

Merveilles, Vallée des *see* MONT-BÉGO.

77 Mont Bégo: Les Vallées des Merveilles et de Fontalba Bronze Age rock engravings *Alpes-Maritimes (06)* ★★

Michelin 84/9–10, 19–20. This mountainous area is reached from Nice by taking the N 202 northwards. Helpful tourist information and suggested itineraries are to be found in the Michelin Green Guide Côte d'Azur, *112–13 and in the* Guide Bleu Provence Alpes Côte d'Azur, *707–8.*

The southern Alpine region was colonized by Bronze Age people in the early second millennium BC. They brought with them a complex polytheistic religion, with a vivid and imaginative iconography. The ruggedly beautiful region around Mont Bégo was clearly seen as one of great sanctity, and it became a cult centre for the entire area. It must have been a place of pilgrimage for people living in lowland regions that were more favourable to human settlement, to judge by the immense number of rock engravings concentrated in the Vallée des Merveilles and other valleys around the mountain.

Cultural upheavals and climatic fluctuation in the second half of the second millennium brought about profound changes in belief and habitat, and the practice of rock engraving for cult purposes was abandoned.

▼ Mont Bégo: general view of the landscape

However, the upland pastures continued to attract shepherds, hunters, outlaws, and visitors in the succeeding centuries, and all left their traces in the rocks. The Vallée des Merveilles has been likened to a giant amphitheatre sculpted by glacial erosion and defined by peaks and crests mirrored in the many mountain lakes. It lies above the tree-line and the vegetation is sparse; for much of the year it is snow-covered. The valley floors are strewn with glacial erratic boulders†, some of enormous size, and with outcrops of rock smoothed by the action of the ancient glaciers. The fine-grained sandstones and schists that make up the geology of the region have weathered into a dazzling range of colours—every shade of violet, red, orange, yellow, and green—as a result of geochemical and microbiological action.

More than 100,000 engravings have been recorded since Émile Rivière and the Englishman Clarence Bicknell began their work in the 1870s. This was taken up by the Italian sculptor Carlo Conti between 1927 and 1942, and has been continuing as an annual systematic recording campaign since 1967 carried out by a multidisciplinary group led by Henry de Lumley (Université de Nice).

The Bronze Age engravings in this region are symbolic pictograms, without any attempt at realism; there is also no indication that they should be evaluated as hieroglyphs or ideographs. Five main groups have been identified:

1 corniforms (animal horns)—46%;
2 weapons and tools (daggers, swords, halberds, sickles, axes, etc.)—4%;
3 anthropomorphic figures (single, multiple, etc)—0.2%;
4 geometric figures (circles, crosses, stars, spirals, etc)—7%; and
5 non-representational figures—42.8%.

The corniforms, to which should be added corniform human and animal representations, are in places grouped in such a way as to imply an act of communal worship. In some case horned animals are harnessed to simple ploughs. They may therefore be identified with confidence as being associated with bovines, which are known elsewhere in the Mediterranean to have had special religious significance (cf. the Minotaur).

The representations of weapons can be related directly to actual Chalcolithic and Early and Middle Bronze Age weapons, which helps to date these engravings.

The rare anthropomorphic figures are highly stylized. Certain of them have attracted popular names, such as the Chief of the Tribe, the Sorcerer, the Little Man with the Torero's Hat, the Dancer, and the Christ. Several show 'stick men' brandishing weapons or using tools.

▲ Mont Bégo: engraving showing plough drawn by oxen

The technique used is that of pecking the surface of the rock with a pointed metal or stone tool. The meticulous technique of the early engravings gave way to more sketchy workmanship. Incised lines are to be found on later engravings, which include some Roman inscriptions and later representations of warriors and boats.

The two main areas of rock engravings are the Vallée de Merveilles, which is reached from Saint-Dalmas-de-Tende via the Lac des Mesces and the Vallon de la Minière, and the Vallée de Fontalba, accessible through the Val de Casterino. The best-known examples are to be found near the southern edge of the Lac des Merveilles. All are difficult of access and for certain groups it is advisable to secure the services of a local guide.

GAF 26; GB Provence 702–8; PBSAF 408–9.

Early man

The mid-C19 was the birth of the study of human origins, now known as human palaeontology, which flourishes to the present day, generating controversy and sensationalism.

It is now generally accepted that the ancestors of modern human beings originated in Africa, spreading gradually across the face of the planet. *Homo erectus* is now thought to have made his first appearance in Europe around 900,000 years ago, in the period known to geologists as the Lower Pleistocene and to archaeologists as the Lower Palaeolithic (Old Stone Age). This species was using crude tools of stone, bone, and antler (and no doubt also of wood, though these have not survived), but appears to have lacked the ability to create fire. Theirs was a nomadic way of life, following herds of game and ripening plants and fruits, in what anthropologists describe as hunter-gatherer societies.

Gradually they improved their way of life, making more elaborate, specialized tools and weapons and mastering the use of fire. Their settlements were no more than transient camps, moving north and south as the ice sheets retreated and advanced. Some more permanent, but still seasonal, settlements are known from Southern France, such as Terra Amata (Nice). They were joined (and perhaps replaced) around 200,000 years ago by another form of hominid, *Homo neanderthalensis* (better known as Neanderthal Man, named for the site in Germany where this species was first recognized). With this began the archaeological period known as the Middle Palaeolithic, when techniques of tool production were refined. A number of sites in Southern France have produced evidence of occupation at this period, notably Orgnac.

Around 35,000 years ago the direct ancestors of modern human beings, *Homo sapiens sapiens*, appeared in Europe and replaced their Neanderthal cousins (and perhaps interbred with them). The Upper Palaeolithic saw rapid developments in tool and weapon production and the mastery of fire. The flowering of cave art is eloquent testimony to the spiritual life of the Upper Palaeolithic. Although its symbolism still remains largely enigmatic, it constitutes irrefutable evidence of an awareness of the supernatural.

78 Nice Roman public buildings *Alpes-Maritimes (06)*   ★
Michelin 84/9–10.

Humans have been living on and around the site of modern Nice, on the Baie des Anges, since the Lower Palaeolithic period, some 500,000 years ago. It first enters history with the arrival of Greek colonists from MARSEILLES, who set up one of their trading posts there and gave it the name *Nikaia*. This was probably located at latter-day Vieux-Nice, below the castle hill. By this time the local Celto-Ligurian tribe, the *Vediantii*, were settled in a hillfort† or *oppidum*† at Cimiez (*Cemenelenum*). The two settlements seem to have coexisted peacefully, since the Vediantii do not figure as enemies in accounts of the defence of the Massaliote communities by the Romans in 154 BC, nor in the list on the LA TURBIE inscription.

With the creation of the new province of *Alpes Maritimae* by Augustus *Cemenelenum* became its capital, and it prospered throughout the Early Empire. It was, however, devastated during the late C4 barbarian incursions, and the site was finally abandoned during the C5, when the urban focus settled definitively on the decayed Greek town of Nikaia, which was not to recover until the C10.

Mont Boron, on the eastern side of the present town, has revealed evidence of Lower Palaeolithic occupation. The Grotte du Lazaret has been known since the early C19; recent scientific excavations there have produced the vestigial remains of an Acheulean shelter, along with abundant stone tools and food remains.

When earth-moving works were carried out on the slopes of Mont Boron to the north-west of the Grotte, a Lower Palaeolithic encampment was revealed and excavated. The remains of several shelters were discovered, together with tools and food remains, which indicated that this was a seasonally occupied site dated to 480,000 years ago. The material is

▼ Nice: plan of Cimiez

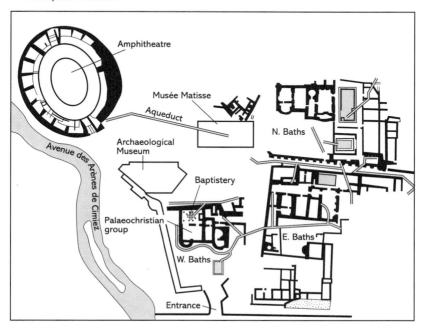

conserved in the **Musée de Paléontologie Humaine de Terra Amata** near the original site, with reconstructions of the settlement.

Major public buildings of the Roman town are preserved and displayed in the **archaeological area** at Cimiez, which covers about 1 ha. The best-preserved features of the monumental Northern Baths are the swimming pool and the colonnaded *frigidarium* or cold room (known in the Middle Ages as the 'Temple of Apollo'). The two *caldaria*† were much degraded by being converted to dwelling houses in the late Roman period.

These baths are separated from the later Eastern Baths, which survive in only fragmentary form, by a buttressed wall lining one of the main streets (*decumanus*†). Another *decumanus* forms the southern limit of this block, which also contains a group of late Roman houses.

The last bath complex to be built in the town was the Western Baths, which may have been reserved for use by women, judging from articles found in the drains. They were converted in the C5 to a church by the removal of the walls between the *caldaria* and the *tepidarium*, the choir being constructed in the *frigidarium*. The baptistery† was built in the area formerly occupied by the two furnaces; the hexagonal baptismal pool in the centre was formerly covered by a canopy on six columns, two of which survive.

The amphitheatre lies just outside the archaeological area. It is small by comparison with those at ARLES or NÎMES, with seating for only five

▼ Nice: the Roman baths at Cimiez

thousand spectators in its two ranks of seats. These were demonstrably built in two phases, one Augustan† and the other Severan†, since they are very different in style and construction: the excavator estimated that the original structure had places for at most six hundred people. The arena is cut out of the solid rock, and so lacks the customary cellars and other underground works to be found in Roman amphitheatres.

The **Musée Archéologique** is located at Cimiez, just to the south of the amphitheatre.

GB Provence 651–74; Bromwich 277–86; PBSAF 394–5.

Olbia *see* HYÈRES.

79 Orange Roman public buildings *Vaucluse (84)* ★★
Michelin 81/12. Musée Municipal: Place des Frères-Mounet.

The high ground overlooking the fertile plain of the lower Rhône valley on which Orange developed provided an ideal location for human settlement. Human settlement was certainly established there in the Neolithic period, and occupation continued, perhaps intermittently, during the Bronze Age. However, the proto-town of the Iron Age lay some 5 km. to the south of the modern town, at Lampourdier; the Colline Saint-Eutrope, now a public park in Orange, was probably the site of a subsidiary *oppidum*†. It was here that a Roman army was annihilated in 105 BC by the invading Germanic tribes, the *Cimbri* and the *Teutones*.

Like its neighbours, AVIGNON and CAVAILLON, *Arausio* was a centre of the *Cavares* and came under Massaliote domination in the C6. With the submission of Massalia to the Romans in 49 BC, a new colony was founded at the lesser site for legionary veterans of the II Gallica, known from the number of their unit as *Secundani*. There is some uncertainty about the precise date of the foundation of *Colonia Firma Iulia Arausio Secundanorum*: the legion was disbanded in 35 BC, but excavations have yielded nothing earlier than 20 BC.

Owing to its commercially strategic situation overlooking the great trade route along the Rhône valley, the colony prospered. Despite being sacked by the Visigoths in 412, it recovered sufficiently to be chosen as the location of a Council in 441. Thereafter its historical development followed the rise and fall of this region, one of military and commercial significance and hence fought over by contenders for power during the Middle Ages. Sadly, much of the Roman remains that had been spared by the barbarians in the C5 were dismantled to provide material for the imposing fortifications built by Prince Maurice of Orange-Nassau in the early C17, and levelled on the orders of Louis XIV.

Traces of the Roman city **walls** indicate that they extended for more than 3 km., enclosing some 70 ha. (including the Colline Saint-Eutrope). The present-day street layout retains the alignments of the main Roman

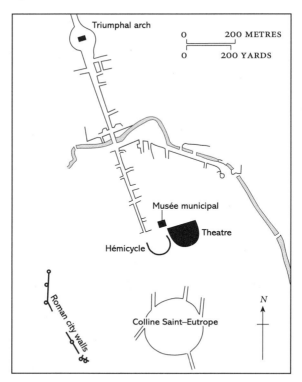

▲ Orange: general plan

streets: the main east–west street (*decumanus maximus*) is now the Rue de la République, whilst the Avenue de l'Arc de Triomphe and the Rue Victor-Hugo are on the line of the north–south street (*cardo maximus*).

Excavations have produced a good deal of information about Roman *Arausio*, although the exact location of the forum† is still not known. However, the town is justly famous for two of the most outstanding and best-preserved monuments in the Roman world.

The **Triumphal Arch** was built to span the so-called Via Agrippa that linked Lyons with Arles, just before it passed through the walls of the town from the north. Its survival is fortuitous, since it was converted into a fortress in the C13, and this was not dismantled until 1811. There is still some debate about when it was built and on what occasion. Current research favours construction during the Augustan period†, to honour the veterans of the II Legion, followed by restoration and reconstruction by Tiberius in AD 26–7 to celebrate the victories of Germanicus over the Germans in the Rhineland.

The Arch is built of large unmortared limestone blocks. It has three arches, that in the centre being larger than the two flanking ones. The

▲ Orange: the triumphal arch

entire structure measures 19.57 m. long by 8.40 m. wide and stands to a height of 19.21 m. Most of what is now visible is original, apart from the western façade, which was reconstructed in the C19. Each façade has four semi-engaged Corinthian† columns.

Much of the grandeur of the Orange arch is due to the remarkable preservation of the decorative motifs on each of its façades. The two long façades celebrate war, with trophies† of arms over the side arches and scenes depicting naval engagements and land battles on the attic storeys†. These are best preserved on the north front. The narrow façades also carry scenes and motifs associated with war—fighting men, barbarian prisoners, and trophies† of arms. Nothing remains of the dedication, which must have spanned the main façades, but the holes in which the bronze letters would have been fixed have been the subject of intensive study and have provided convincing evidence for a dedication to Tiberius.

The **Theatre** is one of the finest and best preserved in the Roman world; only that at Aspendos (Turkey) compares with it in completeness and grandeur. It is a classic example of the Roman theatre, built up against the Colline Saint-Eutrope. Its survival is due to the fact that its structure had been used as the framework for an entire quarter of small houses in the Middle Ages, traces of which can be seen on the Roman building. Unlike the Triumphal Arch, it has been possible to identify the quarries in the vicinity from which the stone was extracted to build the Theatre. It is generally thought to have been built at the end of the C1 BC, when the colony was founded.

The building is orientated towards the north, as dictated by the topography, with the main entrances to the east and west. Its overall diameter is 103 m. and it is estimated that it would have provided places for some 7,000 spectators. The seats in the *cavea*† were divided into three groups: twenty rows at the lowest level, nine in the second, and five in the uppermost. The lowest row, facing directly on the *orchestra*†, still bear an inscription indicating that they were reserved for spectators of higher rank (*equites*).

The main feature of the Theatre, however, is its stage building, which exceptionally survives almost intact. The inner façade (*scenae frons*†) has now lost almost all of the great number of columns with which it would have been embellished originally, but the sheer scale of what lay behind them is staggering. The whole structure is 103 m. long by 36 m. high and is organized on three levels. The lowest of these has three doors, the largest, in the centre, being reserved for royal personages in performances and those flanking it for lesser mortals. The double life-size statue of an emperor (doubtless Augustus) in the central niche would have been just one of many statues representing divinities and emperors that would have filled niches covering all three levels of the façade, and there is evidence that these would have been lined with brilliant mosaics.

The Theatre formed part of a monumental complex, probably dedicated to the Imperial Cult. It is possible to visit what is known as the **Hémicycle**, probably part of a temple. It has been suggested that this might have reutilized the site of an earlier and less impressive theatre, but this is still speculative and awaits confirmation by further excavation. This complex can be seen to best advantage from the Colline Saint-Eutrope, where the plinth of a monumental Roman *capitolium*†, on which three temples would have been erected, have been uncovered, alongside those of a C16 castle.

A visit to Orange must include the **Musée Municipal** in front of the Theatre. It contains a number of interesting finds from the Theatre and elsewhere in Orange, but its greatest treasure is the group of marble plaques which record the land survey carried out in the region around Orange by Roman surveyors. These largely fragmentary tablets, which constitute an official 'land registry', are unique in the Roman world, and

▲ Orange: the temple in the hemicycle

their interpretation (including the identification of certain plots in the modern landscape) was a work of remarkable scholarship.

The Theatre and the Triumphal Arch were inscribed on the World Heritage List by the UNESCO World Heritage Committee in 1981.

GAF 23; GB Provence 674–82; Bromwich 181–94; PBSAF 397–401.

Pont Julien *see* BONNIEUX.

80 Riez Roman and Palaeochristian remains *Alpes-de-Haute-Provence* *(04)*

Michelin 84/5.

This small Gaulish settlement was the capital of the Reii, a Celto-Ligurian tribe. It owes its earlier name, *Alebaece Reiorum*, to the hillfort† that preceded it on the hill now known as Mont Saint-Maxime, which dominates the town. During the reign of Augustus it was created a *colonia latina*†, under the resounding title *Colonia Iulia Augusta Apollinaris Reiorum*. It was something of a backwater during the Early Empire, and does not figure in history until the C5, when it became an important religious centre. In 439, Bishop Maximus (later to be canonized) held a Council there to consider misdemeanours in the neighbouring see of Embrun (*Ebrodunum*). One of his successors, Faustus, a close friend of Sidonius Apollinaris, was born in Britain.

The most notable Roman remains in Riez are the four imposing columns, known today as **Les Colonnes**, which are all that survive of a temple erected in the C1 AD. The 6 m. high columns are made of granite, allegedly imported from Egypt, and are highly polished, with impressive marble Corinthian† capitals and an architrave†, which was brought from an earlier monument. Excavations in the 1950s and 1960s around the columns and the nearby spring suggest that the tetrastyle temple†, measuring 20 × 10.75m., was dedicated to Apollo, who is commemorated in the name of the town. No inscription referring to the god was found, but the relationship with Apollo is supported by an inscription to his son Aesculapius, god of healing.

The excavations demonstrated that the town was well equipped with fine public and private buildings. Remains of a set of baths were found beneath those of the C5 **cathedral**, which had a conventional layout of three naves and a large apse. These are displayed in the archaeological site adjoining the other major monument of Riez, the **baptistery**†.

The baptistery is a rare survival from the Merovingian period. Construction began in the C5, most probably by Bishop Maximus, but it has been considerably modified since that time, most notably with the reconstruction of the dome in the C12. It is a square building enclosing an octagonal interior, with four apsiodoles in the thickness of the corners, one containing the altar. Eight reused ancient granite columns with marble Corinthian† capitals encircle the baptismal basin, now much degraded.

GB Provence 820–1; Bromwich 286–8; PBSAF 401.

81 La Roquebrussane: Grand-Loou Roman villa *Var (83)* ★
Michelin 84/15. 30 km. N of Toulon by N 97, D 554, and D 5.

The villa of Grand-Loou began in the later C1 BC as a group of modest wooden buildings reminiscent of military barracks, which suggests that the builder and proprietor of this small agricultural estate was a time-expired legionary soldier. It was not until the beginning of the C2 AD that it was significantly altered, when the owner of the day built an imposing villa of traditional Roman form. It consisted of a group of rooms round a central colonnaded courtyard, with the obligatory suite of baths and quarters for servants. However, much of the interest lies in the large and very complete winery installation on the northern side of the complex, with vats for crushing by feet, presses, and enormous storage vessels. It is also considered to have been used for the production of olive oil.

GB Provence 318; PBSAF 401.

Roquepertuse *see* VELAUX.

Saint-Blaise *see* SAINT-MITRE-DES-REMPARTS.

82 Saint-Chamas Roman bridge *Bouches-du-Rhône (13)*

Michelin 84/1. 35 km. W of Aix-en-Provence on D 10.

The ancient road system in southern Gaul began after the foundation of the province of *Gallia Transalpina* in 118 BC, when the proconsul Cnaeus Domitius Ahenobarbus constructed the *Via Domitia.* This links Italy with Spain, where the Romans had been established since the beginning of the C2 BC. It runs through FRÉJUS, AIX, ARLES, NÎMES, and NARBONNE. This was the first stage in the creation of a network covering the whole of Gaul, the work of Agrippa at the behest of Augustus.

One of the most important spurs to be constructed, probably at the same time as the main highway, linked Arles with Marseilles; there may well have been a pre-Roman highway on the same alignment. North of the Étang de Berre this road crosses the river Touloubre, where there was originally a wooden bridge. During the Agrippan reconstruction, this was replaced by an elegant bridge of classic Roman form. An inscription recounts that the bridge was built as a bequest in his will by one Flavos, a Romanized Gaulish aristocrat (most probably of the *Avatici* tribe) who was a *flamen* (priest) of the Imperial Cult of Rome and Augustus.

It is a single-arch bridge, built in a buff limestone. The piers are original but the paving and parapets are more recent. At each end there is a ceremonial arch, constructed in white limestone; the western one was reconstructed after collapsing in the C18. Only one of the lions, on the eastern arch, is original.

GB Provence 623–4; Bromwich 200–1; PBSAF 402.

▲ Saint-Chamas: Le Pont Flavien

83 Saint-Cyr-sur-Mer: Les Lecques Roman villa Var (83)

Michelin 84/14. 15 km. E of Cassis on D 559.

The remains of a large villa founded in the C1 AD have been roofed to form the **Musée de Tauroentum** (a possible misattribution, according to some authorities). Three mosaics are preserved, along with finds from the villa and other sites in the vicinity.

GB Provence 384; Bromwich 291.

84 Saint-Mitre-les-Remparts: Saint-Blaise Pre-Roman
and Roman settlement *Bouches-du-Rhône (13)* ★

Michelin 84/11. 8 km. SE of Istres on D 5.

This promontory commanding the Étang de Berre and the wide Crau plain attracted human settlement from at least as early as the Neolithic period (fourth millennium BC), and it continued to be occupied, with some gaps, until the end of the C14 AD. The early settlement was sparse, but this changed around 625 BC, when a substantial defensive wall was built across the neck of the promontory and roughly aligned stone houses were constructed within the enceinte. As at ENTREMONT, there were two distinct habitation areas.

This settlement of the *Avatici* tribe (possibly the *oppidum*† referred to as *Mastrabala* by Avienius) was a centre for trading with the Etruscans, who began their commercial penetration of the region in the mid-C7 BC. Saint-Blaise was especially renowned for its salt production, from the many small lakes in its immediate vicinity. However, the arrival of the eastern Greeks from Phocaea in Massalia (MARSEILLES) around 600 BC severely curtailed, and eventually destroyed, Etruscan commercial links with this region, and so the Saint-Blaise settlement stagnated for several centuries.

Its fortunes were to change dramatically at the end of the C3 BC. The earlier settlement was deliberately levelled and covered with a layer of sand, on top of which a town of stone houses was built on a classic grid layout. It would appear that Saint-Blaise had found a profitable niche in the Massaliote trading network, although it was not incorporated into that city's territories. In the mid-C3 a master-builder was brought in from the Greek world who constructed a massive new wall across the promontory in the best tradition of Hellenistic† military fortifications.

Despite its sophistication, however, this wall was unable to withstand a siege by the Roman army, most likely during the campaign of 125–124 BC. The defences themselves were partially dismantled, and the *oppidum*† itself became almost deserted. The site was not to attract any significant level of occupation again until the turbulent days of the later C3 AD. This town was to grow considerably in the C5–C6, and the Hellenistic walls were rebuilt, with addition of ten towers.

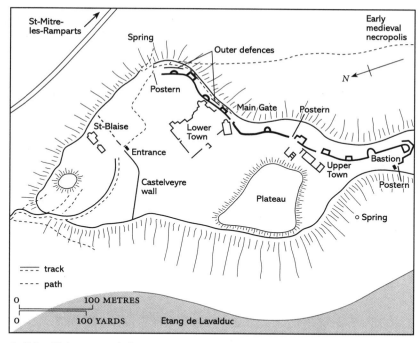

▲ Saint-Blaise: general plan

The final decline of Saint-Blaise (known as *Ugium* after its rehabilitation) began when it was sacked by the Saracen invaders in the C9. A new line of fortifications was built, enclosing a much smaller area, which took the name of Castelveyre, but this, too, failed to flourish, and it finally disappeared, leaving only the surviving Romanesque† church of Saint-Blaise, after being sacked by a marauding mercenary band in 1390.

The most outstanding feature of Saint-Blaise is the line of ramparts running right across the promontory. The Hellenistic work can be distinguished from the later rebuilding by the quality of the masonry. Some of the carefully dressed blocks bear Greek letters, which may have been masons' marks; their meticulous stone-dressing technique is illustrated by the characteristic chevron marks made by their chisels. The Hellenistic walls were built without the use of mortar, which also distinguishes original sections from the later rebuilding, when the earlier masonry was often reused, as, for example, in the square tower projecting at the main gateway.

In the upper town, at the south end of the site, a number of houses have been excavated and remain visible. Some of these contain small mills and olive presses. The postern gate in the well-preserved section of

▲ Saint-Blaise: aerial view

Hellenistic walling here was used to take water from the spring a little lower down the hillside.

GB Provence 621–2; Bromwich 196–200; PBSAF 402.

85 Saint-Rémy-de-Provence: Glanum Pre-Roman and
Roman town *Bouches-du-Rhône (13)* ★★

Michelin 81/12. D 571 17 km. S from Avignon to Saint-Rémy. The site lies 3 km. south of the town. Musée Archéologique: Hôtel de Sade, Rue du Parage, Saint-Rémy-de-Provence.

The origin of this long-lived settlement appears to have been a sanctuary associated with healing, which may date back to as early as the Neolithic period. A small settlement inevitably grew up around the sanctuary, and not surprisingly became involved in the intensive trading activities in the region from the C7 BC onwards, given its situation at the foot of one of the main gaps in the chain of the Alpilles. Pottery and coins found in a deep crevice in the rock show that it had connections with Massalia (MARSEILLES) as early as the C6 BC.

It was, however, in the C2 BC that the town began to grow and prosper, as its role in the complex and profitable trading network developed and expanded. The town underwent serious destruction in the 120s BC and again in the 90s, on both occasions at the hands of the Romans because the town had taken the side of the *Salyes*. On the latter occasion it probably came under direct Massaliote rule, and thereafter it developed, after a short period of virtual abandonment, as a Greek town rather than a Gaulish *oppidum*†, with features such as an agora, a *bouleu-terion* (council house), and peristyle† houses.

The mid-C1 BC saw a strong revival of Glanum's fortunes, character-ized in particular by the erection of a number of lavish urban houses with a fine disregard for earlier planning, which have been interpreted as the assertion of their identity by a local indigenous élite group.

In the first decade of the C1 AD Glanum underwent a process of comprehensive Romanization. The surviving Greek public buildings were swept away and replaced by two forums†, a triumphal arch, Imperial temples, a theatre, a basilica†, and other purely Roman urban elements. The lack of new building in the C2 AD suggests that the town may have been entering a period of economic recession. A devastating raid by Germanic invaders in the 270s appears to have driven the already disheartened citizens out of the town for good. The water channels became blocked and silt washed down from the mountains gradually covered up the remains of the deserted ancient town.

A large area of the town has been excavated and can be visited; it shows admirably the way in which it evolved and expanded. The original core was the **Sanctuary Area** at the southern end of the site. This began at a hollow in the side of the hill, which was the sanctuary dedicated to the native god Glan; there are two inscribed altars alongside the steps leading up to it. Opposite a flight of steps on the Nymphaeum† leads down to an underground spring-head, most likely Hellenistic† in date. The spring is flanked to the south by a temple dedicated to Hercules, which is matched on the other side by a smaller temple, dedicated, according to an inscription, by Agrippa to *Valetudo* (the goddess of health).

There is a number of other buildings in this area, including several houses and what may have been a Hellenistic† bath house. A fortified gateway, of characteristic Greek pattern and similar to that at SAINT-BLAISE, leads to the main settlement.

The first section of this is what is usually known as the **Monumental Area**, containing the remains of a long series of public buildings from the Greek and Roman periods. Immediately inside, on the right, are the remains of a portico with Doric† columns (the bases of two survive), which may have been associated with the 'severed head' cult (see p. 128) and was later adapted for secular use in the Roman period.

Excavations have revealed two different layouts of this area in the Greek and Gallo-Roman periods respectively which are difficult to dis-tinguish on the ground. In the earlier period there was what is thought to have been a double treasury facing the gateway, with a large council house (*bouleuterion*) to the west of it. The latter had tiers of seats on three sides and an altar in the middle, and is similar to other examples at Ephesus and Priene (Turkey).

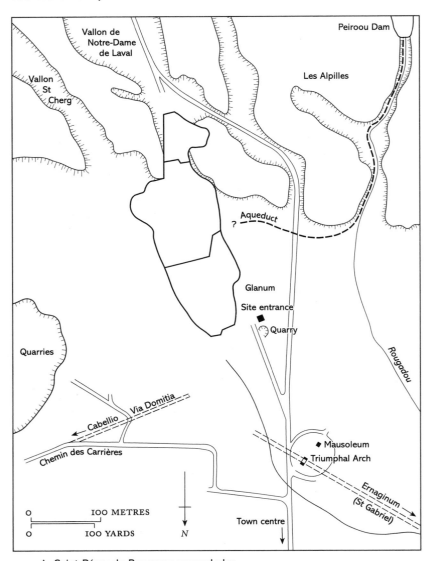

▲ Saint-Rémy-de-Provence: general plan

The Roman forum† was built in the early 20s BC over the flattened remains of a large Greek building with lavishly decorated rooms and a garden. It was remodelled during the second decade AD, and additions and alterations took place until AD 70–80. The structures visible today include the impressive basilica† on the north side of the forum, with a large two-storey apsed building built up against it, probably to act as the meeting place of the town council (*curia*), and stretches of the retaining

▲ Saint-Rémy-de-Provence: general view of the excavations

walls. Just outside are the remains of the Dromos well, probably linked with the neighbouring Tuscan temple. This was used as a dump towards the end of the town's life and has produced a number of important sculptural fragments. Twin temples were built at the beginning of the Roman occupation west of the well. There is no indication of their original dedications, but they were rededicated later to Lucius and Gaius, the adopted sons of Augustus. Their high quality is indicated by many architectural fragments found in their vicinity, most of which are on display at the site. The wall of the *peribolos* (open portico) surrounding both temples also testifies to the quality of the design and execution of the ensemble.

The final section of the Glanum site is the **Residential Area**, further to the north. The public baths, with their pool, were comparatively modest for so important a town. They are early Roman, from the time of Julius Caesar (mid-C1 BC). There are several relatively complete and well-preserved town houses. The so-called 'House of Antes' is in peristyle† form, with a central courtyard, open cistern, and portico and rooms facing inwards on three sides. It is very characteristic of the Hellenistic† period, but shows evidence of an Augustan† remodelling. Next to it is the slightly smaller House of Atys, thought to have been connected with the worship of Cybele, to whom part was to become a cult centre in a later phase.

The junction between the main Roman road from Italy and the spur road to Glanum is graced with two masterpieces of Roman provincial art, at the point known as Le Plateau des Antiques. The **Mausoleum**† still stands to a height of 18 m.; it is in three sections. The cubic podium† base is decorated on all four sides with dramatic carved reliefs, showing scenes of battle and hunting. Above this is a four-sided arched structure (*quadrifrons*), and this is surmounted by a rotunda with Corinthian† columns enclosing two statues.

An inscription on the podium refers to 'Sextus, Lucius, and Marcus, sons of Caius, of the Julian family, to their parents'. This has been interpreted in the past as referring to the Imperial princes to whom the temples in the town were dedicated, but it is now thought to be the work of a local aristocratic family, granted Roman citizenship by Julius Caesar. It is also now considered that this building was a cenotaph† rather than a mausoleum†.

Alongside this remarkable structure is the **Triumphal Arch**, reminiscent of those at ORANGE or Tarragona (Spain), although smaller than either of these. It has lost its attic storey† and much of the decoration has been removed or has decayed sadly. What survives is symbolic of the defeat of its enemies and the triumph of Rome—the bound Gaul on the eastern façade and the goddess of Rome seated on a heap of weapons on the western. It is generally thought to be the work of Agrippa.

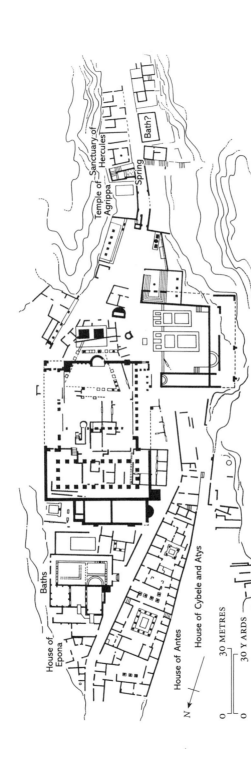

▲ Saint-Rémy-de-Provence: plan of the excavations

House of Epona

Baths

House of Antes

House of Cybele and Atys

Temple of Agrippa

Sanctuary of Hercules

Spring

Bath?

N

0   30 METRES
0   30 YARDS

Material from Glanum is to be seen in the **Musée Archéologique** in nearby Saint-Rémy-de-Provence.

GAF 19; GB Provence 723–6; Bromwich 201–21; PBSAF 403–5.

86 Salernes: Grotte de Fontbrégoua Prehistoric inhabited cave *Var (83)*

Michelin 84/6. 20 km. W of Draguignan on D 567/D 560.

Although not decorated with the rock art that distinguishes many of the southern caves occupied in prehistory, the Grotte de Fontbrégoua, on the limestone hills overlooking Salernes, is one of the most important from an archaeological point of view. The 11 m. of occupation deposits were built up during the later Palaeolithic and Neolithic periods from 10,000 to 3000 BC. It began as a permanent living site at the end of the Palaeolithic, but during the earlier Neolithic it was used only seasonally, on hunting expeditions.

In the fourth millennium BC it was divided into two sections by means of a wall, the outer section being used as a sheepfold and the inner as a living area. As well as providing some of the earliest evidence for farming activities in France, the cave also produced human skulls that testify to occasional cannibalism.

The site may be visited by prior arrangement with the Centre Archéologique du Var, Toulon.

PBSAF 406.

87 Sisteron Roman town *Alpes-de-Haute-Provence (04)*

Michelin 81/6. Take D 3 NE out of Sisteron; the inscription is on the south side of the road, in the Défilé de Pierre Écrite, about 10 km. from Sisteron.

The Roman town of *Segustero* in the land of the Gaulish tribe of the *Vocontii* was built at the foot of the impressive hill on which the modern town of Sisteron now stands, but which must have been the site of a hillfort† in the pre-Roman period. It was an important settlement on the *Via Domitia*, linking Italy with the flourishing Roman towns of the Rhône delta.

The picturesque town of Sisteron is medieval in origin and plan, and its fortifications date from the C16. Limited excavations have produced evidence of the Roman town, but nothing is currently on display to the public. However, the rich ornamentation of the fine late C1 AD mausoleum† discovered in 1946 is on display in the museum on the citadel.

The gorge known as the Défilé de la Pierre Écrite takes its name from the rock-cut **inscription** on the south side of the road. This was cut on the orders of Claudius Postumus Dardanus, who was the civil governor of the whole of Gaul as Praetorian Prefect of the Gauls in the early years of the C5. After listing the many official posts that he had held, and also those of his brother, Dardanus goes on to record the construction of the road through this gorge and the creation of a fortified building on his personal estate, known as *Theopolis* (City of God). Dardanus was a dedicated Christian, and the name of his estate clearly echoes the great work of Saint Augustine of Hippo.

The site of Theopolis is not known, although there are indications that it may have been at Saint-Geniez, a little further up the gorge. It has also been suggested that the Romanesque† crypt of the Chapel of Notre-Dame du Dromon may originally have been the mausoleum† of Dardanus and his wife, Nevia Galla.

GB Provence 762; Bromwich 288–9.

88 Taradeau Pre-Roman hillfort *Var (83)* ★

Michelin 84/7. N/D 565 S from Draguignan, then D 10 W to Taradeau.

Transit between the Rhône valley and northern Italy obliged traders and travellers to follow the valley of the Argens. During the later C2 BC the local Gallic tribe, the *Salyes*, constructed a strong *oppidum*† on a hilltop dominating the valley, in response to threats from Rome or from the Germanic invasion of the *Cimbri* and their allies in 106 BC. It was only occupied for a short period and had been abandoned by the middle of the C1 BC. There was another short period of occupation in the mid-C1 AD. In the later Empire it was the site of a villa establishment during the early C5.

The defences of the *oppidum* consist of a roughly five-sided rampart with a ditch outside; there are three bastions on the northern side. Three

▼ Taradeau: aerial view of the site

entrances large enough to permit the access of wheeled vehicles have been identified; two of these were blocked during the first reoccupation, when small houses were constructed along the inner faces of the walls. There is no evidence of Romanization in the form of public buildings. Of particular interest are the remains of the presses used for the extraction of olive oil, which was produced on a large scale in the region in antiquity.

GB Provence 418; Bromwich 291–2; PBSAF 408.

89 La Turbie Roman triumphal monument *Alpes-Maritimes (06)*   ★

Michelin 84/10. On R 7 between Nice and Menton.

When he assumed power in 27 BC, Augustus was confronted with the problem of subduing the Alpine region, whose warlike tribes threatened the communications between Italy and Gaul. He carried out a series of campaigns between 25 and 14 BC, at the end of which the region had passed under Roman control. To commemorate this decisive victory, the Roman Senate and people decreed in 7 BC that a trophy† should be erected in the new province of *Alpae Maritimae.*

The *Tropaea Augusta* (whence the modern name, La Turbie) was set up at the foot of Mont Agel at the point where the new highway, the *Via Iulia Augusta,* dominated much of the Mediterranean coastline. It is one of the two surviving examples of this type of Graeco-Roman monument (the other, at Adamklissi, Romania, has been over-restored). The first damage to the Trophy is attributed to Saint Honoratus, who is recorded as having found the local people worshipping it. It was badly slighted in the Middle Ages, not least by converted barbarians, who saw in it a monument to the pagan god Apollo, and, like so many other Roman commemorative monuments, such as the Arch of Septimius Severus in Rome, it was converted into a castle. Its robust construction survived an attempt to blow it up by Louis XIV's Maréchal de la Feuillade in 1705. It owes its present form to a combination of meticulous study and painstaking restoration, largely financed by the American, Dr Edward Tuck, in the 1930s.

Construction of the Trophy began with the levelling of a large area on the hillside. The structure itself rests on a base 32.56 m. square built at two different levels. This supports a circle of twenty-four Doric† columns 8 m. high and 1 m. in diameter, only four of which are complete, surrounding a tower crowned with a conical stepped roof, which originally rose to a height of 50 m. It is probable that the roof would have been crowned originally by a statue of Augustus, and this might in turn have been surmounted by a light, to serve both as a navigational aid for sailors and a triumphant statement of Roman Imperial power.

The first podium† is decorated with two Winged Victories presenting their crowns to Augustus and a truly monumental inscription, cut in

▲ La Turbie: the Triumphal Monument

elegant letters. The latter has been reconstructed from no fewer than 136 fragments; fortunately, it had been recorded by Pliny in his description of Italy. It reads:

To the Emperor Augustus, son of the deified Caesar, Supreme Pontiff, in the 14th year of his Imperial Power and 17th year of Tribunician Power, [erected by] the

Senate and People of Rome. To commemorate the bringing of all the Alpine peoples from the Adriatic Sea to the Mediterranean under the dominion of the Roman people. The Alpine people conquered were [then comes a list of 44 defeated tribes].

The first section is cut in letters some 30 cm. high, the remainder in slightly smaller, but equally impeccable lettering. The most complete face is that on the west, along which the Roman road passed. The entrance to the interior of the monument, which originally contained staircases allowing access to all the levels, was on the south face (there is no authority for the existing bronze doors). The degradation of the east and north faces was such that little restoration was possible. The masonry of which the Trophy and the shafts of its columns is composed is of white limestone from quarries some 700 m. away, whilst the marble is from the famous Italian quarries at Carrara.

GB Provence 806–7; Bromwich 270–5; PBSAF 410.

90 **Vaison-la-Romaine** Roman town *Vaucluse (84)* ★★

Michelin 81/2. N 7 S from Orange, then D 950 E, D 977 NE.

Vasio (Vaison) was the capital of the Celtic *Vocontes* tribe, which occupied a large region between the Rhône and Durance rivers from as early as the C6 BC. They were subdued in 124–123 BC by the Romans, whose aid had been sought by the Greek city of *Massalia* (MARSEILLES) and its daughter colonies. Some time in the early C2 BC Vaison became the administrative capital of one of the *civitates†* of the new Roman province of *Gallia Narbonensis*, with the privileged status of *civitas fœderata* ('federated town') which conferred a considerable measure of autonomy on its citizens (though not exemption from taxes); this is thought to have been to ensure the support of the *Vocontes* against their somewhat uncertain northern neighbours, the *Allobroges*.

Painstaking analysis of the remains by scholars has revealed three main phases in the evolution of the Roman town. The earliest phase (from *c.*50 BC) is represented by buildings in Roman style but constructed using native techniques and widely scattered. A period of construction in the second decade of the C1 AD saw a process of Romanization, with large urban villas equipped with bath suites being built using high-quality Roman techniques. This process saw its apogee at the end of the century, with a formal grid pattern of streets and central facilities (water supply, drainage, etc.). Excavation has revealed that there was considerable destruction in the late C3, probably as a result of barbarian incursions, but the urban structure was strong enough for this to be made good quickly.

Vaison continued to play an important administrative and religious role even after the quadripartite division of this *civitas* in the C4, when it

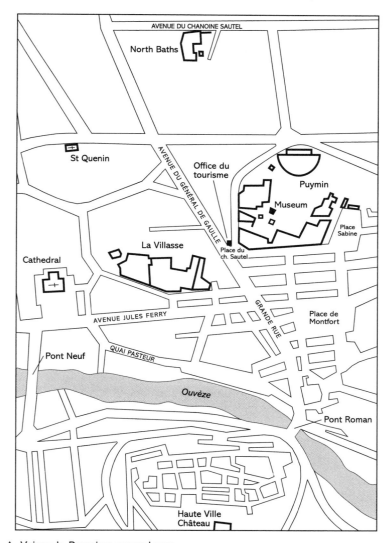

▲ Vaison-la-Romaine: general map

appears to have contracted somewhat in size. Little is known of its history from the C6 until the Middle Ages, though the influence of its bishops is attested by a number of documents. What is undeniable is the fact that the ravages of warfare in the Middle Ages led the inhabitants to desert much of the area on the right bank of the Ouvèze in favour of the more easily defensible area below the castle, built by the Counts of Toulouse in the later C12. A large part of the Roman town reverted to farmland, and was not built on again until the C19 and early C20.

Nonetheless, considerable areas remained accessible for archaeologists to explore over the past hundred years.

The pre-Roman *oppidum*† of Vaison is generally believed to have been on the hill now crowned by the medieval castle, overlooking what is now known as the Haute-Ville. It has been difficult to confirm this, since the upper slopes have been drastically eroded by human action and nature and the Haute-Ville itself retains most of its medieval and Renaissance buildings.

The Roman town developed on the north side (right bank) of the Ouvèze river. Unlike other Roman towns in the region, Vaison was never enclosed by a town wall, and so its extent can only be judged by the location of the cemeteries on its outskirts, their traditional location in Roman towns. They suggest that it covered 60–70 ha., making it smaller than NÎMES but larger than ARLES or FRÉJUS, which lends weight to the description of the town by Pomponius Mela in the mid-C1 AD as one of the most opulent towns (*urbs opulentissima*) of the province.

Systematic excavation of the ancient town (though not necessarily to acceptable modern scientific standards) began in 1907 and continued until 1955 under the direction of Joseph Sautel, a local cleric. These have continued since that time in the capable hands of two distinguished French archaeologists, Christian Goudineau and Yves de Kisch. As a result, some 15 ha. have been explored and opened for public viewing, whilst observations in later buildings have permitted more information to be garnered. However, the centre of the ancient town lies beneath its present-day successor, and so little is known about the forum and the grand public buildings that would have surrounded it.

There are two principal areas of excavated remains. For the most part, these represent the town as it was in the C2 AD, since Sautel's excavations did not go deeper: it is therefore a powerful evocation of *Vasio Vocontiorum* in its prime. Further excavation in these areas is inhibited by the fact that large quantities of concrete, which would be difficult and expensive to remove, were used to consolidate the remains.

La Villasse

This area, the more southerly of the two, is on a steep slope and traversed by a narrow street. To the east there is a wide street, known, from the many small structures that line it, as the Street of Shops. At its southern end there is a large structure, originally identified by Sautel as a basilica†, but more likely to have been a set of public baths.

Opposite the Baths is the entrance to a large town house, known from its most striking find (now in the museum) as the **House of the Silver Bust**. The plan is highly irregular, and it has been suggested that it was originally a public bath that was converted when the establishment on the other side of the street was opened, a view that is strengthened by

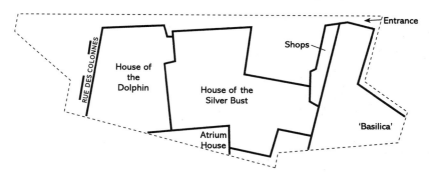

▲ Vaison-la-Romaine: plan of La Villasse

the impressive group of latrines. Parts of two other houses abutting directly on this building have been uncovered, with evidence of mosaic floors and painted walls.

On the far side of this area is the **Street of Columns**, which takes its name from a portico that borders it, still retaining its columns; it is dated to the end of the C1 AD. It was obviously a pedestrian street, since there are steps at one end, and it is surfaced with gravel. Some small shops open out on the street, from which access is gained up two steps to the *atrium*† of the **House of the Dolphin** (which takes its name from a sculpture found there and now in the museum).

This is a fine example of a late Roman town house, resulting from several stages of rebuilding. The *atrium*† contains a pool fed with rainwater from the roof and a reception table (*tablinium*). The visitor passes through one of the rooms into the central part of the house, arranged round a garden with a colonnaded portico fronting a series of formal rooms. The existence of an upper storey is attested by the bases of staircases. To the south of the main building there was another, larger garden with a portico and in front of it a broad pool originally equipped with fountains. Among other components of this villa (which is as large as some of the grandest in Pompeii) are service rooms, a suite of baths, and latrines.

Puymin

The Puymin quarter is to the north-east of La Villasse. The first structure encountered by the visitor is the House of the Messii, another extensive town house which takes its name from the family cited in two inscriptions found during excavations and believed to have been its proprietors. Only some 2,000 sq. m. has so far been excavated: an area equal in size lies beneath the modern town. There are substantial remains of wall paintings and decorated floors in several of the rooms: particularly impressive is the floor of the main

▲ Vaison-la-Romaine: general view of the excavations at La Villasse

▲ Vaison-la-Romaine: the 'Silver Bust'

reception room, with marble tiles imported from Italy, Greece, and North Africa.

Alongside this house is the **Portico of Pompey**, which takes its name from an inscription found there referring to a woman called Pompeia. It consists of a range of Tuscan columns fronting a sturdy back

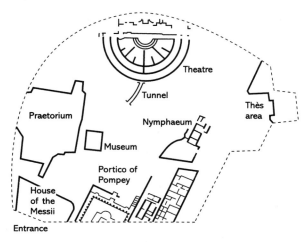

▲ Vaison-la-Romaine: plan of Puymin

wall with niches inset into it. These are occupied by casts of statues found in other parts of the town. Behind there is a colonnaded garden, only part of which has been excavated. Visitors are warned that this monument was heavily 'restored' in the years between 1920 and 1950.

Next comes a row of modest tenements, with nearby a confused group of ruins variously interpreted as a *nymphaeum*† (a monumental fountain dedicated to water spirits) and as a *castellum divisorium* (the central source of water distributed by pipe to other parts of the town). To the east lies the Thès area, where scientific excavations have been carried out in recent years. These brought to light the remains of the **Villa of the Peacock**. Only part of what must have been a large establishment of the later C1 AD have been uncovered. The high quality of the mosaics, one of which depicts the peacock that gives the building its name, testifies to the wealth of the owners in the late C2, when these are believed to have been laid. A group of small shops and a wall thought to be the base of a C1 BC temple complete the visible remains in this area.

The street on which these shops were built leads directly to the **Theatre**, which was built into the hillside in the C1 AD. This is a relatively large (95 m. diameter) theatre, excavated by Sautel between 1907 and 1926 and very extensively reconstructed in the mid-1930s: photographs taken during the excavations show that all that survived was a confused heap of rubble that had been extensively quarried after it went out of use in the C5. The thirty-two rows of seats, divided into four blocks by three staircases, provided places for some 7,000 spectators; the first three rows were reserved for local notables. Only rough foundations of the stage (*scenae frons*†) survive, but it is clear that it rose to more than

25 m. in height, like that in ORANGE. Trenches carved into the rock to accommodate the stage machinery are well preserved.

A path climbs the western flank of the hill from the Theatre to the building identified by Sautel in his 1927–9 excavations as the **Praetorium**. The scale of the building, with its many rooms, colonnades, courtyards, and gardens, led him to believe that it must be the palace of an official grandee, such as the *praetor*† who governed this part of the province. Subsequent discoveries, such as that of the House of the Silver Bust, have shown that this is more likely to have been no more than the residence of one of the wealthy citizens. It lies outside the main town and appears to have been surrounded by fields and orchards.

The Puymin area is the site of the fine **Musée Théo-Desplans**, which is reached on foot from the Praetorium. Its collections, all from Vaison itself or its immediate surroundings, are outstanding, in particular the collection of Imperial statues discovered in the Theatre.

GAF 1; GB Provence 811–16; Bromwich 221–37; PBSAF 411–13.

Roman cemeteries

The oldest code of Roman law, drawn up in the mid-C5 BC and known as the Law of the Twelve Tables (*lex duodecim tabularum*), lays down that the dead may not be buried or cremated within the boundaries of a town. For this reason Roman cemeteries are always to be found outside the settlements to which they belong, most commonly lining the roads leading into it, so as to create a link between the dead and the living. The most spectacular example is probably the many splendid mausolea† that line the Old Appian Way (*Via Appia Antica*) outside Rome.

The monuments to the more illustrious and affluent dead, which are those that are still visible today, take many forms, including mausolea in the form of temples or domestic houses, commemorative arches, and columns, often lavishly decorated and bearing inscriptions eulogizing the dead. Family tombs, often in use for a century or more, are also known, such as the Tomb of the Scipios on the Appian Way, in which the ashes of six generations of this influential Roman family were deposited. As time passed, such tombs would be constructed in a second or even a third line behind the earlier ones.

The graves of the poorer citizens are not visible nowadays, but these come to light whenever the land in which they were dug is disturbed for new buildings or road-making. Such operations also bring to light from time to time the catacombs in which the bodies of Christians were buried.

The graves of early Christian martyrs are often commemorated by the erection of a chapel, around which a monastic complex or even a whole new community sometimes developed. In some cases (e.g. St Albans, Mainz) the medieval city evolved from the nucleus of the martyr's tomb in preference to the site of the abandoned Roman town.

91 **Velaux: Roquepertuse** Pre-Roman sanctuary *Bouches-du-Rhône (13)*

Michelin 84/2. D 20 W from Aix-en-Provence, then D 10 to Velaux. The site is on the south side of the railway line 1.5 km. NE of the town.

The archaeological site of Roquepertuse was found in a natural hollow set into a low cliff at Velaux, and was excavated in the 1920s, and again in the early 1960s. The religious function of the remarkable finds, which are now on display in the Musée d'Archéologie Méditerranéenne in MARSEILLES, showed it to have been a Celto-Ligurian sanctuary established in the C3 BC, possibly by the powerful *Salyes* tribe. It was associated with the 'severed head' cult (see p. 128); most notable were the seated figures that are believed to have been set up in a portico. Catapult arrows, ballista bolts, and stone missiles point to the Romans having been responsible for the eventual destruction of this centre of a bloodthirsty cult, but it is not clear when this took place. The sanctuary was isolated, with only a handful of small buildings nearby; it is located, however, roughly at the centre of a number of known *oppida*† of contemporary date.

The scanty remains still visible on the site show that there had been a monumental façade, erected on a 22 m. long wall some 2 m. thick, which bordered a platform on which the main sanctuary was built. On a lower terrace the presence of worked and carved stones has been taken to demonstrate the existence of a stone portico.

GB Provence 179; Bromwich 194–6; PBSAF 414.

92 **Vernègues: Château-Bas** Gallo-Roman temple *Bouches-du-Rhône (13)*

Michelin 84/2. N 7 NW from Aix-en-Provence, then D 22B after 27 km.

The remains of a Gallo-Roman temple built into a hillside are all that can be seen of this small settlement. The sacred precinct is semi-circular, some 60 m. in diameter, and is enclosed by a well-built stone wall that still survives to a height of fifteen courses. A flight of steps 8 m. long gives access to a porch defined by four columns leading to a sanctuary (*cella*); the ensemble is well known throughout the Roman Empire. Traces of a second temple were found to the west of the main temple, and it is postulated that another lay to the east, but was demolished to permit the construction of the apse of a small Carolingian chapel, of which the main temple formed the nave.

The dedication of the temple is not certain, but inscriptions found in and around the enceinte make reference to Jupiter, Minerva, Neptune, and Mercury. An altar dedicated to Rome and Augustus raises the possibility that it was at some period devoted to the Imperial Cult.

▲ Vernègues: the sanctuary

The temple is in the grounds of the Château-Bas wine-growing estate.

GB Provence 744; Bromwich 237–9; PBSAF 415.

Rhône-Alpes

93 Alba-la-Romaine Medieval town on Roman foundations *Ardèche (07)*

Michelin 80/9. On D 107, 12 km. NW of Viviers.

Alba Helviorum is first mentioned by Pliny in his account of Gaul as one of the *oppida Latina* in Narbonensis, a status that was doubtless conferred upon it in recognition of the loyalty of the *Helvii* during the Gallic War. It seems likely that this was a new implantation after the creation of the province in 100 BC, although there was a minor settlement earlier on the site of the modern village.

At its greatest extent, in the C2 AD, Alba appears to have covered *c*.30 ha. The town benefited from the introduction of viticulture in the C1. Unlike a number of other Roman towns in the region, it was never fortified, either as a matter of prestige in the C1 AD or during the troubled C3, when it went into an economic decline from which it never recovered. The episcopal see created towards the end of the C4 was short-lived, being transferred to Viviers around 475. The town suffered grievously during the barbarian invasions and it did not recover until the Middle Ages, when it took its present form, that of a fortified medieval settlement round a strong castle.

Excavations have revealed that Roman Alba was laid out on the typical chequer-board plan. It is situated on the opposite bank of the river Escoutay to the modern village, and much of it lies beneath fields and vineyards.

The monumental centre, covering 3.2 ha., has what is believed to have been the forum† at its core. This is flanked by the area traditionally known as 'Le Palais', which was probably a temple complex or sanctuary. Several luxurious urban villas have also been revealed by excavation, but nothing is to be seen now. The only building that is properly conserved is the **Theatre**, developing in three stages from a simple *cavea*† built into a natural slope in the Augustan† period through a mid-C1 AD expansion into its final, massive form in the C2. The semicircular seating area (*cavea*†) is 70 m. in diameter and would have provided places for 3,000 spectators. An exceptional feature of the theatre is the fact that a small stream was channelled through the space between the *orchestra*† and the back of the *proscenium*†.

The town walls have largely disappeared or have been incorporated into later structures. However, there are substantial sections surviving along part of the Place Neuve (L'Esplanade) and the Rue du Barry.

There was a small indigenous settlement to the north of the Roman town that became one of its suburbs, now known as Bagnols, which

▲ Alba-la-Romaine: Roman theatre

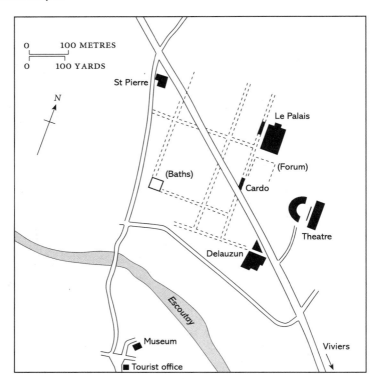

▲ Alba-la-Romaine: plan

suggests the existence here of baths of some kind. It is interpreted as having been an artisan quarter, judging from the modest scale of the buildings and the material recovered during excavations.

An unidentified Roman building was beneath the remains of a group of early Christian churches and other religious buildings (dating from the late C4 to C12) to the north-west of the Roman town.

GAF 5; GB Rhône-Alpes 132; Bromwich 17–21; PBSAF 180–1.

94 **Bourg-Saint Andéol** Bas-relief of Mithras *Ardèche (07)*

Michelin 80/10. N 86 between Viviers and Pont-Saint-Esprit.

Little is known about the small C2–C3 Roman settlement at Bourg-Saint-Andéol, which developed at the site of a ford across the Rhône, linked with the Helvian tribal capital at ALBA. It is best known for the monumental bas-relief of Mithras slaying the bull carved into a rock face in a small valley, the only example of its type in France.

It depicts the god Mithras in the traditional pose, with his knee in the bull's back and pulling back its head, ready to slash its throat with

▲ Bourg-Saint-Andéol: the Mithras relief

the sword (now disappeared) in his right hand. Around the central subject are carved symbols—the sun god Sol, the moon goddess Lunar, animals such as a dog, a snake, a raven, and a scorpion—associated with the Mithras cult. There is a three-line inscription, but this is almost illegible: it has been interpreted as a dedication by Greek traders.

Excavation has revealed that this relief forms part of a small temple or *mithraeum†*, some 10 m. in length and with the traditional Mithraic appurtenances of a central well and benches on the side walls.

GB Rhône-Alpes 671; Bromwich 21–3; PBSAF 184.

95 Die Roman defensive walls *Drôme (26)*

Michelin 77/13. On D 104/93 50 km. E of Loriol-sur-Drôme on N 7. Musée Municipal: 11 Rue Camille Buffardel.

Before the Roman conquest in 125–118 BC, the Gallic *Vocontii* tribe occupied an extensive area to the east of the central Rhône valley, in the Alpine foothills. The tribal capital was in all probability at *Vasio* (VAISON-LA-ROMAINE), in the southern part of the Vocontian territory, but there were other important *oppida†*, where Roman towns were established following the creation of the province of *Gallia Transalpina*. In the north-western quadrant the first main settlement was at Luc-en-Diois (*Lucus Augusti*); the appearance of the name of Augustus in the name suggests that the town was founded during the reign of this Emperor at the end of the C1 BC.

Little is known of the Roman town here, but the sparse archaeological evidence and documentary sources suggest that it was superseded in the late C2 AD by *Colonia Dea Augusta Vocontiorum*. The name refers to the tribal goddess *Dea Augusta Andarta*, whose name appears in numerous inscriptions found in and around Die, many of them now in the Musée Municipal.

There is a good deal of evidence of the Roman town preserved in the cellars of more recent structures (consult the Museum for details of access), and excavations have revealed the existence of public buildings, such as an impressive public baths facility and an amphitheatre. However, the walls and defences of the Roman town still survive to a remarkable extent. The original perimeter was nearly 2 km. in length; not all the walls survive as such, but their alignment can be traced in later roads, created when sections were demolished, or in stretches of medieval walls that were erected on the Roman foundations.

The best-preserved section of Roman wall is in the north-east of the town, along the Rue de la Citadelle. In the east, the lower portion of the Porte Saint-Marcel is late Roman work, with circular towers flanking an imposing archway 4.10 m. wide and 7.40 m. high beneath a frieze showing a sacrifice to Cybele. There is another excellent stretch of Roman walling, with a number of towers of late Roman type, along the Boulevard du Cagnard.

The small **Musée Municipal d'Histoire et d'Archéologie** contains finds from the town and its vicinity, including important prehistoric material from Charens and a large collection of Gallo-Roman material.

GB Rhône-Alpes 380; Bromwich 23–6; PBSAF 188.

96 Donzère Roman villa and wine presses *Drôme (26)*

Michelin 81/1. 10 km. S of Montélimar on N 7.

Gaul was recognized as a major producer of wine before the Roman conquest. It was, however, not until the Gallo-Roman period that production began on a large scale in establishments devoted entirely to this industry. The Le Molard villa, discovered just south of Montélimar, is one such establishment. It was built in the mid-C1 AD and continued in use for more than a century. Two large grape presses were excavated, with between them an immense cellar 70 m. long and 15 m. wide, containing no fewer than 200 *dolia* (large storage jars) lined with pitch to make them watertight, half set into the ground, and neatly ranged in six rows. It has been estimated that they would have contained about 2,500 hectolitres of wine; details of their capacities were inscribed below their necks. This capacity is such that it would have provided storage for more than one harvest, suggesting that the proprietor was producing a high-quality wine that could be given time to age, while at the same time

▲ Die: the ramparts

holding a buffer stock that allowed the owner to survive fluctuations in price.

There is a small site museum. The **Musée des Amis du Vieux Donzère** in the Grande-Rue contains material from various sites in the region dating back to the Neolithic.

GB Rhône-Alpes 674; PBSAF 189.

Jastres, Plateau de *see* LUSSAS.

97 Lussas: Plateau de Jastres Pre-Roman hillforts Ardèche (07)

Michelin 76/19. 76 km. E of Aubenas on D 259 from Eyriac.

The Col du Pal was one of the major routes into the Massif Central in antiquity. It was controlled by the Gaulish tribe of the *Helvii*, who had preserved a considerable measure of autonomy when the Roman province of Narbonensis was created. Significantly, they failed to respond to the appeal for aid sent out by Vercingetorix when Caesar began his invasion of Gaul.

Two successive hillforts† were built by the *Helvii* on the Plateau de Jastres to protect the Col du Pal. Jastres-Sud dates from the end of the C2 BC, but it was superseded in the early C1 BC by Jastres-Nord. This *oppidum* was abandoned when the Roman town of ALBA-LA ROMAINE was founded, but it was reoccupied and its defences were strengthened around 60 BC. It is not established whether this is attributable to an unrecorded revolt or whether it indicates a special privilege accorded to one of the leading Helvian aristocratic families.

Jastres-Sud (also known as Camp-de-César) encloses some 12 ha. within its double ramparts that stretch more than 1 km.; they enclose three sides of the hillfort, the fourth being defended by a steep cliff more than 180 m. high. The hillfort has two entrances. No traces of permanent occupation have been found within the enceinte, but many broken *dolia* (large storage jars) and stone missiles up against the insides of the walls suggest temporary use as a refuge.

Jastres-Nord is a promontory fort (i.e. a spur with fortifications on the side not protected by steep slopes), much smaller than its predecessor. The first defences were double banks-and-ditches, as at Jastres-Sud, with two entrances; its defensive purpose is once again confirmed by slingshots and other missiles. During the second half of the C1 BC a new defensive rampart was added, to be followed shortly afterwards by yet another. The later defences were massive stone-faced walls with square towers of an advanced Iron Age type, most probably Greek in origin. Unlike Jastres-Sud, this *oppidum* contained permanent buildings laid out on streets and lanes. The diversity of the material found during excavation reinforces the view that the role of this settlement was to control a major trading artery.

GB Rhône-Alpes 853; Bromwich 44; PBSAF 192.

▲ Lussas: the ramparts of the *oppidum*

Vercingetorix

Vercingetorix, a member of the ruling family of the *Arverni*, raised the standard of rebellion in 52 BC, and was elected to lead the combined forces of most of the western Gaulish tribes. Caesar, who had been in Rome when the rebellion began, hurried back to Gaul and defeated Vercingetorix in a series of pitched battles.

Vercingetorix then changed his tactics, systematically attacking the lightly protected Roman supply columns and challenging Caesar to attack him on impregnable *oppida*. Emboldened by two successes, he ventured another attack on the Roman forces in the open field, but was decisively defeated, his cavalry being destroyed.

He then retired with his remaining forces to the *oppidum* of Alésia (Alise-Sainte-Reine, between Auxerre and Dijon). Caesar set his troops to surround this forbidding hillfort with siegeworks and two parallel lines of trenches (a circumvallation). This enabled him not only to defeat the Gallic army recruited to raise the siege of Alesia but also to compel the defenders to surrender. The victor was generous to the Gallic warriors, but he seized Vercingetorix, whose qualities he acknowledges in his *Gallic War*. However, this did not prevent him from taking his captive back to Rome and exhibiting him in his triumph in 46 BC, after which he was strangled.

98 Orgnac-l'Aven: L'Aven d'Orgnac Palaeolithic occupation site *Ardèche (07)*

Michelin 80/9. 3 km. N on N 86 from Pont-Saint-Esprit, then D 901 10 km. W to Laval-Saint-Roman, D 174 7 km. W to Orgnac and continue 3 km. to the cave (L'Aven d'Orgnac).

L'Aven d'Orgnac is one of the largest and best-known cave systems in the world. A prehistoric occupation site was discovered at the bottom of a hollow some 600 sq. m. in area, resulting from the collapse of an underground pothole. Its 7 m. of deposits are testimony to its long period of occupation during the Palaeolithic period.

The finds from this site, along with those from the many other prehistoric sites in the region, such as the small but spectacular Abri des Pêcheurs, and a number of site reconstructions can be seen in the attractively located **Musée Interrégional de la Préhistoire** in Orgnac-l'Aven.

GB Rhône-Alpes 203; Rigaud 85; PBSAF 196

99 Le Pègue Pre-Roman *oppidum Drôme (26)*

Michelin 81/2. 7 km. NW of Nyons on D 538, then 2 km. N on D 538.

The important ancient road linking MARSEILLES with Vienne passed along the foot of the escarpments of the Montagne de la Lance, where a hillfort† was established in the Early Iron Age on the Colline Saint-Marcel. It has had only limited archaeological investigation, but has produced an outstanding assemblage of Greek and Massaliote ceramics of the C6 and C5 BC. It is still debatable whether this was a rich native settlement, importing costly materials from Marseilles, or whether it was a Greek-Massaliote trading station. It later became a small Gallo-Roman town, the remains of which overlie the earlier evidence.

Bromwich 44; PBSAF 197.

100 Le Pouzin Roman bridge *Ardèche (07)*

Michelin 77/11. 25 km. S of Valence on N 86 (Le Pouzin), then 1 km. W on N 304.

There is a well-preserved single-span Roman bridge over the Ouvèze, a tributary of the Rhône. It is in the same style as the bridge at VIVIERS. It has been suggested that there was a posting station (*mansio†*) here.

Bromwich 44.

101 Saint-Paul-Trois-Châteaux Pre-Roman and Roman settlement *Drôme (26)*

Michelin 81/1. N 7 N from Orange to Mondragon, then D 26 to Bollène, D 71 to Saint-Paul.

The Gallic tribe of the *Tricastini* occupied a small territory to the west of VAISON-LA-ROMAINE. The heart of the pre-Roman settlement was the large hillfort† at Barry, just south of Saint-Paul-Trois-Châteaux, in the commune of Bollène (which cannot be visited). As was customary, it was replaced by a new Roman town after the conquest, and this was given the name *Augusta Tricastinorum* (it was elevated in status in the later C1 under the name *Colonia Flavia Tricastinorum*).

Very little of the Roman town remains visible today, apart from the doorway of one of the public buildings, to be seen in the Rue Saint-Jean. The **Musée de Saint-Paul-Trois-Châteaux** contains some of the abundant material from the excavation of a large cremation cemetery at Valadas, just outside the walls of the ancient town.

GB Rhône-Alpes 767; Bromwich 45; PBSAF 200.

102 Valence Museum with important collections *Drôme (26)*

Michelin 77/12. Musée des Beaux-Arts: 4 Place des Ormeaux.

Although *Valentia* was one of the main towns of Roman Gaul, as the capital of the powerful *Segovellauni* tribe, very little is known about it. There is no evidence that this site was occupied by a settlement before the Roman conquest: it would appear to have been an Augustan† foundation, to replace the main tribal *oppidum*† at Soyons (Ardèche). Excavations and chance discoveries have located a theatre, and the line of the walls with their gates is known as a result of excavations of ramparts and cemeteries, but the street pattern has been only approximately established.

For the archaeologically minded visitor, the main attraction is the excellent **Musée des Beaux-Arts**, which contains several impressive mosaics.

GB Rhône-Alpes 784; Bromwich 26–8; PBSAF 201.

103 Vassieux-en-Vercors Prehistoric flint-working sites *Drôme (26)*

Michelin 77/13. Leave Valence eastwards on D 68, then D 70, D 199, and D 76 to Vassieux (55 km. on winding mountain roads).

The Plateau de Vercors, some 1,100 m. above sea-level, possesses a high-quality flint which attracted Neolithic settlers in the second half of the third millennium BC. A large number of flint-working sites, producing long, slender flakes used for making tools and weapons, were found during archaeological survey work in the early 1970s. It has been suggested that these people came from the Grand-Pressigny region in Touraine, some 600 km. to the west.

One of the large excavated flint-working areas has been covered, to form the **Musée-site Préhistorique de Vassieux-en-Vercors**. Associated with it are several reconstructions of Neolithic buildings.

GB Rhône-Alpes 824; PBSAF 202.

The beginnings of farming

In another, more philosophical, context the Romans believed in the saying that *ex oriente lux* ('enlightenment comes from the East'). European prehistorians will assert the correctness of this aphorism on the basis of their observations, since all the most important elements of human cultural and social development emanate from farther east. In no respect is this more true than in relation to the introduction of farming, both agriculture and stock rearing.

As early as the eleventh millennium BC there were small settled communities in the Fertile Crescent of the Near East subsisting on cereals that they had grown themselves. Sheep and goats had been domesticated by the ninth millennium BC, and cattle and pigs followed two millennia later. These practices progressively diffused into Europe, through the Mediterranean and up the Danube. Farming reached Southern France by the former route around the beginning of the sixth millennium BC, spreading slowly northwards and westwards until it met the same movement coming into the Parisian Basin from central Europe. These were not major migrations of peoples but the result of trading and other contacts which led to the adoption of new techniques by Mesolithic groups, whose existing way of life made them receptive to innovative ideas.

As in the Near East, the first evidence of the advent of the Neolithic (New Stone Age) took the form of small houses and other structures that were stoutly constructed, favouring permanent rather than seasonal or transient occupation. They were equipped with secure enclosures for livestock and surrounded by fields demarcated by walls or ditches. These settlements gradually coalesced into small communities of hamlets or villages, and these in turn evolved into larger communities resembling towns, surrounded by impressive earthen and stone defences in less peaceful times. Excess and specialized production resulted in the development of trade between communities, and the release from unremitting hunting in order to survive gave the opportunity for specialized craftsmen to appear, producing pottery, basketry, textiles, and other goods for barter.

In regions with climates less favourable for agriculture, stock rearing became economically more viable. Vast herds of beasts were assembled that would produce meat, wool, hides, horn, and other products much sought after by sedentary farming communities. The necessity of finding suitable grazing lands throughout the year for such large flocks and herds militated against the establishment of permanent settlements, and so nomadic pastoralism became a central feature of the way of life in the great steppe lands of eastern Europe. In less extreme environments such as the mountain massifs of the Alps and the Pyrenees another form of farming developed. Large flocks would spend the winter in lowland pastures and then move to high upland meadows for the winter, a practice known as 'transhumance', still to be found in the Pyrenees at the present day.

104 Viviers Roman bridge *Ardèche (07)*
Michelin 80/10. On D 107 from Viviers.

Viviers is known to have been a Roman foundation, and it became the see of a bishopric in the C5, but otherwise virtually nothing is known about its early history or layout. There is a bridge over the river Escoutay just north of the town, with nine semicircular arches, the foundations and lower courses of which are known to be Roman.

GB Rhône-Alpes 669; Bromwich 45.

Chronology

Chronology

Upper Palaeolithic

35,000 BC	Emergence of modern humans (*Homo sapiens sapiens*)	Nomadic hunter-gatherers	Warm climate
30,000 BC	Aurignacian and Châtelperronian Cultures	Nomadic hunter-gatherers	Climate deteriorating
25,000 BC	Gravettian Culture	Nomadic hunter-gatherers	Full Ice Age
20,000 BC	Magdalenian and Solutrean Cultures	Nomadic hunter-gatherers Flowering of cave art	Climate improving

Mesolithic

10,000 BC	Azilian Culture	Semi-nomadic culture	Cold interval

Neolithic

5000 BC	Danubian Cultures (from east)	First agriculture, villages, pottery, deforestation	Temperate climate
3000 BC	Megalithic Culture (in west)	Large collective burials, stone circles and settings	Colder climate
2500 BC	Beaker Culture	Transitional, some use of imported copper	Colder climate

Bronze Age

2500 BC	Chalcolithic, Early Bronze Age	Introduction of metal production (gold, silver, copper, bronze). Increasing trade, more complex social organization
1500 BC	Middle Bronze Age	Specialized metal-producing communities
1000 BC	Late Bronze Age	Development of warrior aristocracies, production of high-grade metal artefacts. Construction of hillforts.

Iron Age

750 BC	1st Iron Age (Hallstatt Culture)	Continuation of Late Bronze Age culture, with introduction of iron metallurgy. Trade with Mediterranean lands (Etruria, Magna Graecia, Carthage, Greece)
600 BC	Establishment of Greek colonies in Southern France	
450 BC	2nd Iron Age (La Tène)	Advent of *oppida* (proto-towns)
125 BC	Beginning of Roman occupation	Romanization of southern Gaul
52 BC	Completion of conquest of Gaul	
AD 190	First Germanic raids	
AD 350	Barbarian invasions - Alans, Suebi, Vandals.	
AD 418	Establishment of Visigothic Kingdom in Aquitania	
AD 476	End of the Western Roman Empire	

Climate of present period

Glossary

acanthus: stylized representation of the leaf of the acanthus plant (*Acanthus mollis*) on **Corinthian** (q.v.) capitals.

*aedile***:** an elected magistrate in Rome (and later in provincial towns) responsible for public works, markets, policing, etc.

*allée couverte***:** French term for **passage grave** (q.v.).

*alveus***:** a hot bath in a Roman baths suite.

amphitheatre: a large structure, elliptical in plan, with rising tiers of seats around a central arena, used for large-scale spectacles such as gladiatorial performances and chariot races. It developed in the Roman period, and in form it consists essentially of two theatres joined together. The best-known example is the Colosseum in Rome.

amphora **(pl.** *amphorae***):** large pottery vessels used for transporting foodstuffs such as wine, oil, and **garum** (q.v.).

aqueduct: channel to convey water from a distant source to a town. It is applicable to simple channels cut into natural rock, but is more commonly associated with structures built to span areas of low-lying land (e.g. LE PONT DU GARD).

architrave: the lowest part of the **entablature** (q.v.) of a classical façade, resting directly on the capitals.

ashlar: dressed (and often squared) stone used for facing walls.

*atrium***:** the open space at the entrance of a Roman villa.

attic storey: low storey above the cornice of a classical structure, usually with square columns or pilasters instead of pillars.

Augustan: pertaining to the reign of Augustus, 23 BC TO AD 14.

aurochs: the extinct wild ox (*Bos primigenius*), ancestor of domestic cattle.

baptistery: in early churches the sacrament of baptism took place by means of total immersion in a separate building, usually circular or octagonal in plan, with a baptismal tank in the centre of the interior.

barrel vault: simple hemicylindrical roof constructed of stones set in concrete and built using a wooden framework.

basilica: large rectangular hall, usually with a nave and two side aisles separated by rows of columns and with apsidal ends, used for administrative and judicial purposes in the Roman period. These were often converted for use as Christian churches, and the term is also used for palaeochristian churches built to the same plan.

*basilica thermarum***:** a larger room in a Roman baths suite, used for social intercourse.

*bouleuterion***:** the council chamber of a Greek or Hellenistic town.

breccia: a conglomerate rock composed of angular fragments.

*calanque***:** deep inlet, often with very steep sides, on the Mediterranean coast of France.

caldarium **(pl.** *caldaria***):** rooms in baths heated by means of **hypocausts** (q.v.).

capitolium: the area in the heart of a Roman town, either on a natural feature or elevated by means of an artificial *podium*, on which the temple of the Imperial Cult and other administrative buildings were located.

cardo [*maximus*]: one of the main axial streets in a Roman town, crossed at right-angles by the *decumanus* [*maximus*].

cavea: that part of a Roman theatre containing the seating for spectators.

cella: the central sanctuary of a Roman temple in which the statue of the divinity to which the temple is dedicated is located.

cenotaph: a commemorative funerary monument without burials.

chambered tomb: a tomb, whether rock-cut or above-ground, with a large central chamber in which the dead were placed. Some were used over long periods to receive the remains of a family or clan group. When above-ground tombs are reached by means of a stone-lined corridor they are known as **passage graves** (q.v.).

cist: simple box-shaped grave formed by means of stone slabs set on edge, either below or above ground.

civitas (pl. *civitates*): Latin word meaning 'citizenship' that was applied to non-Roman communities (in most cases pre-Roman tribes) and by extension often used incorrectly to describe their central administrative towns.

colonia: town whose inhabitants possessed full citizenship, often created for retired legionary soldiers.

Corinthian: ornate order of classical architecture in which the columns are elaborately carved with an *acanthus* (q.v.) motif.

cryptoporticus (pl. *cryptoportici*): a colonnaded structure set into a hillside.

curia: the meeting place of the municipal council of a Roman town (cf. *bouleuterion*).

decumanus: see **cardo**.

dolium (pl. *dolia*): very large earthenware jars, usually globular, used for the storage of grain, wine, oil, etc, and often set into the floors of storehouses, shops, or taverns,

dolmen: general term for megalithic chamber tombs and passage graves, now obsolete in English but still used in French.

Doric: the earliest order of Greek architecture, characterized by the plain capitals and the absence of bases on its columns.

drystone: technique of wall construction without the use of any form of bonding or mortar.

entablature: that part of a classical façade immediately above the column capitals.

fanum: small Gallo-Roman temple, with a single sanctuary (*cella*—q.v.) surrounded by a colonnaded portico.

forum: central open space of a Roman town where official administrative business and trading took place.

frigidarium (pl. *frigidaria*): the unheated room first entered in Roman baths in which initial washing took place.

garrigue: secondary vegetative cover on calcareous soils in the Mediterranean region following the removal of primary forest, consisting of aromatic shrubs and other plants, with scattered oak trees (much less dense than the *maquis*).

garum: a sauce made of fermented fish and other sea products much prized by the Romans.

glacial erratic boulders: boulders, often enormous, brought down by glaciers during the last Ice Age and deposited when the glaciers receded.

graver: small stone tool used for incising designs.

Hellenistic: pertaining to the period of Alexander the Great and his successors (C4–C1 BC).

hillfort: a fortified hilltop enclosed by one or more earthen or stone banks and ditches. Hillforts are generally distinguished from ***oppida*** (q.v.) by the lack of permanent habitations within them, being used as temporary refuges rather than proto-towns.

hornworks: curving, pointed outworks flanking gates in defensive walls.

horreum (pl. ***horrea***): granary.

hypocaust: heating system for rooms or baths in Roman public and private buildings, using hot air ducted beneath the floors and up the walls.

ibex: the European long-horned wild goat (*Capra ibex*).

impluvium: shallow pool in the centre of the ***atrium*** (q.v.) of a villa fed by rainwater draining down from the sloping roof of the **peristyle** (q.v.).

insula (pl. ***insulae***): the square or rectangular building block resulting from the classical urban grid-pattern of streets.

macellum: market-place for foodstuffs in Roman towns.

maeniana: horizontal divisions of seating in amphitheatres.

mansio: posting station, to be found at distances of roughly one day's journey by horse, on major Roman roads.

mausoleum: a large tomb or funerary monument (from the tomb of Mausolus at Halicarnassus in Asia Minor, one of the Seven Wonders of the Ancient World).

menhir: single vertical standing stone, usually from the Bronze Age.

mithraeum: temple dedicated to the cult of Mithras.

murus gallicus: earthen ramparts strengthened with interlaced timbers.

nymphaeum (pl. ***nymphaea***): ornamental fountain dedicated to water nymphs.

oppidum (pl. ***oppida***): distinguished from a **hillfort** (q.v.) by the fact that it encloses a permanent or semi-permanent settlement.

orchestra: the semicircular space between the lowest rank of sets and the stage in a Roman theatre.

palaeochristian: term generally applied to the period up to the C8 AD.

palaestra: an open courtyard in a Roman baths suite, used for exercise.

passage graves: so-called 'megalithic' (large stone) tombs of the Neolithic period consisting of stone-built burial chambers approached by narrow passage-ways, also stone-built, and covered with an earthen mound (see ***allées couvertes***).

Pax Romana: The 'Roman Peace' is the term applied (often with some measure of irony) to the process of rapid Romanization that was adopted, not always voluntarily, by the inhabitants of its conquered provinces.

pediment: the triangular section surmounting the **entablature** (q.v.) on the façade of a classical building.

pendentives: in a Byzantine or later domed structure, the elements inserted at corners to enable a round-section dome to be supported on a main structure built on a square plan.

peribolos: an open courtyard surrounding a temple.

peristyle: range of columns enclosing a building or open space.

Phrygian cap: a soft conical cap with the top tilted forwards.

piscina: a cold plunge bath in a Roman baths suite.

podium: the raised base upon which classical temples were built.

praefurnium: the furnace providing hot air for the **hypocaust** (q.v.) system of a Roman baths suite, often surmounted by a bronze tank for providing hot water.

praetor: a Roman magistrate, below the level of consul. The governors of Roman senatorial provinces were often selected from the praetors, but could also be designated as proconsuls or propraetors.

pronaos: the vestibule through which access is gained to a temple or palaeo-christian church.

proscenium: the stage area of a Roman theatre.

protohistoric: derived from French *protohistoire*, used to describe the period between the later Neolithic and the establishment of Roman rule in Gaul (equivalent to the Bronze and Iron Ages in Britain and other European countries).

quadrifrons: see *tetrapylon*.

Romanesque: style of architecture transitional between Roman and Gothic, characterized by rounded arches and vaulting.

Samian ware: see *terra sigillata*.

sarcophagus (pl. *sarcophagi*): stone coffin, often elaborately decorated.

scenae frons: the interior architectural façade of a Roman theatre which served as the fixed backdrop to theatrical performances.

Severan: pertaining to the reigns of Septimius Severus (193–211), his sons Caracalla and Geta, and their successors (to 235).

slipware: pottery coated with fine clay in suspension before firing, but not fired to temperatures high enough to form a glaze.

spear-thrower: notched wooden shaft used for increasing the range of spears.

sudatorium: a small chamber in a Roman baths suite, usually containing a heated plunge bath, with very high temperatures.

tablinium: a fixed stone table in the *atrium* of a Roman villa.

tepidarium: a room in a Roman baths suite in which a gentle heat was produced by means of a **hypocaust** (q.v.).

terra sigillàta: moulded red slipware (plain or decorated) produced successively in southern, central, and north-eastern Gaul in the C1–C3 AD and traded widely in the western provinces of the Roman Empire (also known as **Samian ware**).

tetrapylon: a monumental structure composed of four arched sides, the corners being in the form of massive pillars, and often surmounted by a statue or other symbol (the Latin term *quadrifrons* means essentially the same).

tetrastyle temple: a temple fronted by four columns.

triclinium: the dining room of a Roman villa.

trophy: ornamental group of the spoils of war (skulls, weapons, etc.). The term is used both for decorative elements on monuments and for monuments themselves (e.g. LA TURBIE).

tuff: a soft, easily worked, volcanic rock (also known as tufa).

velum: the fabric awning over all or part of the seating in Roman amphitheatres and theatres.

villa rustica: the complex of buildings in a Roman villa establishment used for industrial and domestic purposes.

villa urbana: the part of a villa used for residential and ceremonial purposes.

vomitorium (pl. **vomitoria**): passages by means of which access was gained to the seating in amphitheatres.

wattle-and-daub: form of walling consisting of clay plastered thickly on a framework of interwoven branches and twigs.

Museums

Southern France has many museums, ranging from grand regional establishments to small local collections. The following are museums with archaeological materials, listed alphabetically. It is difficult to provide reliable information about opening times or entrance fees, since these vary widely. One word of warning: most museums and art galleries in France are closed on Mondays! This list does not pretend to be exhaustive; it also omits reference to site museums.

Agde: Musée Agathois, Rue de la Fraternité. Two rooms devoted to finds from prehistory and classical antiquity.

Aix-en-Provence: Musée Granet. This large, imposing museum contains some outstanding archaeological collections from Aix and its region, in particular Entremont (with relics of the 'Severed Head' cult).

Antibes: Château Grimaldi (Picasso Museum), Place du Barri. A small display of Gallo-Roman finds.

Antibes: Musée d'Histoire et d'Archéologie, Bastion Saint-André. Of especial importance are the finds from the many ancient shipwrecks off the Provençal coastline.

Arles: Musée Lapidaire d'Art Païen, Place de la République. Housed in a C17 church, this museum contains many sculptures, mosaics, and architectural elements from the Roman city.

Arles: Musée d'Art Chrétien, Rue Balze. Noteworthy for its magnificent collection of early Christian sarcophagi.

Avignon: Musée Lapidaire, Rue de la République. An outstanding collection of Greek and Roman art from Avignon, Vaison-la-Romaine, and the region.

Beaucaire: Musée de la Vignasse, Rue de Roquecourbe. Small general collection of archaeological material.

Béziers: Musée du Biterrois-Saint-Jacques, Caserne Saint-Jacques. Important collection of prehistoric and Gallo-Roman material from the Béziers region.

Bordeaux: Musée d'Aquitaine, Cours Victor-Hugo. Important prehistoric and Gallo-Roman material from the region (especially tombstones and other inscribed stones).

Bordeaux: Musée Paléochrétien, Place des Martyres-de-la-Résistance (in the crypt of the Basilica of Saint-Seurin). Wall paintings, sarcophagi, and other early Christian material).

Cabrerets: Musée Amédée-Lémozi. Finds from prehistoric sites in the Quercy region, including the Grotte du Pech-Merle.

Cap d'Agde: Musée d'Archéologie Sous-Marine et Subaquatique (Musée de l'Ephèbe), Mas de la Clape. Modern museum housing an important collection of material from underwater excavations.

Carcassonne: Musée des Beaux-Arts, Rue de Verdun. The museum contains a small collection of archaeological finds from the locality.

Carcassonne: Musée Lapidaire, in the Château Comtal. One of the rooms is devoted to Gallo-Roman material.

Carpentras: Musée Lapidaire, Rue des Frères-Laurent (for access, contact 234 Boulevard Albin-Durand). Prehistoric and Gallo-Roman material from the town and its surroundings.

Cavaillon: Musée Archéologique, Cours Gambetta (Porte d'Avignon). Interesting collection of prehistoric material from the area, with Gallo-Roman finds from the town.

Dax: Musée de Borda, Hotel Saint-Martin-d'Agès, Rue Cazade. Important Palaeolithic collection, with Gallo-Roman finds.

Die: Musée Municipal, Rue Camille-Buffardel. Collection of local antiquities, largely Gallo-Roman.

Donzère: Musée des Amis du Vieux Donzère, Grande-Rue. Collection of local prehistoric and Gallo-Roman antiquities.

Foix: Musée de l'Ariège, in the Château Comtal. Prehistoric and Gallo-Roman material.

Forcalquier: Musée de Forcalquier (for access contact Syndicat d' Initiatives). Material from local excavations.

Fréjus: Musée Archéologique, Place de Formigé (access through the cloisters of the cathedral). Gallo-Roman material from the town.

Gap: Musée Départemental, Jardin Public de la Pépinière. Prehistoric and Gallo-Roman finds from the region.

Hyères: Musée Municipal, Place Théodore-Lefèvre. Small display of prehistoric and Gallo-Roman material from Olbia and the region.

Istres: Musée du Vieil-Istres, Place du Puits-Neuf. Material from local prehistoric and Gallo-Roman excavations, including underwater finds.

Île-Sainte-Marguerite: Musée de la Mer, in the Fort-Royal. Material from excavations of ancient shipwrecks.

Lattes: Musée Archéologique. Small but important collection of protohistoric and Gallo-Roman material.

Luzech: Musée, Maison des Consuls. Small collection of prehistoric and Gallo-Roman material, including finds from L'Impernal.

Marseilles: Musée d'Histoire de Marseille, Centre Bourse (access from Jardin des Vestiges). Modern museum containing material from recent excavations in the city, including an almost complete Roman merchant ship.

Marseilles: Musée d'Archéologie Méditerranéenne, Centre de la Vieille-Charité. Major collection of material from Egypt, Cyprus, Greece, and the Roman Empire, including a gallery devoted to finds from Roquepertuse.

Marseilles: Musée des Docks Romains, Place Vivaux. Modern display of material from the excavated ancient docks.

Martigues: Musée Ziem, Boulevard du 14 Juillet. One section of this art museum is devoted to finds from local prehistoric excavations.

Marvejols: Musée Archéologique, in the Hôtel de Ville. Small display of material from local excavations.

Le Mas d'Azil: Musée de la Préhistoire, in the former *Mairie*. Excellent collection of Palaeolithic material and photographs and drawings of non-accessible caves.

Menton: Musée Ancien, Rue Lorédan-Larchey. Regional museum with important prehistoric collection, including the skull of the celebrated Menton Man.

Millau: Musée Archéologique, Hôtel de Pegayrolles, Place du Maréchal Foch. Outstanding collection of *terra sigillata* from the Gallo-Roman potteries nearby.

Montmaurin: Musée Archéologique. Small collection of local finds, including those from the Gallo-Roman villa.

Montpellier: Musée de la Société Archéologique de Montpellier (visits on application to the Bureau de Tourisme). Good collection of native and imported materials from prehistory and classical antiquity.

Montréal: Musée Archéologique. Small collection of finds from the Gallo-Roman villa at Séviac.

Murviel-lès-Montpellier: Musée Municipal, in the *mairie.* Material from the neighbouring hillfort of Castellas.

Nages: Musée Municipal, in the *mairie.* Material from the nearby hillfort of Les Castels.

Narbonne: Musée Archéologique, entrance through the Palais des Archevêques, Place de l'Hôtel de Ville. Fine collections of material from archaeological excavations in and around Narbonne.

Narbonne: Musée Lapidaire, former church of Notre-Dame de-Lamourgier. Important collection of inscriptions and other lapidary material from Roman Narbonne.

Nice: Musée Archéologique, Rue Monte-Croce, Cimiez. Modern museum housing collections based on excavations in and around the town.

Nice: Musée de Paléontologie Humain de Terra-Amata, Boulevard Carnot, Mont Boron. Material from the Lower Palaeolithic nearby.

Nîmes: Musée Archéologique, former Jesuit College, Boulevard Amiral-Courbet. One of the most important and extensive collections of Gallo-Roman material in France.

Nîmes: Musée d'Histoire Naturelle et de Préhistoire. Interesting collection of pre- and protohistoric finds from the Nîmes area.

Orange: Musée Municipal, Place des Frères-Mounet. Finds from the Gallo-Roman town, including the famous land-allotment plans (*cadastres*).

Orgnac-l'Aven: Musée Régional de Préhistoire, at the site of L'Aven d'Orgnac. Modern museum presenting the art and way of life of early Man.

Le Pont de Montvert. This *Écomusée* contains displays relating to the prehistory of the Mont Lozère region.

Riez: Musée Municipal, located in the Baptistery (for access, contact the Syndicat d' Initiatives). Small collection of Gallo-Roman material from the Plateau de Valensole.

Saint-Bertrand-de-Comminges: Musée Archéologique. A specially constructed building housing material from the excavations that have been in progress since 1913.

Saint-Martin-des-Brômes: Musée Gallo-Romain, in the tower of the parish church. Small collection of finds from the Plateau de Valensole.

Saint-Raphaël: Musée d'Archéologie et de Préhistoire, in the former presbytery of Saint-Pierre, Rue des Templiers. Remarkable collection of amphorae from ancient shipwrecks.

Saint-Rémy-de-Provence: Dépôt Archéologique, in the Hôtel de Sade, Rue Parage (guided tours only). Graeco-Ligurian and Gallo-Roman finds from the Glanum excavations.

Sault: Musée Municipal. Prehistoric and Gallo-Roman finds from the Plateau de Vaucluse.

Tautavel: Musée de la Préhistoire. Modern museum presenting the early prehistory of this region.

Toulouse: Musée-Saint-Raymond, Place Saint-Sernin. Major collection of prehistoric and Gallo-Roman material from Toulouse and its region.

Vaison-la-Romaine: Musée Archéologique Théo Desplans, Puymin quarter. Fine modern museum housing an outstanding collection of finds from the Roman town.

Valence: Musée des Beaux-Arts, Place des Ormeaux. Three rooms in this art museum contain finds from excavations in and around Valence.

Vassieux-en-Vercors: Musée de la Préhistoire, enclosing an excavated flint-working area, with displays.

Viols-le-Fort: Musée Préhistorique. Small display of material from the prehistoric settlement excavated at Cambous.

Maps, Guidebooks, and Further Reading

Maps

For visitors to any part of France, the familiar yellow Michelin 1:200 000 maps are essential. The area that is the subject of this Guide is covered by the following sheets:

75 Bordeaux, Périgueux, Tulle
76 Aurillac, Le Puy-en-Velay, St-Étienne
77 Valence, Grenoble, Gap
78 Bordeaux, Dax, Biarritz
79 Bordeaux, Agen, Montauban
80 Albi, Rodez, Nîmes
81 Montélimar, Avignon, Digne
82 Mont-de-Marsan, Pau, Toulouse
83 Carcassonne, Montpellier, Nîmes
84 Marseille, Toulon, Nice
85 Biarritz, Lourdes, Bagnères-de-Luchon
86 Bagnères-de-Luchon, Andorre, Perpignan

The Michelin *Atlas Routier de la France* is at the same scale as the maps (1 cm. = 2 km.), but its size (29 cm. by 39.5 cm.) makes it suitable only for use by motorists.

For the more conscientious visitor, the maps at a scale of 1:100 000 produced by the Institut Géographique Nationale (IGN) are available. These maps, equivalent to those of the Ordnance Survey in the United Kingdom, are obtainable from bookshops in the major towns.

Guidebooks: General

The finest general guidebooks for France that are currently available are the series of *Guides Bleus* published by Hachette. They are not inexpensive (at current rates of exchange around £15/$22 each) and are only available in French, but they are indispensable when visiting France, since they contain much information about every aspect of the country and its heritage.

More familiar are the well-known series of Michelin 'green' guides. Those for the area of Southern France covered by this Guide are the following (most are now available in English as well as French):

Périgord Quercy
Pyrénées Aquitaine
Pyrénées Roussillon
Gorges du Tarn
Auvergne

Vallée du Rhône
Alpes du Sud
Provence
Côte d' Azur.

There is a plethora of guidebooks to France in English. One of the best remains the *Shell Guide to France*, though this is for reading with a glass of *pastis* in one hand rather than taking on site. The flavour of the Midi is well reproduced in Archibald Lyell's *Companion Guide to the South of France*, and there are volumes in the *Rough Guide* and *Lonely Planet* series for the more adventurous (and impecunious) travellers.

Guidebooks: Archaeological

For some of the best-known sites and monuments there are volumes in the excellent series of *Guides archéologiques de la France*. Those so far published include guidebooks to the following:

1 Vaison-la-Romaine
5 Alba-la-Romaine
8 Narbonne
17 Arles antique
19 Glanum
23 Orange antique
26 Le Mont Bégo
27 Nîmes antique
28 Ensérune
33 Saint-Bertrand-de-Comminges.

The booklets in this fine series, published by the Imprimerie Nationale, are all written by experts, in many cases those responsible for the excavation and management of the sites, and are very well produced, with photographs and plans.

The most comprehensive guide to the prehistoric (Palaeolithic and Neolithic) sites in France is undoubtedly *Les Haut Lieux de la Préhistoire en France* edited by Jean-Philippe Rigaud (1989: Bordas, Paris). A succinct account is given of all the major sites, including many caves with important rock art in Southern France. It also has the advantage of being truly pocket-size.

Those with a special interest in the Roman period of the Midi are admirably catered for by *The Roman Remains of Southern France: A Guidebook* by James Bromwich (1993: Routledge, London and New York). It is written for a readership with a more than passing knowledge of provincial Roman archaeology, but its wealth of plans and general information, combined with the author's felicitous style, make it highly readable as well as authoritative.

The 'Guide-Album' entitled *Les Plus Beaux Sites archéologiques de la France* (1993: Eclectis, Paris) is in essence a coffee-table book, not least because of its sheer bulk, but also because of its general presentation. It is, however, well illustrated and informative on general matters of archaeology as well as the individual sites. As such it provides an excellent basis for planning archaeological tours and excursions, in association with the more specialized works of Rigaud and Bromwich.

Further Reading

The work that is fundamental to an understanding of France and its history is by the great French historian, Fernand Braudel. *L' Identité de la France*, and in particular the first part of *Les Hommes et les Choses* (1986: available in English as *The Identity of France*, published in paperback by Fontana in 1990), is an eminently readable work of immense scholarship.

The current state of archaeological research in France is summarized in *Archéologie de la France* by Jean Combier *et al.* (1990: Flammarion, Paris). This contains a series of period surveys by French experts, though its value as a work of reference is reduced because of its irritating lack of an index. On a more lavish scale is *De Lascaux au Grand Louvre: Archéologie et histoire en France* (1989: Errance, Paris), edited by the two leading French metropolitan archaeologists, Christian Goudineau and Jean Guilaine. This sumptuous publication, written by specialists and containing many superb illustrations, covers all the major archaeological projects in France (many of them in the area covered by this Guide) in the period following the end of the Second World War up to the Bicentenary in 1989.

The prehistory of France is covered in two excellent works, one in English and the other in French. Christopher Scarre edited *Ancient France, 6000–2000 BC* (ND: Edinburgh University Press), which is an excellent survey of French prehistory by a group of younger British scholars. The chapters on the Neolithic Period in Southern France (Nigel Mills) and the French Pyrenees (Paul Bahn) are of direct relevance to the region covered by this Guide. For French archaeologists, prehistory ends during the Neolithic (for the purists *la préhistoire* covers only the Palaeolithic period). In his *La France d'avant la France: Du néolithique à l'âge du fer* (1980: Hachette Littérature, Paris) Jean Guilaine provides a masterly synthesis of current knowledge of what is generally known in France as *la protohistoire*.

The impact of the classical civilizations of the eastern Mediterranean is admirably described by Barry Cunliffe in *Greeks, Romans and Barbarians: Spheres of Interaction* (1988: Batsford, London). This is a brilliant analysis and highly readable account of the transformation of the social and economic structures of southern Gaul following the Greek settlements beginning in the C7 BC. It provides the transition to the Romanization of the region, a period that is well covered in both French and English works.

The standard academic work is Albert Grenier's massive multi-volume *Manuel d'archéologie gallo-romaine* (1931 onwards: Picard, Paris). However, a large number of works in French on all aspects of Gallo-Roman life have appeared over the past decade.

In English there is nothing to compare with *Gallia Narbonensis: Southern Gaul in Roman Times* by A. L. F. Rivet (1988: Batsford, London). This is, however, a work of high scholarship and erudition, for only the most dedicated students. Much more accessible to the general reader is *Roman France* by Paul MacKendrick (1971: Bell, London); it is in this author's inimitable style, at the same time authoritative and highly readable. Although written more than a quarter of a century ago, it deals competently with most of the main sites of the southern part of Roman Gaul.

A more up-to-date picture is given by Anthony King's *Roman Gaul and Germany* (1990: British Museum Publications, London), which is a workmanlike survey with a broad canvas. Those interested in the social and economic framework of Gaul should read *Roman Gaul* by J. F. Drinkwater (1983: Croom Helm, London), a good introduction to Roman provincial administration and society.

Illustration Acknowledgements

Photographs and drawings on the following pages reproduced with kind permission:

15 (top):	Landesmuseum Trier
15 (bottom):	CNRS—Centre Camille Jullian
34:	Droits réservé
39:	M Lorblanchet
44:	DIAF—D. Lerault
48:	Toulouse, Yan
50:	Norbert Aujoulat—Centre National de Préhistoire
69:	Dessin de F. Souq
70:	J.-C. Joulia
74:	M. Lugand
78:	D. Garcia
83:	A Chéné, Ph. Foliot et G Réveillac
85:	ICOMOS
86–7:	F. Jalain
91:	Alain Aigoin
95:	ICOMOS/Musée Archéologique de Nîmes
96:	ICOMOS/Musée Archéologique de Nîmes
97:	ICOMOS/Musée Archéologique de Nîmes
100–1:	Aquarelle de J.-C. Golvin, cliché Errance
104:	C. Goudineau
105:	C. Goudineau
114:	ICOMOS
115:	ICOMOS
121:	SCOPE—J Guillard
123:	CNRS—Centre Camille Jullian—Chéné
128:	CNRS—Centre Camille Jullian—Chéné-Réveillac
131:	Cliché Lapie, Photothèque française
140:	CNRS—Centre Camille Jullian—Chéné-Réveillac
143:	Cl. D. Ponsard
145:	Cl. H. De Lumley
148:	DIAF—D. Thierry
151:	ICOMOS
155:	C. Goudineau
158:	CNRS—Centre Camille Jullian—Réveillac
161:	SCOPE—J. Guillard
165:	CNRS—Centre Camille Jullian
172:	DIAF—J.-C. Pratt—D. Pries
173:	Centre C. Jullian (A. Chêné Ph. Foliot, G. Réveullac)

177:	CNRS—Centre Camille Jullian
179:	R. Lauxerois
181:	G. Barruol
183:	Photo Archives photographiques
185:	C. Goudineau

Index of Places

General Index

References in italic are to illustrations.